Acknowledge

As with most works of this nature, I am indebted to many others for assisting me in the research and development of this volume. First and foremost, my wife Dennise, who provided love and support in so many different ways throughout the 10 odd years I have been working on this project; my children, for making every day better than the last; my parents, who were the first to teach me the importance of reading, and gave me an unyielding will to learn (special thanks to my Dad for his editorial insight); Tracy Callis, whose dedication to the research of fight records is unparalleled; Bob Carson, who kept me on the straight and narrow, and may be the only other human on this planet who shares my passion for the pre-1930 black prizefighter; Ben Hawes, the only possible exception to my last statement, Dave Bergin, who has shared with me over the years some of the most rare and unique items I have ever seen—his picture of Bob Smith being the only one I know to exist; the members of IBRO, who are true historians, and an unequalled faction of knowledge pertaining to the squared circle; Mike Delisa of the CyberBoxingZone, who was one of the first outside sources to take an interest in my work, and whose support has been inspirational; the staff of the Boston Public Library who have always done their best to assist me in my research; Dave Gentleman and Mark Bedard for giving me the kind of encouragement that comes only from true friends; Tim Sullivan for making me believe that the world just could not survive without this book. Clay Moyle, Don Koss, Dan Cuoco, Chuck Hasson, Don Cogswell and to the many who I have forgotten—I thank you as well.

Prologue: The Vanishing

"…Down there in the hollow square of faces in the lantern's light, the white faces on three sides, the black faces on the fourth, and in the center two of Sutpen's wild Negroes fighting, fighting naked, fighting not as white men fight, with rules and weapons, but as Negroes fight to hurt one another quick and bad."

—William Faulkner's *Absalom, Absalom!*

I have always enjoyed prizefighting. To me it represents the ultimate test of individual strength, both mental and physical. It is the essence of sport, modern day games stripped of their balls, bats, gloves, rackets, pads, helmets, sticks and other ancillary devices, down to the bare essence of competition. It is simply, one man against another, using only what "God hath given" to either conquer or be conquered. Of course, fighting with one's fists was originally a necessity and viewed by ancient civilizations as a must have for any young man. Warfare then was characterized by hand-to-hand conflicts of a far more personal nature than today's technological combat. The ability of a soldier to handle himself well with his fists might have been the difference between victory or defeat, life or death.

Despite its early practical uses however, fighting has always been a sport. As early as man's discovery of the joy of wagering, prizefighting, or the act of men fighting for a prize, has been existent. The Greeks, who trained all of their young warriors to fight with their fists, also featured boxing as a part of their Olympic Games. Winning boxers were treated as human Gods and in essence represented the early manifestation of the sports hero. That the sport has survived for a millennium speaks to its purely visceral nature.

However, the relationship between prizefighting and modern boxing is much the same as the brotherhood shared between cricket and baseball. Though both contests are based in similar principles, each has their own unique and wholly different characteristics, making them entirely their own sport. Though rooted in the same basic activity, in the case of baseball and cricket, hitting a ball with a bat, they are in essence more different than alike. Prizefighting and boxing share the same distant relationship

Although commonly called the predecessor of modern boxing, prizefighting was not boxing. It was human combat with the body as the sole weapon, governed for almost 100 years by seven simple rules. These concise and direct rules, (see appendix B), and the observation of them, were the only barriers that separated prizefighting from the realm of the barbaric.

Unlike boxing, where combatants are restricted to the use of gloved fists, prizefighting incorporated and allowed for a plethora of martial arts. Gouging, hair pulling, grappling, wrestling, choking and in some cases biting and scratching, were all acceptable during the early years of the prize ring. Hitting with the fist was the main choice of attack, but it was often times these other manners of assault that separated the victor from the vanquished. Men fought for hours on end, in open-ended, fight to the finish contests that in many cases balanced not on who was the most skilled man, but who was the greater glutton.

This initial volume of the *Caramel Colored Kings: Black Genesis* is the story of the black prizefighter, from his entrance into the game up through the end of the true bare-knuckle era (1760-1870). Encompassing roughly 100 years, and several different nations, the tale of the black prizefighter is one of curious inclusion, systematic segregation, grand victory and harsh defeat.

In 1897, Richard K. Fox published the first known history of the black prizefighter entitled *The Lives and Battles of Famous Black Pugilists*. This magazine style work, printed on Fox's own *Police Gazette* press, was basically a collection of

Black Genesis

Black Genesis

✦

The History of the Black Prizefighter
1760–1870

Kevin R Smith

iUniverse, Inc.
New York Lincoln Shanghai

Black Genesis
The History of the Black Prizefighter 1760–1870

iUniverse, Inc.

For information address:
iUniverse, Inc.
2021 Pine Lake Road, Suite 100
Lincoln, NE 68512
www.iuniverse.com

ISBN: 0-595-28884-7 (pbk)
ISBN: 0-595-65928-4 (cloth)

Printed in the United States of America

For Dee, The Duke, Bo-Bo and the Little Man

Contents

biographical sketches gleaned from Pierce Egan's *Boxiana*, Henry Miles' *Pugilistica* and the *Police Gazette* itself. Commendable in its intent, *The Lives and Battles of Famous Black Pugilists*, was little more than re-hash of old hat, hastily put together by an over ambitious editor. Its main focus was not historical accuracy but rather fanciful biography; Fox trying mainly to sell more of his "sheets" to the boxing crazy public. However, despite its shortcomings, Fox's volume was the earliest of its kind and the first real attempt by anyone to detail the lives and careers of the sport's black practitioners.

The second attempt to chronicle the journey of the black pugilist was Nat Fleischer's far more ambitious *Black Dynamite* series that began publication in 1938. Released in five volumes, Fleischer's work was both heavily flawed and repetitious. Nat, using the same sources as Fox, and in some cases simply plagiarizing directly from *The Lives and Battles of Famous Black Pugilists*, brought little to the table in terms of historical research. His first volume, which covers the bare-knuckle period, is shameless in its un-credited reiteration of Fox's work and in essence was a cheap re-write of *The Lives and Battles of Famous Black Pugilists*. Fleischer was also unabashed in his use of poetic license, making up sources and fictionalizing events when unable to unearth the true facts. Some of his conclusions are downright ludicrous and have done more to further mystify and confuse the history of several of these fighting men than to clarify their lives, careers and impact. (Examples of Fleischer's lack of true research and dedication to his subject are glaring in some portions of his work. In his chapter on Sambo Sutton, he intertwines the career of Sutton with that of Young Sambo, in essence claiming that they were one in the same. Sambo Sutton and Thomas Welsh, aliasYoung Sambo were two different fighters in two separate weight classes. In another chapter he lists Bob Travers birth name as Charley Jones, when in fact Travers was merely trained early on in his career by an old time pugilist named Charley Jones. These very same mistakes were found, verbatim, in Fox's *The Lives and Battles of Famous Black Pugilists*, further illustrating Fleischer's lack of true research). Despite his supreme dedication to the sport of boxing, and his reputation as one of the sport's great historians, Fleischer's work on volume one of the *Black Dynamite* series was less than adequate. Never the less, *Black Dynamite* remains popular even today, and although now known to be inaccurate, still used as a reference point for anyone studying the history of the black prizefighter.

Arthur Ashe's impressive three-volume set, *A Hard Road to Glory*, published in 1988 was the next work to recount the history of black pugilists. Initially broken down into three separate volumes, each covering the participation of black athletes in a plethora of sports over a specific time period, Amistad press later issued single volume works dedicated solely to one sport. Thus, in 1989, *A Hard Road to Glory: Boxing* was published and represented only the third work to devote itself entirely to the history of the black prizefighter. (In 1991 Dr. Charles Saunders published his work *Sweat and Soul* which was devoted to the history of the black boxer, but focused mainly on those from Canada). Ashe's work was commendable but far from complete. The main issue dogging Ashe and his staff was their choice of resources. Relying heavily on Fleischer's *Black Dynamite* and other secondary sources, such Ociana Chalk's *Pioneers of Black Sport*, as well as glossing over some of the more important black careers of prizefighting's early days, *Hard Road to Glory: Boxing* failed to bring any new perspective or clarity to the subject.

It was my frustration with the lack of accuracy and overall availability of information regarding the early black prizefighters that led me to research and write *Black Genesis*. It was not my aim to make this book the end all, be all of black boxing history. Rather, it was my intention to pry from primary sources what I could of the facts and put them in a readable history. I did my best to flesh out the fact from the fiction and where necessary leave blank those points that I could neither substantiate nor explain. Through this methodology, I hope to both inform and entertain, and in the end, add a chapter to the history of boxing that has largely been ignored for a better part of two centuries.

1

Stepping into the Light

Modern prizefighting has always been an English sport. Although introduced and practiced for several hundred years by the ancient Greek Olympic boxers and that of the Roman Gladiatorial boxers, prizefighting's modern genesis occurred in the British Isles in the early part of the 18th century. James Figg, who in 1719 opened his famous amphitheatre where he taught sword and single stick exercises as well as the "noble art of self defense", re-introduced the sport to the world, and began what has now been an English passion for close to three hundred years. But the recorded entrance of the black prizefighter into this world of modern prizefighting would not occur for nearly 70 years after Figg first brought the "art" back from extinction. This could hardly be considered strange for it was not until late in the 17th century that many blacks could even be found on the shores of the British Isles.

The history of black people in Britain certainly goes back many centuries—well before the reign of Queen Victoria. There were Black people in Britain in Roman times, and there has been a continuous black presence in the British Isles since 1555. But it was not until the end of the 17th century that this presence would become significant. Slavery—"the trade in black people and the fruits of their labor"—became a lucrative trade, and its affects on the social landscape were widespread and easily visible, especially in London and in the port cities. London had several pedestrian thoroughfares named for African peoples: Black Boy Alleys, Black Boy Court, Blackamoor's Head Yard, Blackamoor Street, and many Blackamoor's Alleys. Sometimes the street names reflected the nature of the businesses found there; other times, the people living there. Slaves were sold at auctions and Africana decorations (busts of 'blackamoors') were popular. African servants, freedmen, and fugitive slaves were common in seaside towns, and Bristol, Liverpool, and Cardiff had black communities. Freedmen and runaway slaves created vibrant free black communities. In London, the possession of young black slaves as pages—the darker the better to contrast with the artificially-enhanced whiteness of their owners—had become both a fad and a badge of elitism. Given classical Roman and Greek names and dressed in silks and satins, black slave pages paraded behind their owners, especially women, carried their owners' small dogs, and attended to the whims of their masters and mistresses. Their likenesses also appeared in their master's portraits to show their owner's status level and wealth. Such badges of prosperity were not confined to the aristocracy and elite, however. In a 1765 publication, *The Character of a Town Misse*, the author states that the "town misse" or "'the fashionable high-class whore of the period hath always two necessary Implements about her, a *Blackamoor*, and a little *Dog*; for without these, she would be neither *Fair* nor *Sweet*.'" Interracial marriages were not unusual, since the numbers of black men far outpaced the black female population. Cultural evidence abounds—from paintings, prints, and engravings to popular novels and plays—that working-class white women, during the eighteenth-century, at least, were not averse to marrying black men.

By the 1760s, the Black population in Britain had grown to somewhere between 20,000 and 40,000; Granville Sharp estimated the number of black servants in London alone at 20,000, in a city of 676,250 people. Many had attained freedom—or run away from their masters. In 1772, Lord Chief Justice Mansfield's historic decision in the case of runaway John Somerset ruled that a slave could not be deported from Britain against his or her will. This was the beginning of the end of slavery in Britain itself, and an encouragement to Black people and to abolitionist campaigners. An Act of Parliament confirmed the abolition of slavery in 1806.

As the 18th century drew to a close, Britain's Black population was well established, breaking free from slavery—but remained as a unit very poor and sometimes destitute. The first-generation immigrants were overwhelmingly male, supplemented by arrivals of Black sailors, plus 4,000 Black Loyalists who had fought for George III against the United States during the American Revolution. Black people integrated and intermarried into poor white urban populations, and entered the nineteenth century sharing in the misery and historical anonymity of the British poor.

Into this cauldron of strife strode the black prizefighter. Obviously from the re-popularization of the sport of fighting in the 1720's until late in the 18th century, boxing was dominated almost exclusively by white men, a few bouts between women the only exception to the rule. The written history of pugilism did not record one instance of a black man participating in an organized prize-fight until 1791. This is not to say that no black man had ever taken part in a boxing match, but these deeds, if they had occurred did not hold any significant meaning to the men who chronicled the storied history of the sport. So then the question must be asked; who was the first black prizefighter?

In answering this question it must be admitted with a certain amount of humility, that no such question could ever truly be answered. Black men no doubt took part in organized fighting in the ancient civilizations of Africa, Rome and possibly even Greece, but no record survives which could truly place such an appellation on any one man. However, even narrowing our query to modern times and location (which in the case of modern pugilism's infancy the location would be England) the true answer may never be known. The following list of men and their accomplishments attempts to bare out the facts of the lineage of the black pugilist, but still, it cannot be considered beyond reproach.

For many years the man who held the distinction as history's first black prize-fighter was Joe Lashley, whose name appears in both Pierce Egan's *Boxiana* and in Dowling's *Fistiana*. However, closer examination fleshes out that history had recorded a few earlier pugilistic encounters in which a black man had been a participant, the first of whom was a French mulatto.

Chevalier de St. George

Joseph Boulogne, more commonly known as Chevalier de St. Georges, was born to a member of the French Parliament and an African mother. St. Georges, who was birthed in Guadalupe but reared and educated in France, was known as a consummate violinist and composer, a superb athlete, swordsman, military commander and huntsman. Though his name held the title of French nobility, his African heritage made him ineligible to claim the spoils of such a title. Today he is better known for his musical talents, the fruit of which bore assorted sonatas, string quartets, and some of the more popular love songs of his day, however it was his athletic prowess that earned him a unique place in the history of pugilism.

St. Georges visited England for a six-month period sometime between the years of 1765 and 1767. There he was treated to a grand reception and feted on by some of the more important citizens of London, including the Prince of Wales, later to be known as King George IV. St. George treated his hosts to fantastic displays of shooting skill, dancing and ice skating as well as solo violin concertos which he was said to have performed with his riding whip as opposed to a traditional bow. But, Georges' most masterful displays were those he performed with the sword and cudgels. A feared and revered swordsman, Georges had taken part in several duels before he had turned 21 and had also beaten such illustrious masters as Faldoni of Italy, the Chevalier d'Eon and Captain Telfer in organized matches. By the time he came to England he was considered to be unparalleled in the use of the sword. But even though most of those who met Georges found him both humble and fantastic, there were those who found fault in his color. According to JA Rogers in his book *The World's Great Men of Color*, St. George was, "a master at everything and his conduct was so perfect withal that his enemies could find but one thing to pin their meanness on, and that was his birth and racial descent." St. George had been the victim of racial slurs for most of his life. In one instance while walking on the Rue de Bac a passerby called Georges a "moricaud", which was the French equivalent of "darkey". According to Rogers, Chevalier responded by grabbing his antagonist by the collar, thrashing him, rubbing his face in the dirt on the street and remarking, "there you are now, as black as I am."

It was a racial slur that prompted St. Georges' entrance into the pages of boxing history. An English Dragoon had seen Chevalier work with his sword and figured that as a cavalryman his swordplay was a notch better than the black Frenchmen's. He asked St. George to have a go with him but the latter declined insisting that he had no desire to combat any of the "King's men." The Dragoon took offense and in turn called Chevalier a "black scoundrel". St. George, who did not stand for such offenses, immediately agreed to the challenge and the two men, along with a host of onlookers, retired to a private gymnasium to settle the dispute. St. Georges' had little difficulty in mastering his foe and within a few short moments had disarmed his man and placed his blade at his neck. Outraged, the soldier challenged Chevalier to fight with his fists, commenting that the latter would stand little chance in a test of the "English Art". To this trial St. Georges gladly agreed. The men neither bothered to strip nor remove their wigs but instead immediately took to fighting. St. Georges astonished the entire collection of onlookers by smashing the Dragoon to the floor with two quick blows. So mastered was the Englishman that he immediately surrendered the contest. The fight so intrigued one onlooker, an artist known as Austin, that he immortalized the event in a sketch entitled, "St. George and the Dragoon." Despite his impressive triumph, St. Georges' left England shortly thereafter and never again tried his hand at pugilism.

St. Georges' impromptu mill with the English soldier may not be the first true occasion of a black man involved in battle of the "English Art". However, it may be considered the first recorded instance, for even though the details of the fight are a bit vague and the story a bit romanticized, the drawing of the event is no doubt proof of its occurrence.

Higgins 1778

There are only two references to the man named Higgins, one listing him as *black*, the other making no mention of his color. In the 1841 edition of *Fistiana: The Chronology of The Ring*, as well as subsequent versions, a fighter by the name of Higgins, listed as a black man, fought and was defeated by Joe Wood, The Weaver on July 23, 1778. Eagan's *Boxiana* also discusses the bout between Higgins and Wood but states that Higgins was a native of Birmingham, England who had won fifteen prize ring contests without a defeat prior to his bout with Wood. He further adds that Higgins was a "bottom" fighter evidently meaning he relied on his strength and durability as opposed to science in winning his contests. Egan makes no note of Higgins color. This would lead one to believe that Higgins was in fact not a black man. It would be rather odd for such an important characteristic to be left out of a fighter's description. Egan was known for his attention to detail and to believe that he would overlook such a significant fact is nearly impossible.

Unknown Black 1786

Indicative of the difficulty in naming the earliest black prizefighter to leave his mark on the sport is the following excerpt from the *The Times* (London), April 27, 1786.

"Yesterday afternoon a most desperate battle was fought in the Ring, in Hyde Park, between a butcher's apprentice of St. James Market, and a black stripling, who was lately a servant to the celebrated Mr. Katterselto, which lasted upwards of three quarters of an hour, during which time the successes of the combatants was as dubious as it was obstinate. The Honorable Mr. Booth by happening to pass at the time, the crowd took his attention time enough to see a sufficiency of the conflict, to prove to him, that the parties were obstinately bent on each side not to yield. Struck with the ferocious obstinacy, he stepped into the ring, parted the lads, and gave them a guinea each to make up the quarrel. The Black, though he bears the character of meekness and sobriety, has been unfortunate enough to have been obliged to fight no less than five scuffling battles within this week, all with young men of superior strength and proven victorious."

No mention of the "black stripling's" name is made by the *Times*, but it was evident that he was called upon to fight quite frequently. That he had won these contests, five in all, was proof that he was a "fighting man" and possibly a pugilist of some merit. His trade was obviously that of a servant or valet and not a prize-fighter; however, it was not uncommon for men to settle disputes with public fistfights. These fights were in many cases, neither impromptu nor unorganized. In fact, in England during this time, the prizefight had replaced the far more dangerous and morbid duel, as the manly way of settling disputes. The cause for such disputes could range from the inane, such as stepping on another man's shoe, to the severe, perhaps bedding another man's wife. Undoubtedly the above fight was just this sort of affair: a grudge being settled. Why the black had to fight five times in one week, while obviously being a man with a reputation of "meekness", is difficult to ascertain. The most likely answer is the color of his skin often times made him the target of insults and charges. That this man chose to stand up for himself is also interesting, considering that at the time, slavery was still legal in England, and even free blacks were considered citizens in name only.

Joe Lashley "The African Black" 1791

Perhaps the first truly recorded instance of a black man participating in a prize-fight comes from Pierce Egan's *Boxiana*. In his small chapter on Tom Treadway, brother of the less successful Bill Treadway, Egan tells of the former's battle with Joe Lashley.

> "In Marylebone Fields, Treadway fought an African Black, of the name Joe Lashley on June 13, 1791. It proved a desperate conflict for thirty-five minutes, when Treadway was taken senseless from the scene of action. Lashley, during the battle, evinced great activity, skill and game, portraying knowledge of the art superior to most amateurs. Treadway never properly recovered from the effects of this severe contest."

Not much about Lashley can be derived from Egan's reference. Even his nationality, although listed as African, must be questioned. It is doubtful that Egan had the opportunity to interview or speak with Lashley himself, and his information on Joe's heritage was most likely second hand. It is therefore not beyond reason to assume that Lashley, because of the color of his skin, was simply considered or called an African. However, judging from the result of the bout and the fact that Treadway, who up until his bout with Lashley had never been defeated, it is evident that the black man could fight. Egan took mention of both his skill and his "game" or his fortitude—sighting that Joe understood and practiced "the art" better than most amateurs (who were in essence men who trained in the "art of self defense"). This was fairly high praise indeed, for it was thought and believed that only those who trained in the science could truly be successful in the prize ring. A novice, such as Lashley, was not expected to dominate a man such as Treadway, who had taken part in six prize-ring encounters without defeat and undoubtedly had been taught the science of fighting by a qualified teacher.

Unfortunately, Lashley's debut in the prize ring is the only surviving record of his fighting activity. Neither Egan nor later books, such as the highly detailed *Fistiana,* mentions his name outside of the Treadway affair. Judging from Egan's description, I find it doubtful that the Treadway mill was Joe's only contest, but undoubtedly it is the only one that remains on record. (Nat Fleischer, in the first volume of his *Black Dynamite* series, claimed that Lashley did fight again, killing his opponent "Stewey the Breakman" in a 1796 fight, but no other source supports this assertion. If Lashley had in fact killed Stewey, then he would hold the distinction of being the first black fighter to have killed another man in a recorded ring contest.)

2

The Black Terror

"But if there were no men at the tables who could have held their own against Jackson or Jem Belcher, there were others of a different race and type who had qualities which made them dangerous bruisers. A little way down the room I saw the black face and woolly head of Bill Richmond, in a purple-and-gold footman's livery—destined to be the predecessor of Molineaux, Sutton, and all that line of black boxers who have shown that the muscular power and insensibility to pain which distinguish the African give him a peculiar advantage in the sports of the ring. He could boast also of the higher honor of having been the first born American to win laurels in the British ring".

—Sir Arthur Conan Doyle's *"Rodney Stone"*

It is Bill Richmond who today is generally considered the first black fighter of note to make a true mark on the sport of prizefighting. Richmond must also be regarded as the catalyst by which so many other black prizefighters came to the fore. Through his combination of science, skill, wits, guile and bravery the road had been paved in England for all who would come after him. And it was under his sage guidance that many of the black fighters who postdated him entered the ranks, knowing well that to have Richmond in their corner was always an advantage.

Richmond could not have come from more humble beginnings. Born a slave in Cockhold's Town, now Port Richmond Staten Island, NY, August 5th, 1765, Bill lived under the cruel hand of bondage throughout the early years of his childhood. A wealthy loyalist preacher who called himself Charlton owned his mother and until his pre-teen years, young Bill lived under his rule as well. Around 1776, Richmond came to the attention of British general Hugh Percy, who was then the commanding general of British forces in New York during America's War of Independence.

Percy took Richmond in after the lad had acquitted himself nicely in a tavern brawl with several Redcoats. The fight took place in the horse yard of the Red Lion, a tavern on the Kill van Kull waterfront. Percy's own dispatches reveal what happened, "A young Blackamore was ostling the officers' mounts, and fetching water to the horses, when a corporal of the Brunswicke division chaffed the black boy and he did make sport of the ostler's colour. Two more Hessians joined in the folly, and one of them tripping the black boy a-purpose so that he dropped his water-can, spilling the lot. The stable-boy fetched his right hand sidelong to the corporal's great beak of a nose, then he layed into the other two Hessians with both fists set flailing. The three men were taller than the Blackmoor boy, and their arms more prodigious of reach. Still he easily payed them in full for their merriment, and laced his right fist again and once more into their ears and shoulders, his left arm parrying and blocking their efforts to hit him in turn until at the last, two of the Hessian rogues gave flight and ran, as the Brunswicke corporal fell to bleeding hard by the horse-trough. The Blackamore warrior triumphant, he fetched his water-can and went again to his work as if nought had occurred."

Richmond's success supposedly continued in contests, arranged by Percy as entertainment for his guests, against New York-based British soldiers. Although this may be true, it is difficult to believe. In 1776 Richmond would have been a boy of only twelve years of age, and it is highly unlikely that he would have been purposefully pitted against grown men in physical combat. Nevertheless, at some point, either by purchasing Richmond or by claiming him in the "name of his majesty's service", Percy took young Bill under his command as an attaché and servant.

Bill's association with the Percy led to his involvement in one of the more famous events of the time. On September 26, 1776 Nathan Hale, the now celebrated American spy, was executed by the British in New York for spying. Young Bill Richmond was one of the hangmen, his responsibility being that of fastening the rope to a strong tree branch and securing the knot and noose. Sketches and engravings of the event portray a rather youngish black man in the crook of the tree fastening the rope as soldiers prepare to hang Hale.

In 1778, Percy returned to England and brought with him young Bill Richmond. He enrolled Bill at a school in York where the latter spent five years gaining a rudimentary education. After "graduating" Richmond became an apprentice to a cabinetmaker and served out his two-year stint in such a capacity. Bill excelled at his work and his employer was quite fond of his hardworking assistant, both treating and paying him fairly well. Upon his release from his apprenticeship, Richmond stayed in the field as a journeyman, making himself a fine living in the process. Although his lot in life had turned out to be a rather fortunate one, and certainly much better than he could have expected had he stayed in America, there were still those who found the color of his skin a problem. In fact as it would turn out, Richmond's skin color was really what started his fighting career.

Sometime in the mid 1790's, Bill took employment as a personal valet to the infamous Lord Camelford, who was well known as a sporting man. Camelford was an ex-Navy captain who had been honorably discharged from her majesty's Navy after he was found not guilty of murdering his second in command after the latter had refused to carry out an order. Camelford was not only a fancier of the fights but a horse and dog man as well. He liked to watch the horses race but he loved to watch dogs fights. His own bull terrier, "Trusty", was famous by his own right. "Trusty", who later was known as "Belcher", after the famous pugilist Jem Belcher, had won 104 straight fights and retired undefeated in the "pit". Camelford was rarely seen in public without "Trusty" in the lead. The Lord was also known as a "swell", that liked to both dress and drink in style, Camelford frequented the horse tracks of York and with him he brought Richmond in tow. Being in the service of a Lord, Bill was often dressed in rather loud, colorful clothes upon his trips to town and to the races. This combined with the color of his skin often left him open to heckling and insults. Being rather level headed and often times simply not wanting to insult the reputation of his employer; Richmond always did his best to remain oblivious to his verbal assailants. However, one day at the races a bully became so threatening that Richmond had little choice but to defend himself. The ruffian was named Dockey Moore and he was known, as most bullies were and are, to pick on the weak and the meek. Moore, because of his great size, and the diminutive stature of Bill, took the young black man for an easy target and challenged him to a fight. Richmond, with the grace of Lord Camelford, accepted the challenge. The men "peeled" instantly and set to on a flat piece of lawn adjoining the racetrack. Twenty-five minutes later, Moore, after taking a fearful beating, called that he had "had enough". Richmond had settled one bully but he would find that beating one man would not be enough. Moore was a soldier by trade and when his comrades had heard of the thrashing that Richmond had placed on Dockey they vowed to find a man to take the measure of the "black". On his next visit to the races, Richmond found the challenges of two Inniskilling Dragoons awaiting him. He accepted and defeated both with little issue. Bill Richmond was now earning himself a reputation as a fighter.

Bill also had his troubles in town, however. On one occasion while walking the streets of York Richmond was accosted by a blacksmith who after verbally abusing Bill, proceeded to kick him in the thigh. Richmond kept his composure and told the blacksmith that if he wanted a fight he would be accommodated but in an appropriate place. The two men met the next morning at a mutually agreed location and Bill conquered his attacker in less than three minutes. On another occasion Richmond, accompanied by a woman friend, was attacked by a Frank Meyers. Myers, after calling Bill a "black devil", turned to his victim's companion and chastised and insulted her for being in the presence of a black man. Richmond again insisted that the men not fight on the street but at a more appropriate time and place. Myers agreed and the two men made arrangements to meet at "The Groves"(which was a local field area) the next morning. That next day, Richmond and a mob of curious onlookers waited nearly a full hour for Myers to show up only to be doomed by disappointment. As the crowd began to disperse, figuring that Meyers had thought the better of fighting, Bill remembered the cruel words that Frank had cast upon not only him but his female companion as well. Richmond figured Myers had to suffer more than a simple dent to his reputation and convinced the group to follow him up to Myers home, where Bill would induce him to fight or be branded a coward in front of a town full of witnesses. The mob found Myers at his home and shamed him into returning to the Groves in order to keep his engagement. Richmond and Frank set to and after only a few minutes, Myers was beaten to a pulp only to be saved by his wife who interrupted the slaughter.

Although Bill had proven more than capable of handling himself in street fights and "semi-professional" encounters, his ring escapades up until this time were little more than rough and tumble experiences. Richmond had yet to meet a true fighter in what would be considered a legitimate match but he did have a fair amount of exposure to the Prize Ring. As early as 1801, when Richmond was seen in the company of Camelford at the Joe Berks-Jem Belcher fight, Bill had been attending matches and learning a great deal about his trade. Camelford never considered Bill a prizefighter, but certainly valued him as a bodyguard of sorts. When England and France declared peace in 1801 after nearly a century of non-stop war, all of England celebrated. In display of jubilation for the war's end all of England placed lit candles in their windows; all that is except for Lord Camelford. He publicly denounced the peace treaty, stating that it was dishonorable to England and point blank refused to light a single candle in his home. The mobs of people who had taken to the streets for close to a week in celebration took exception to Camelford's snub and decided to storm his home. Camelford, keenly aware and prepared for trouble, had beforehand placed Bill Richmond in charge of gathering up a force of pugilists to defend his estate. When the mob attempted to storm the house, Richmond and the other pugilists fought them back stubbornly until the group of frenzied citizens realized that Camelford's hide was not worth such a price.

Richmond's entrance into the professional prize ring was a rather impromptu and chance happening. Having set out on the morning of January 23 1804 to Wimbledon Commons to witness a bout between Hen Pearce and Joe Berks, Bill made his first appearance to the "fancy". Because of the locality of the fight and the importance (Pearce and Berks were in essence fighting a sort of elimination contest to see who was to succeed Jem Belcher as Champion), the crowd who attended the fight was large and important. All of the big London sports were present and most of the "sporting money in England" could be found amongst the spectators. After Pearce had defeated Berks and George Maddox had disposed of a novice named Seabrook in three rounds, Richmond presented himself to the crowd and stated that he should like to "have a turn with a professional pugilist". Maddox, who was still stripped to the waist, looked at Bill and replied, "well coom Massa, thou needn't goo furder, for I'll take thee on meeself." Richmond, upon the prompting of Lord Camelford, accepted. Maddox was not a man to be taken lightly. A veteran of considerable success who had been fighting since 1792, George stood a head taller and weighed 20 pounds more than Richmond. From the first call of time the bout was a mismatch and when Bill received a fearful smash just under his right eye in the third round, which both blinded and dazed him, he quit. It was an inauspicious start for the young fighter and it took him nearly a year to find the confidence to re-enter the ring.

However, Bill did not spend his time brooding, but improving. Richmond studied the art of fighting and by practicing this art for hours upon end he developed a system that best suited his physical stature. At some point he realized that his speed and agility were his best assets and that they could be used in a manner to offset a stronger or larger man. He also was a true believer in the benefits of a good defense. Thus, Richmond developed a "strike and duck" or a "hit and get away" style that was quite revolutionary for its time. In an environment where men often times slugged away at each other in morbid contests of attrition, Bill Richmond devise methods that were truly ahead of their time. Lord Camelford was not blind to Richmond's action and after watching the pugilist working on his "system" of fighting for close to a year, Camelford felt Bill was ready for another crack at the Prize Ring.

In the spring of 1805 Lord Camelford convinced Richmond that he had enough natural skill to make some real money in the prize ring. He armed his young black attendant with a letter of introduction and descriptions of Bill's fighting prowess and sent him off to London in order to seek out a Mister Fletcher Reid. Reid was a wealthy member of the Fancy who, if willing enough to risk a few guineas on the young black man, could provide Bill with the proper backing and contacts to get a real fight. Upon finding Reid, Richmond proved sufficient evidence of his fighting prowess by stepping a few rounds with a local novice. Reid then backed Richmond for a few guineas against a London whip maker named Green. It proved to be money well spent for Reid as Richmond polished off his opponent in less than ten minutes.

Despite his performance against Green, Richmond found difficulty in finding another match. Most of the Fancy had remembered the beating he had taken at the hands of Maddox, and even Reid was reluctant to back Bill against big game. It was by happenstance then that Richmond would find his next opponent. As a member of a large crowd that had traveled to Blackheath on May 21, 1804 where Cribb and Ikey Pig were to battle for 100 pounds, Bill had little idea that he would be fighting by the end of the day. After Cribb had forced Pig into submission in less than 25 minutes, the crowd, who was largely Jewish, was both dismayed and dis-satisfied with the day's activities. A purse of ten guineas was raised and offered to any man who would "set-to" with another Jewish fighter by the name of Young Youssop(Joseph). Richmond, without hesitation accepted the fight. A newspaper of the day reported the particulars of the bout as such:

"The men stripped, shook hands, and set-to without loss of time. The battle was well contested, neither man flinching from his work or falling without a knockdown. For the first and second rounds Youssop showed off his dexterity, and this superiority he particularly displayed in the third round when he stopped Richmond neatly and followed him up till he drove him nearly out of the ring. He did not however, seem to mark or hurt his man. In the fourth round Richmond improved and following up his opponent in turn gave him several desperate blows in the face, sadly to the disfigurement of the Mosaic countenance. Youssop gave way altogether, and at the close of the sixth round declared, like Ikey Pig, "He'd have no more of it". Richmond accordingly was proclaimed the conqueror, and pocketed the stakes."

Richmond's apt destruction of Youssop earned him both a reputation and a ring sobriquet, "The Black Terror". His performance also earned him the renewed interest of the wealthy Fletcher Reid. Reid's confidence was fully displayed when he agreed to back Bill against Jack Holmes that summer at Cricklewood Green. Richmond, displaying all of his "science" mastered the tough Holmes and put the quietus on him in less than 50 minutes of fighting. So extraordinary was Richmond's victory, and so impressed were the Fancy with both his skill and his uncanny ability to handle a larger man, that nary a lip curled when Richmond next challenged a young heavyweight named Tom Cribb.

Cribb was not yet at the pinnacle of his powers as a prizefighter when the fall of 1805 rolled around, however he was considered a game and tough up and comer. Richmond at this point was nearing 42 years of age: an age that was by and far considered to be well past that of a prime athlete. Cribb also constituted a strange challenge for Bill, for he was not only 20 pounds heavier and some 20 years the younger man, but also a fighter of "science". Tom Cribb was noted for his ability to "mill on the retreat", which in essence was a system of fighting that counted heavily on defense and counterpunching. Up to this point in his career, Richmond had made mincemeat of men who came to him: aggressive fighters who stressed the importance of attack at the sacrifice of defense. Like Bill, Cribb used angles and defensive tactics when he found that brute strength could not get the job done. That styles make fights could not have been more evident in the case of Cribb and Richmond. The question was whose skill and system would prove to be more effective?

Cribb and Richmond met at Hailsham, Sussex on October 8, 1805. The fight lasted 90 long and arduous minutes. Those customers who may have come to see blood shed were surely disappointed for the fight lacked anything that could be considered fierce action. Void of any real "milling" the battle was more of a chess match than a fight. Both men found it difficult to reach the other with any damaging blows and neither was willing to simply bore in and attack. Richmond, when he found that he could not penetrate Cribb's guard began, "hopping and dancing about the ring". Cribb for his part could not be persuaded to force the issue and steadfastly refused to lead, choosing instead to "stand in puzzlement". Documentation on the bout itself is scarce and in no chronicle of the Prize Ring does it state how the bout ended other than the simple fact that Cribb was declared the victor after 90 minutes. Whether or not Richmond failed to come to scratch, fell without a blow (which was an infraction of the rules at that time) or simply quit is unclear. What is clear is that any aspirations Bill Richmond had of fighting for the championship evaporated with his loss to Cribb. Tom Cribb, would go one to fight for the championship in his very next bout and win it, defeating Jem Belcher in just over 35 minutes (almost one third of the time it took Cribb to beat Richmond).

After his defeat at the hands of Cribb, Bill Richmond, retired from the prize ring and focused himself on teaching others. Fletcher Reid, who had both won a considerable amount of money on Richmond, and gained a great deal of confidence in his ability as a fighter, used Bill as both a trainer and a "second". In this capacity, Richmond was considered one of the best and he figured prominently in the training and seconding of such notable pugilists as Bob Gregson, John Gully and even Tom Cribb himself. Sometime before 1807 Richmond also became a "publican" or a saloon or Innkeeper when he opened the Horse and Dolphin on Saint Martin Street. This was a very successful venture for Bill and his opening and operation of the "House" demonstrated more than a few things about Richmond's mental capacities and ability to notice and take advantage of an opportunity. The Horse and Dolphin was located next door to the famous "Fives Courts", which was built in the mid 18th century to house games of "Fives" and tennis. In the late 1770's, Thomas Higginson who owned and operated the Courts, turned to sparring exhibitions as an added attraction. Although Higginson died in 1783, the Fives Court continued to be a gathering place for the Fancy and sparring matches and benefits thrived. Richmond's opening of his Horse and Dolphin Inn directly across the street from such an institution virtually ensured it success in catering to the fight crowd. But Richmond was also an active participant at the many Fives Courts benefits and sparring matches. In fact, it was Richmond who was responsible for two innovations whose effects can still be seen in modern boxing. When the Fives Courts began hosting sparring exhibitions, the matches would take place on the courts themselves, and the majority of the customers would stand at the same level straining to get a good view of the fight. It was Richmond who suggested that a 4ft tall raised stage be made so that all could see the action without interruption. The Court in turn built a removable stage that could be dismantled immediately after a night's sparring so that tennis matches could resume the next day. Bill was also the first fighter to spar without a vest or shirt. He announced that he chose to do this so that the spectators could gain a true appreciation for the muscular development of the fighter and the skill and agility of his movements.

During his retirement Richmond also became quite a gambler, winning far more than he lost, amassing himself a small fortune in the process. In these capacities, Bill made his living for close to three years when for one reason or another he decided to enter the ring again on April 14, 1808 at Epsom Downs against a man named Carter (not the famous Jack Carter, but a "country man from Nuneaton"). Richmond although well into middle age had little trouble with his foe and polished him off in less than a half an hour. Richmond must have liked the taste of success for he again entered the ring in the year 1808, on June 11 near Hendon where he fought and defeated a non-entity by the name of Atkinson in 20 minutes. Richmond's rekindled interest in the prize ring also brought about a new fire to settle old scores. He knew he had little chance of getting Cribb, who had since ascended to the championship, in the ring again, but Bill's first conqueror was a different story. In January of 1809, Richmond publicly challenged Maddox to a match but the latter, who was retired an 51 years old, declined. Undaunted, Bill continued to challenge Maddox but took a fight with an unknown named Ikey Wood who he thrashed at Combe Wood in lest than 20 minutes. Finally Maddox accepted Richmond's challenge and the two men met for the second time at Reculvers on Aug 9, 1809. So well respected was Maddox that even though he was over half a century old and had not fought in over two years he was a 6 to 4 betting favorite when the fight began.

The fight itself was as terrible a mismatch as the first Maddox-Richmond contest some five years earlier. However, this time it was Bill who was in control of the situation. From the first call of time Richmond mastered his man: and so badly beaten was Maddox in the first round, that upon the call of time for the second stanza, 4 to 1 was being laid on Richmond. The contest lasted 52 minutes, which was a great testament to the courage and pluck of Maddox for Bill Richmond practically butchered him. When the fight ended George was so dazed that he attacked Richmond when the latter had crossed the ring to shake hands. Maddox grabbed the unsuspecting Bill by the throat with one hand and punched with the other until exhausting himself and collapsing. For Richmond it was a great victory and one that firmly established his reputation as a first class ring practitioner.

Richmond did not again appear in the ring for nearly a year, and again it was an impromptu event. On May 1, 1810 Bill, along with Tom Cribb, John Gully, John Jackson and Tom Belcher had dinner at Bob's Chophouse in Holborn. It was a very festive night and after dinner the men enjoyed a good deal of spirits and ring chat. A few pair of mufflers were produced and some of the men began to spar. Growing bored with the stale action of the sparring, the men raised a subscription purse of 20 pounds for any two men to engage in a real contest. Tom Cribb's brother and Dogherty accepted the terms and agreed to set-to. Tom Cribb seconded his brother and Bill Richmond took care of Dogherty. The battle was a good one and lasted close to an hour before Cribb threw in the towel. At the end of the contest the noted pugilist Jack Power entered the Chophouse and offered to fight Richmond for a subscription purse of 18 Pounds. Bill although he was somewhat extended from his duties in the prior encounter, agreed. He and Power had never liked one another and both surely would have fought for free. The battle was not a very good one. With the exception of the first round, when Power had the better of the fighting, Richmond was always in control. He had little trouble avoiding the blows of the larger and stronger Power and repeatedly smashed him with left hand counters. It took less than 45 minutes for Richmond to settle Power and win his small purse. Power claimed that his defeat was the result of a drinking binge that had left him drunk and ineffectual upon setting to with Bill. But those who had seen the fight, including Tom Cribb who had seconded Richmond during the battle, refused to accept Power's excuses. It was generally accepted that even stone sober, Power's bull rush style would have little chance against the science, quickness and pluck of Richmond.

It was at this point in his life that Richmond again retired from active participation in the prize ring. He focused his attention on running the Horse and Dolphin as well as seconding and training other fighters. Bill also continued to spar at the Fives' Courts on a regular basis and began appearing at such prestigious theatres as Olympic Pavilion and the Regency Theatre. His reputation as a teacher was second to none and some of the more wealthy and famous people in London sought him out as a teacher. It was about this time that perhaps Richmond's most famous pupil walked into the Horse and Dolphin. He was a black slave from America named Tom Molineaux. He was uneducated, alone and knew little of the British art of fighting. Possibly because Richmond felt some sort of kinship with his fellow black American, or perhaps because he saw something in his eyes, he took in this big, black American and help turn him into one of the most ferocious fighters of his time.

Not only noted for his fighting skill, Bill Richmond was also well respected as a man and a member of society; looked upon as not only one of the great fistic minds of his time but also esteemed for his character and his knowledge of other subjects. Egan wrote, "We cannot omit stating that of our hero that he is intelligent, communicative, and well behaved: and, however actively engaged in promulgating the principles of milling, he is not so completely absorbed with fighting as to be incapable of discoursing upon any other subject; in fact he is rather facetious over a glass of noveau; his favorite wet with a swell."

Egan, in his many passages on Richmond, also noted that Bill was to be considered a very levelheaded and even keeled man. He ascertained from both his own dealings with Bill and from the many stories he had heard, that Richmond was unique in his ability to calmly deal with the very unique situation he was in. "In being a man of colour" Eagan wrote, "from the taunts and insults which he has received upon that account, particularly in his capacity as a publican, when he kept the Horse and Dolphin, Richmond must be considered good tempered and placid, even to a degree that could not be expected."

Bill's character and reputation was such that many viewed him with reverence and most considered him a credit to England and to the "noble art". This was fully evident when the George, the Prince of Wales, invited Richmond, among several other champions including Cribb, Belcher, Oliver and Gentleman John Jackson to exhibit before visiting dignitaries, including the Czar Alexander and the King of Prussia in April of 1814. George, who was a fan of the fights, extended an even greater honor to Richmond when he invited him, as well as several other prominent champions, to serve as ushers at his coronation as King of England in 1820.

Richmond must also be considered somewhat of a fitness guru. In the early 19th century men, even athletes, were not particularly noted for their training regimes. Bill on the other hand seemed to be a man of unique fitness. Egan noted, "Although 50 years of age(a length of years that few boxers arrive at), his appearance to a common observer portrays no more than 35, enjoying a good state of health, and not unmindful that it is necessary to preserve it. And what appears rather singular is, that at a time of life when other pugilists have long previously retired from the scene of action, the spirits of Richmond seem in such trim, that, with all the ardency of youth, he is still eager for a fray; and of whom, there is little doubt, if he were in possession of that quality(which must be served) youth—he would not be wanting of the support of the most distinguished of the Fancy, to become a leading boxer."

The sense of restlessness that Egan spoke of was not of the impetuous kind. Bill Richmond was anything but reckless and he knew that there was a time to fight and a time to resist. Bill stayed away from anything that could have been considered a real fight for close to four years. However, he maintained his strength and vigor by training daily and remaining active in the sparring and exhibition circuit that boomed in the London area at the time. However, in May of 1814, when the newly created Pugilistic Club had its initial meeting at Combe Wood, it was Bill Richmond who stepped forward to battle Jack Davis "The Navigator" for a purse of 50 pounds.(NOTE: The Pugilistic Club was one of the first attempts to organize a boxing league or organization. The Club was formed in the hope that all crosses and fixes, which were threatening to ruin boxing at the time, could be done away with all together. The club had its own ring stakes, a club secretary, a treasurer and consisted of about 120 subscribers, who paid an annual membership sum, which in essence paid for all the fight purses and the officials salaries. Purses were regulated, depending upon the quality of a particular contest and the men who were involved. The highest purse was fifty pounds and the lowest 10 guineas). Richmond's decision to fight was beforehand known only to him and there was great surprise when he announced his intention to set to. Bill weighed in at around 170 pounds while Davis weighed about ten pounds more. Jack was 24 years old, Richmond was 52. The first round was not a good one for the veteran. Davis, full of confidence, moved forward without fear of retaliation, and although struck several times by Bill, landed a tremendous blow to the latter's temple. Richmond was immediately grassed by the blow and visibly shaken. In the second round, Davis again overpowered Richmond and floored his older antagonist with another temple blow. It was not until the third round that Richmond's tactic of hitting and getting away began to take affect. Although the round ended with Davis throwing Bill, the latter had done the greater damage in the frame. From then on, Richmond's greater science and skill held the advantage over Davis' youth and strength. Describing the bout in *Pugilistica*, Henry Miles wrote, "The Black kept punishing, but received nothing; retreating, retreating and retreating again, and at almost every stop made woeful havoc on the nob of his adversary, completely showing the spectators what might be accomplished by scientific movements. At length he suddenly made a stand and his distance proving correct, with his right hand hit the mouth of Davis with such uncommon severity, that he went down like a log of wood."

The bout lasted just 13 rounds that were spread over 20 minutes. Bill was nearly unmarked, yet Davis was so brutally beaten that he had to be carried from the grounds. Once again Bill had proven his worth as a fighter as well as demonstrated the artistry and effectiveness of his ring craft. His reputation had been well intact prior to the match but it now soared to new heights. Those who were close to the sport now considered Richmond a nonpareil. Of his skill Egan wrote, "In the ring, in point of activity, he(Richmond) stands nearly unrivalled, and is considered to excel every other pugilist in hitting and getting away, and dealing out severe punishment with his left hand. It is also said of Bill, that for half an hour there is no danger in backing him with any of the fighting men."

Richmond continued to school new, would-be, prizefighters in the noble art and turned out some very good men. Not all of his men appreciated his strict ways however, and not all truly respected Bill Richmond the fighter. One of his students, the tough Tom Shelton, whom Richmond had introduced to the Fancy and backed in the latter's initial ring appearance, found Richmond's confidence annoying and openly accused the latter of being a "fake". Shelton insisted that he could beat "the old man anytime ole Bill wanted to try his druthers". Richmond, who could not be easily provoked, despised Shelton's talk, but did not take the bait. As Shelton's abuse became more public, Richmond simply banned him from the Horse and Dolphin and denounced him as dis-honorable scourge. Bill also knew that Shelton was fond of the drink and sooner or later his act would be looked upon by all as tiresome. Unfortunately, Tom Shelton would not go away. After being attacked physically by Shelton and a group of his cronies outside the Horse and Dolphin one evening, 53 year old Bill Richmond agreed to fight the 26-year-old Shelton.

The Shelton-Richmond contest took place at the popular Mousley Hurst on August 1, 1815. More than 10000 people had come from far and wide to see the grudge match. Shelton was attended to by Tom Cribb and Clarke, and Richmond was looked after by Tom Oliver and Ned Painter. The fight from the beginning was a brutal affair. Shelton was mad with rage and controlled the early rounds by rushing Bill with such force and ferocity that the latter could not escape. It was this system of fighting that soon proved the downfall of Shelton, for Richmond was known for his ability to use his adversaries advance to his own advantage. In the middle rounds, with his eye cut and swollen grotesquely, Bill began to take control of the match. He used his left hand to perfection and continually stabbed the head of Shelton as the latter attempted to rush. Soon the old veteran was hitting Tom with two and three punch combinations that were dreadfully effective. By the 23 round Shelton was a spent and beaten pulp. Miles noted, "It was distressing to see the punishment that Shelton brought upon himself from the rushing system he pursued. The right of the Black was at work like a sledgehammer…Richmond now had it all his own way and with the utmost sang froid planted so tremendous a blow upon Shelton's temple that he went down. The effects of the blow were so severe that Shelton appeared quite stunned and when time was called Tom could not quit the knee of his second. Richmond, elated with the success of victory, jumped out of the ring."

That Richmond was pleased with the thrashing he gave Shelton was evident, but he also knew that his body could no longer stand the rigors of such fierce combat. Bill again turned to training fighters and teaching at the Horse and Dolphin. In this role, he would again contribute greatly to the legacy of the black prizefighter. After the success and notoriety gained by Tom Molineaux (whose life and career will be discussed in the next chapter), a few black fighters appeared in London seeking the counsel and leadership of Bill Richmond. The veteran would serve them well, leading men such as Harry Sutton, Sam Robinson, Joe Stephenson and Jemmy Johnson, the next wave of black champions, into combat well versed in the art of prizefighting. As we examine their careers in future chapters, the influence and involvement of Bill Richmond will be both prominent and well evident.

Hereafter, Bill Richmond's life remained rather quiet. In 1818, he had one more fight that could be considered a prize ring appearance. Jack Carter, the Lancshire Hero would be his antagonist. Carter was a heavyweight prizefighter of some note, as well as a champion runner. He had made for himself quite a career of fighting, and defeating black men, all of whom had some connection to Richmond. In 1816, Carter had defeated two of Richmond's black pupils, Sam Robinson twice and Joe Stephenson once. Upon beating Robinson for the second time, Carter exclaimed that he was "king of the blacks". Richmond, who found Carter to be annoying and idiotic, did not like the statement and publicly answered by stating that, "Carter has not beaten all the blacks". Carter never took up this veiled challenge and Richmond never pursued the issue. It was not until two years later that the two would have the occasion to settle their differences. It was at a tavern in Chancery Lane, where both Carter and Richmond were enjoying the company of the friends and a few drinks. Inexplicably, Carter began announcing to the room that he could beat any man in the world, bar none. Most of those present laughed Carter off at first but he soon became violent and had to be bounced from the tavern. Upon the group, one of whom was Richmond, turning him out into the street Carter exclaimed, "is there any one among you who will dare to fight Jack Carter?". Richmond stated emphatically that he did not fear Jack in the least at which the latter challenged Bill to an immediate fight. Richmond accepted. The men, without ceremony, set to in the back yard of the tavern with maybe 100 spectators now present. The bout was quick and decisive, Bill Richmond ending matters with his famed right hand in the third round. Upon being floored and having a few of his teeth knocked from his mouth, Carter looked up at Bill and stated, "I've been finely served out this evening".

In 1818, Richmond closed the Horse and Dolphin and moved his gymnasium down to the Whitcom Street, Haymarket. It was there that Bill trained and taught Lord Byron the finer points of the game. Byron describes some of his time with Richmond in his "Life and Journals" and it is quite evident that the Lord, who had also taken lessons from the famed and revered Gentleman John Jackson, felt that Richmond was one of the finest pugilist he had ever seen.

Not much is known about Bill Richmond's personal life. He did at one point marry, but to whom and when is not known. He had at least one son, who after a brief and disastrous prize ring career, turned to teaching boxing full time. Young Richmond eventually taught sparring to England's student elite at both Cambridge and Oxford Universities. Bill lived out the remainder of his life in relative peace. His gym prospered and like always he never wanted for patrons. His impact would continue to be felt in the Prize Ring as he occasionally consented to training or seconding a young fighter. It is important to note almost every black fighter who appeared in the English Prize Ring during the years 1810-1829, had some contact with Bill Richmond. He was in a sense the pioneer for the black fighters who came only a few years after his twilight and decades later. He led an exemplary life, carried himself as a gentleman and earned the respect of a nation who was not used to equality for non-white people. Richmond died at his home, now on Titchbourne Street, Haymarket on December 28, 1829. He was sixty-six years old.

3

The Tremendous Man of Color

If there were a more tragic figure in the history of the Prize Ring than that of Thomas Molineaux, it would be difficult to unearth it. His was a tale of bondage and freedom, of poverty and success, of grand victory and tragic defeat, of heroic stature and human frailty. Tom Molineaux was more than simply a black pugilist, he was a complicated bundle of irony; a man both made and destroyed by his own simple ignorance and fiendish vanity, a soul both tortured by its own lack of discipline and bathed in its own jubilee of freedom. Tom, as he was known to those close to him, was anything but a uncomplicated "black buck": for no ordinary man could have crossed the Atlantic without money, friends or the fondest hint of a plan, with the sole purpose of picking a fight with the world's best pugilist. And certainly, when he arrived in England, Thomas Molineaux was, as Pierce Egan noted, "unknown, un-noticed, unprotected and uninformed".

Molineaux's life began sometime around 1784 in the southeastern part of the United States. His place of birth has been variously reported as Baltimore, Georgetown, New York and Virginia, but may never truly be known. It is likely that Tom was born as a slave in the southern United States, most likely Virginia as he claimed. (NOTE: Most of what is known today of Molineaux's early life came from the fighter himself, and must be considered to be based in some truth, yet not wholly accurate. Pierce Egan, the author of *Boxiana*, and perhaps the only contemporary chronicler of Tom Molineaux's life, never published an "interview" of Tom, but judging from the information that he provided in his sketches of the fighter, surely had interviewed him on several occasions. Most secondary works, including Nat Fliescher's 1938 *Black Dynamite*, gained a great deal of their information on Molineaux from the work of Egan. Without his labor most of what is now known of Tom Molineaux's character and early life would indeed be lost. However, even Egan was subject to the whimsical memory of an un-educated Molineaux, whose character was not beyond the stretching of the truth, when and where it was applicable; or simple fiction in place of true memory. Again, all of what is today known of his life and career prior to his arrival in England, was undoubtedly told to Egan and others by Tom himself and therefore subject to some scrutiny and doubt as to its authenticity).

Tom himself proclaimed to be an ex-slave. Not a runaway, but a "free man". His freedom, as he told it, was won by fighting. He claimed to have been "set free" after winning his master a considerable amount of money by defeating a fighting slave from a neighboring plantation. It is a rather difficult story to believe as well as one that is nearly impossible to substantiate. "Slave fighting" of the nature that Molineaux spoke of, where men were maimed and sometimes killed, was surely present but not abundant. Slaves, especially strong, young males, were a commodity in the South during that time and it seems unlikely that pitting them against one another would be a good business practice for their owners. However, this story has been generally accepted throughout the written history of Tom Molineaux's life as being at least based in some fact. But, compounding these bare facts are decades of writers using poetic license to juice up and/or romanticize the Molineaux story even further. Fred Henning in his sometimes fanciful, *Fights for the Championship* went as far as to state that Tom and his young master Algeron Molineaux were boon companions. Henning lists the details of their relationship and claims that Algeron hired a British Sailor named Davis to assist Molineaux in learning the "British art of fighting" and training.

According to Henning it was Davis that then brought Tom to New York, where the latter won several battles, and convinced the black pugilist that he could make some real money fighting in England. Nat Fleischer, the founder of "Boxing's Bible" *The Ring* and one of the sport's great historians, claimed in his *Black Dynamite* series to have found proof that Molineaux's father, Zachary, was a fighter and so too were his four brothers. Fleischer takes his assertion a step further by insisting that it was Zachary Molineaux who was the first prizefighter in the United States! Mr. Fleischer, although well respected as both a publisher and boxing historian was often times prone to both fits of acute egoism and storytelling. He provides quotes from his supposed sources but never identifies them by name. It is safe to assume that Fleischer, like later writers, pieced most of what he wrote on Molineaux together from Egan's work adding his own spicy embellishments. But however unlikely the details of Fleischer's and Hennings' description of Tom Molineaux's early life may be, it seems that Tom himself claimed to have come from a fighting family.

Egan, in his initial description of Molineaux, referred to the latter as, "descended from a warlike hero…feeling all the animating spirit of his courageous sire", obviously stating that Tom had claimed to have come from fighting stock. Fliescher wrote that Tom's father had been both a soldier and a bare-knuckle fighter; statements that may have been true but remain unsubstantiated by factual sources. Regardless of whether or not he had come from a fighting lineage or had won his freedom in such a manner, by 1804, it appears that young Molineaux was in New York fighting for a living. It is likely that Molineaux made his way to the Catherine Market, which was known as an area where "colored sports" could ply their trade. Filled with a motley mix of seamen, street performers, businessmen and lowlifes, the Catherine Slip at that time was one of the busier ports in New York. It is believed by this author that Tom won himself some sort of acclaim participating in the "rough and tumble" style of fighting popular in America at the time. These bouts were truly devoid of any science, ceremony, or skill and were rather crude and brutal. Nevertheless, fighting was fighting and somewhere along the line Tom Molineaux must have proven himself to be quite a battler. It is likely in fact that Molineaux first got the idea to travel to England from an English sailor who had seen him fight and thought him a worthy pug. However, this is mostly conjecture for his career in America has been lost with time. Who Tom fought, where exactly, and for what money and laurels is unclear. However, his opponents and his victories must have been of some importance, because when he did decide to leave for England, he carried with him the title of "Champion of America". Whether or not this was an honor bestowed upon Molineaux by others or a title he claimed for himself is also unknown. What is fact however is that Tom Molineaux was the first man to ever claim such a prize.

How Tom Molineaux, a man of no education, little money and few friends, made his way to England is also a point for debate. Some suggest that he stowed away on a sailing ship, and worked as a cook and porter when discovered while deep at sea. Others maintain that Tom took his ring earnings and paid for his own passage across the big pond, taking part in a few improtu matches with several of the crew during the month long voyage. It is more likely however that Tom "signed" on as a crewmember with some ship and "earned" his passage in that capacity. (Several sources claim that Molineaux sailed upon the ship *Bristol*, but again this fact has never been substantiated). In the end it may be unimportant how Tom got to England, for it is clear that he made it to the British Isles by the winter of 1809. Once there he sought out, or was told to seek out, Bob Gregson a top notch English heavyweight at the popular, Bob's Chop House a standard gathering place of the fight crowd. Gregson, either seeing no future for the black American, or figuring he had a better chance making it through the leadership of "one of his own", sent Tom to Bill Richmond.

Richmond was not impressed with Molineaux, for the latter was probably a ragged mess, and by no means in any position either socially or physically to present himself as a wanting fighter to the well respected Bill. However, feeling some sort of kinship for his fellow black American, Richmond took Tom in. When Molineaux expressed his intentions to challenge Tom Cribb, Richmond scoffed. He figured Tom for a simple fool and initially considered him nothing more than a novelty. However, Bill Richmond was anything but a dupe and figured if Tom was so willing to fight there would be no harm in making a little money off his new student. Bill took to training Tom and was even less impressed with what he saw from the American.

It must be assumed that Tom Molineaux was a crude fighter in the literal sense of the word. His physical makeup was impressive, but his skills were lacking. The differences between the American style of "rough and tumble" fighting and England's "pugilism" were as distant as possible. When Molineaux first sparred for Richmond, he undoubtedly displayed some of his more unsophisticated techniques, one his most glaring inadequacies being the manner in which he threw his right hand punches. Tom knew the rudiments of jabbing, but when he threw his right hand behind it, it was neither straight nor effective. He would instead close with an opponent and bring the blow down in a hammer type motion, striking with the bottom of his clenched fist as opposed to his knuckles.

It was a maneuver that spoke volumes of the kind of fighting Tom Molineaux had done in America.

Richmond did his best to straighten out some of Tom's bad fighting habits prior to matching him in a true fight, but Molineaux was still displaying some of his makeshift techniques shortly before his first "official" bout. In the spring of 1810, Richmond decided to match Tom with some second rate pugilist so that he could measure his man's abilities. He threw down the gauntlet by announcing that he "would match his new dark horse against any inferior man". This in essence meant that Richmond was willing to back Tom against any fighter besides the obvious top-flight men. Nothing was heard from any quarter until Tom Cribb himself approached Richmond with an offer for Molineaux to fight Cribb's unknown novice. This novice was in fact a man known as Jack Burrows, who although he had never shown in a real prize ring contest, had displayed an adequate knowledge of fighting at the Fives Court in several sparring exhibitions. Richmond agreed to Burrows as an opponent and the two sides agreed on a stake of 50 pounds per side with the battle to be held at Tothill Fields in Westminster on July 24, 1810.

Neither Richmond nor the rest of the some 300 "Corinthians, amateurs and sports" who gathered at the aforementioned location knew what to expect from "the new black" as Tom was now being called. The physical makeup of the men gave little indication to the outcome of the battle as when stripped Burrows stood nearly six feet and weighed close to 210 pounds, his skin pasty yet firm. Molineaux, his skin glistening, was in top shape, and his muscles bulged beneath his dark skin, their every movement in plain sight for the bustling crowd to study. It was noticed that in size, Molineaux was far outdone by the Bristol man, but in muscle and development, Tom Molineaux had no peer. When the men were called to scratch, Tom Cribb and his brother George attended to Burrows, and Bill Richmond and Clarke seconded Molineaux. There must have been a great sense of curiosity by all those involved, for nothing like Tom Molineaux had ever been seen in the English Prize Ring before. How would this man bred on "American" fighting fare against a learned novice of the "noble art"?

Most of the initial questions about Molineaux's abilities were answered in the first minute of the fight. Boring in on Burrows at the call of time, Molineaux walked through a fearful smash straight on his forehead and sailed into Burrows with both fists. Tom knocked his adversary to the grass with his "hammer blow" which he "used to great affect upon closing with Burrows ". In the first round of his very first trial in England, Molineaux, in the space of a few moments had proven himself to be a man to reckoned with. Not only had he displayed a great ability to deal out punishment, but he also demonstrated that it would take a man with considerable strength and power to hurt him. His bout with Burrows dragged on for an hour, more or less because of Molineaux's inability to finish the tough, game Burrows, and his inexperience in fighting under a new set of rules. It is safe to assume that when Tom fought in America there were no true "rounds", meaning that when a man was sent to the ground his adversary was allowed to set upon him and punish him until either the floored man escaped or gave in. In the British ring such tactics were not allowed and when a man was floored that ended the hostilities for thirty seconds. Molineaux's unfamiliarity with such a format probably explains the duration of his bout with Burrows, for it is more than clear that Molineaux had little difficulty in mastering him. Eagan noted that, "Molineaux punished his opponent so severely that it was impossible to distinguish a single feature in his face". After Burrows eyes had been closed and the breath literally beaten from his body, Tom Cribb threw in the sponge signaling the defeat of the Bristol man and the virgin victory of Tom Molineaux on English soil.

It was also the first time that Molineaux was to meet Tom Cribb in person. After knowing him only by name, Tom could now place a face to the name that had brought him nearly 3000 miles from home. Cribb undoubtedly was not too impressed or intimidated by what he saw of Tom Molineaux on that day. Cribb probably was confident, after watching Molineaux in action that he had little to fear from the black invader. However, in an odd twist of irony, Molineaux too had a chance to size up the champion. After the fight had ended, Cribb approached Richmond and apparently complained that Tom had fouled Burrows. Bill took offense to the remark and the two men began to fight. The battle did not last long as neither man was inclined to fight long for free, but it lasted long enough for Tom to see Cribb in action.

Richmond was pleased with Tom's performance and by many accounts so too were many of the wealthy "Corinthians" who witnessed the contest. One such man, Lord George Sackville a younger brother to the Duke of Dorset, claimed that Molineaux was the equal of any man on the British Isles and offered to back Tom in his quest to unseat Cribb. Bill Richmond was far more temperate in his assessment of Tom's performance and stood firm by his own theory that Molineaux needed more "seasoning". Bill was indeed hopeful that Molineaux had the ability to cope with Cribb, but felt that he needed a better gauge on Tom's overall fighting aptitude. For this he would need a man that could truly push young Tom. Burrows had proven to be a tough man, but he did not have the resume or the fighting ability to extend Molineaux. Richmond also wanted more time to work with his young protégé' in the hope of changing some of his poorer technique.

While Richmond sought out the correct opponent for Tom's next appearance, Molineaux worked daily on his skill and enjoyed a bit of celebrity. Being housed at the Richmond's Horse and Dolphin, Tom had the opportunity to mix with some of the Fancy and talk to them about his intentions of meeting and beating Cribb. At Richmond's watering hole, every part of society was represented, rich, poor, old and young, but all had one thing in common: the love of sport. The "new Black's" rather impressive defeat of Burrows had given Tom a bit of notoriety about town. Coupled with the fact that he was a rather, large imposing black man, Molineaux stood out wherever he went. Mostly Tom was a curiosity: a boisterous, black American prizefighter who rather fancied himself and his accomplishments. For the most part, the Fancy regarded Molineaux as "spice". That is to say, he brought a new life and new interest into a sport, which had recently seen some of its slower days in England. Cribb had been champion for several years and had, for all intents and purposes, cleaned up his challengers. Without a worthy challenger for the champion, the game had fallen into a small decline. Great fighters make great eras—great champions with mediocre challengers make for modest interest. So in the weeks after the Burrows contest, Molineaux was being viewed as "good for the game". No one, with the exception of a very few, thought that Molineaux's defeat of Burrows signaled him as a worthy challenger to Cribb. In actuality, it was because they did not see Tom as a threat that his popularity was such. Tom, who had probably never known any true celebrity, was surely smitten by the attention and basked in it whenever he could. Bill Richmond new there was danger in all of the interest being shown his new man, but cared little enough at the time to prevent it.

But if the men of England were to be labeled as curious about Tom Molineaux, the women must be labeled as enamored. Many women, most of little or ill repute, made no bones about their desires to "learn" about the "new black". Tom was not shy and partook of the pleasure that his newfound status brought. It was here, after his first victory that the seeds of Tom Molineaux's downfall were planted.

Bill Richmond worked with Tom diligently to try and fine tune his fighting style. He instructed him on how to properly fight "at a distance". Molineaux, who had a quick, powerful straight left hand, learned from Bill the technique by which he could "break a man's guard down" and deliver powerful, straight blows with his right hand. In practice, Molineaux learned quickly and thoroughly. His footwork improved, as did his guard.

A suitable opponent was found in short order. He was a rough, experienced man who would test the "black" like few, short of Cribb, could. His name was Tom Blake, nicknamed "Tom Tough". His appellation was appropriate and besides a keen knowledge of the game he had the ability to absorb tremendous amounts of punishment without yielding. In the spring of 1805 he had battled Cribb for an hour and half before yielding and in 1804 had beaten the well-known Jack Holmes over the course of 60 rounds. Although close to 40, and past his prime fighting years, Blake had spent the past several years at sea and upon returning was "as hard as nails, with a composition unimpaired and splendidly preserved by seafaring life". Blake also undoubtedly took part in more than one or two battles while at sea, and upon hearing of Molineaux and Richmond's challenge, was eager to give the "new black" a try. The largest obstacle for Blake was money. Richmond had sent his challenge out with a 100-guinea stake needed for those who accepted. Unable to raise the funds on his own, Blake visited Tom Cribb, who by now himself was curious about the black man's true abilities, in the hope that the latter could help him raise some funds. Cribb assured Blake that he would handle the money end and told the veteran to accept the challenge. The parties met at the Castle Tavern and agreed to fight for 100 guineas at Epple Bay near Margate on August 21, 1810.

The crowd who showed up to witness the Molineaux-Blake battle was considerably larger than that which had attended the "black's" previous mill with Burrows. There was a great deal of curiosity surrounding Molineaux's abilities, and much of the Fancy were keen to know how good he really was. It was a blistering hot day, and Molineaux was described as seemingly "reveling in the sunshine", while Blake "literally mopped his forehead with his bandana". In the first minute of the fight Molineaux displayed his new footwork and "distance" fighting when he and Blake sparred lightly. Tough Tom made the first move when he stepped in and broke down Molineaux's guard and planted two hits to the face. Molineaux fired off a return but Blake blocked it contemptuously. The men then closed and fought on the inside with Molineaux gaining the upper hand by seizing Blake and attempting to throw him. The veteran Blake was too experienced to be caught in such a trap and slipped away only to be caught on the back of the head by Molineaux's "hammer" blow. Seeing that his adversary was stunned, Tom repeated the blow and felled Blake. Molineaux's strength was again superfluously evident, as his awkward blow had nearly knocked Blake senseless. But when Tom returned to the knee of Richmond, he was scolded for using his favorite punch. Bill pleaded with Tom to straighten out his deliveries and use the "science" he had been taught. In the next round Tom did just that. Blake opened the round by landing three straight punches through Tom's guard, which although well placed, did not knock the American off his feet. According to Miles' Pugilistica, Molineaux, "received the hits with great Sang Froid and at length beat down his opponents guard with his left hand and with a degree of quickness and dexterity in which Dutch Sam or Tom Belcher would be considered an astonishing effort of science brought Blake down by a most severe blow with his right".

This exchange fairly settled the contest for it demonstrated that Blake did not have the power to hurt Molineaux (the first two blows of the fight, when Blake was at his best were landed flush) and did not have the ability to absorb the blows of the American black. The bout lasted another few rounds during which Blake was out crafted and out toughed. At one point in the fifth round Molineaux placed Blake under his left arm and punched him mercilessly with his right hand until the latter had fallen near insensible. The bout ended in the eighth round when Molineaux chased Blake into a corner and, after taking an ineffectual punch on the cheek, knocked Blake unconscious with a straight right hand punch.

If the Burrows battle had been Tom Molineaux's introduction to the English prize ring, the Blake bout was indeed his "coming out party". His display on that hot summer day truly elicited a sounding response. Henry Miles wrote in *Pugilistica*, "In this battle Molineaux evinced great improvement in the science of pugilism, particularly in the art of giving, while nature seemed to have endowed him abundantly with the gift of taking, his body being almost callous to fistic punishment. It was generally considered that should he be able to combine an equal degree of skill with his gluttony, he would mill the whole race of modern pugilists."

Miles sentiments echoed those of Pierce Egan, who wrote of Molineaux after his conquest of Blake, "In the above battle the amateurs were completely astonished at the improvement exhibited by Molineaux, and the punishment he dealt out was so truly tremendous and his strength and bottom so superior, that he was deemed a proper match for the Champion."

After the battle Tom was fairly un-marked despite the blows he had taken. Blake had managed to cut him underneath one of his eyes, but for the most part he was unscathed. Bill Richmond was more than pleased with Molineaux's performance, and perhaps because he was swept away in the moment, or truly feeling his man was ready—he instructed Tom that it was now time to officially challenge Cribb. The Blake victory however, did not hold only a bounty of good fortune, for it was now that Tom Molineaux, the foreign black "invader", became a serious threat to Tom Cribb. Some saw this as good for the game. Others were threatened by it. And Tom, who before the match had been viewed by most with curiosity and amusement, now became something of a more ominous symbol. Molineaux's race was not the only strike against him, for the fact the he was an American pulled at an even more delicate issue for the British. Those two qualities combined made for an almost unbearable thought: a black American becoming the Champion of England. Egan wrote of this phenomenon in *Boxiana* stating that after the Blake victory, "It was now the jealousy commenced, and the aspiring ambition of Molineaux to obtain the Championship of England, excited considerable anxiety and interest in the sporting world; the honor of the country was at stake,"

Richmond and Molineaux made their challenge of Cribb public not more than two months after Tom's defeat of Blake. Cribb however, maintained that he was indeed retired and had no plans of "coming back". Bill mounted a campaign to, in essence, goad Cribb into fighting and at one point Molineaux even publicly claimed the championship of England. It is interesting to note that although the honor of England was at stake, no fighter other than Cribb was considered worthy to contend with "The Terrible Black". Furthermore, most of the Fancy were so impressed with Molineaux's destruction of Tough Tom Blake, that even if another fighter felt he could defeat the American he would never be able to find a backer who shared that confidence.

Tom Molineaux again basked in his status. He thought himself near invincible at this point. He could often be found drinking and carousing at Richmond's tavern, telling anyone who would listen how he would thrash "Massa Cribb" if the two ever met in the ring. There were again those who found Molineaux likeable and considered his boasts to be founded in undeniable truth. Still there were many more who found him to be an uneducated animal with little grace and disgraceful social habits. Tom spent his time and his money on women, drink and fancy "duds". He paraded himself about town in colorful clothes, flashing his newfound wealth with childlike audacity. Bill Richmond, who knew well the racism he had encountered because of the color of his skin, must have warned Molineaux that such behavior would lead to bad things. But Tom was both ignorant and stubborn. He probably viewed all the attention he received as genuine and good-natured. He only knew that he was the center of attention, and as he would demonstrate later on in his career, Tom Molineaux had little time to consider the consequences of his behavior. Miles noted in *Pugilistica* that Molineaux was viewed by many as being, "in the highest state of confidence; indeed his vaunting bordered upon insolent braggadocio".

This excess of confidence not only had a negative affect on Molineaux's public persona but on his private training as well. Bill Richmond, who up until the Blake fight had found it challenging but not impossible to control Tom's extra-curricular activities, was now finding his young charge nearly incorrigible. Molineaux's training regime obviously suffered, but he was so confident in his own physical prowess that he did not feel the need to put in the extra work that Richmond demanded. Bill understood that Cribb would take Molineaux to places he had never been and make him extend himself beyond anything he had ever experienced in his life. But Tom was blinded by his own arrogance. He truly felt that he was ready for Cribb as he was—and that no man, not even the champion, could beat him in a prizefight. It must be considered again the background from which Molineaux came. If he had truly taken part in fights against other slaves, it is likely that training was rarely part of his preparation. The same could be said of his "rough and tumble" bouts in New York. Most of those fights were probably organized and settled in a time span of less than a few days, so again training was probably a foreign and insignificant part of the proceedings. Add this to the fact that Tom had won both of his English prizefights with relative ease, and his arrogance as well as his contempt for training is nearly understandable. To Tom, Blake and Burrows probably represented a mere step below the challenge he would face from Cribb. If this was indeed the case, Molineaux was clearly misjudging the abilities of the champion.

Tom Cribb remained quiet on the matter of Tom Molineaux for quite some time. Molineaux and Richmond did their best to try and pick a fight, but for many weeks their insults and verbal jabs fell on deaf ears. Finally, late in the fall of 1810, Tom Cribb broke his silence and announced that he would fight the black American. He demanded the two men fight for 200 guineas a side and that he be given ample time to work himself into shape. Richmond did not like the fact that Cribb's demand included such a lengthy time period, for he knew that Molineaux would find a better level of comfort fighting in the warmer months. However, at this point it would have been considered ludicrous, after all the goading they had done, for Bill and Tom to refuse Cribb's terms. The fight was set to take place on December 18, 1810 at Copthall Common, near East Grinstead about halfway between London and Brighton.

Tom Cribb was a fighter of great character. His rise to fame was filled with tough battles against the likes of George Maddox, Bob Gregson, Jem Belcher and Bill Richmond himself. His skill was uncommon and he was known for mastering what was then referred to as the art of "fighting on the retreat". But it was Cribb's ability to withstand punishment that set him apart from the rest of the great pugilists of his era. It was once said that Cribb would have to be carried from the ring before he would admit defeat. On one occasion such a scene did occur for Cribb had been defeated once early in his career. But his subsequent battles had placed him in a high standing among the fight followers, to a point where, when Molineaux appeared on the scene Tom Cribb was considered unbeatable.

Cribb trained for Molineaux as he would have for any contest although there were whispers that the Bristol man was taking the black lightly. Miles noted that "although Cribb considered that the conquest of such a beginner in the art as he supposed Molineaux to be, would be mere child's play, he was still wise enough not to throw a chance away and got himself into good condition, although he was, perhaps, a bit too fleshy". Indeed, Cribb thought of Molineaux as an "ebony imposter", but he was not so foolish as to fully neglect his training. Cribb's supporters were confident of their man's ability and there were large odds offered that "The Black" would not last 15 minutes with the champion.

As the day grew closer, the anticipation, and in some quarters the tension, grew to a fevered pitch. Seemingly all of England was interested in the outcome of the match. One contemporary scribe noted, "In London clubs and sporting taverns, on the stock exchange and in the village alehouses, amongst West-end swells and East-end roughs, nothing was talked of but the fight between Cribb and Molineaux". Miles wrote, "The affair excited the most extraordinary sensation, not only in the pugilistic world, but also among the classes who had hitherto considered boxing as beneath their notice and who now, thinking the honor of their country was at stake, took a most lively interest in the affair.

Both combatants made their way out to the neighborhood of Grinstead the night before the battle, Cribb and his backers staying at the Crown house and Molineaux and Richmond at the Dorset Arms. When the morning of the fight arrived it could not have been a more miserable day for combat. The rain fell in sheets while the high winds pushed the pellets sideways. Gentleman John Jackson, who almost always served as the master of ceremonies at big events, was in charge of "pitching the ring" (a phrase which in essence meant that he was in charge of selecting an area to rope off where the combatants would meet. Jackson pitched both an inner ring, where the battle was to take place and an outer ring, which kept the masses from encroaching upon the battle.) Jackson attempted to shield the fight spot from the elements as best he could but even the shallowest part of the common provided little shelter from the elements.

Molineaux stepped out the carriage that had brought him from his quarters at 11:45am. He bowed to the crowd who greeted him with a curious silence and then sauntered towards the ring where he took from his head a borrowed traveling cap and hurled it into the ring. Cribb appeared shortly thereafter and the sight of him brought a large roar from the nearly 10,000 people who had braved the elements to witness the historic mill. The champion made his way to the ring where he greeted Molineaux; the two shook hands and returned to their corners to strip for battle. As the cheers died down only the intermittent shouting of odds could be heard from the crowd. Sir Thomas Apreece, the referee conferred with the umpires, Lord Archibald Hamilton and Colonel Barton. Molineaux stood in his corner with his seconds, Richmond and Paddington Jones and Cribb in his, seconded by John Gully and Joe Ward.

As they stood at the scratch, all could now analyze the contrast of the two men. Cribb was taller and by a small margin the heavier man, but Molineaux appeared as the better physical specimen. Miles noted, "upon stripping the appearance of the men was really formidable; Cribb, who stood five feet ten inches and a half, weighed fourteen stone three pounds, while Molineaux, who was five feet eight inches and a quarter, was only a pound lighter, and consequently looked more muscular. His arms were of wondrous length and roundness of form. He looked confident and fierce, rather than smiling, and nodded his head as the two men again shook hands."

As the men eyed each other and awaited the call of time there was an eerie silence that fell over the crowd. Almost as in expectation of some great event, they held their collective breath waiting the few excruciatingly long moments for the fight to begin. And finally, at approximately noon, it did.

At the call of time both men walked sprightly from their corners and greeted each other with some light sparring. Molineaux made the first play to land a real blow, which he did in the form of a right hand to Cribb's left side. The champion made his challenger pay for his impudence by returning a right and left to the head followed by "one to the body for good luck". Molineaux then attempted to close with Cribb and the champion threw him. The first round had ended with little damage done to either man. In the second round Cribb frustrated Molineaux by superior science in the art of hitting at length. The Black was so discouraged that he attempted to close with the champion and land his "hammer" blows. These proved virtually ineffective as Cribb beat Molineaux to the punch consistently. The American however, was able to slip one of his "rough and tumble" blows through Cribb's guard and draw "first blood"("drawing blood" was one of the first major events in any prizefight of the late 18th and early 19th century. It was an event that was almost always wagered on and was deemed to be of some importance as to predicting the outcome of a match). In rounds three through seven both men received a fair amount of punishment, although it was Cribb who was in charge. Up to this point in the fight, Molineaux had been forced to try and out-muscle Cribb because of the champion's superior boxing skill. Cribb was landing two and three punches to every one the American landed, but Molineaux's blows, even those thrown in the archaic hammer fashion, were far more powerful. By the eighth round Miles noted that both men had "been taught discrimination and had discovered each other's physical prowess. Cribb learned that the notion of beating the black off hand was truly fallacious as he was really an ugly customer." At the end of the eighth round, those who had bet that Molineaux would not last 15 minutes were returned losers.

At the beginning of the ninth round Egan wrote, "Cribb's head was terribly swelled on the left side and Molineaux's nob was also much worse for the fight…. The battle had arrived at that doubtful state and things seemed not to prove so easy or tractable as was anticipated, that the bettors were rather puzzled to know how they should proceed with success". Molineaux had stood up under the gruel as few had expected. Doubt now crept into the minds of even Cribb's most ardent supporters. "On Cribb's displaying weakness, the flash side were full of palpitation—it was not looked for and operated more severe upon their minds on that account", stated Eagn, noticing the worried almost confused look on the faces of the crowd. Their confusion would quickly turn to disbelief when in the ninth round Molineaux broke through Cribb's guard and with a straight right hand sprawled the champion headlong on the turf. Egan again noted the crowd's reaction, "it would be futile here to attempt to portray the countenance of the interested part of the spectators, who appeared, as it were, panic struck…" The crowd's reaction to the events transpiring in the ring, truly reflected the tone of the bout. As expected, Cribb was by far a better scientific fighter than Molineaux. What was not expected was the American's ability to absorb Cribb's best blows and land his own, far more damaging punches. However, despite the crowd's utter shock at the true ability of Molineaux, the contest continued to ebb and flow as each round progressed. Molineaux certainly appeared to be the stronger of the two, but he was being hit with such a multitude of blows, that one had to wonder how long he could stand such punishment without yielding. Cribb employed his "milling on the retreat" to perfection and Tom continued to chase the champion about the ring, taking any blow sent his way only to return his own fire. It was truly a brutal and magnificent display.

By the end of the eighteenth round neither man had shown any true dominance and both were near exhaustion. Molineaux, despite the repeated blows he had received, seemed the fresher of the two, but as Egan noted, "to distinguish the combatants by their features would have been utterly impossible, so dreadfully beaten were both their faces."

It was here in the nineteenth round that the first of several queer moments occurred in the fight. Egan described the incident as such, "Cribb acting upon the defensive, and retreating from the blows of his antagonist, though endeavoring to put in a hit, was got by Molineaux against the ropes, which were in height about five feet, and in three rows. Molineaux with both his hands caught hold of the ropes, and held Cribb in such a singular way, that he could neither make a hit or fall down: and while the seconds were discussing the propriety of separating the combatants, which the umpires thought could not be done till one of the men fell down, about two hundred persons rushed from the outer to the interior ring, and it is asserted, that if one of the Moor's fingers was not broken, it was much injured by some of them attempting to remove his hands from the ropes: all this time Molineaux was gaining his wind by laying his head on Cribb's breast, and refusing to release his victim; when the Champion, by a desperate effort to extricate himself from the rude grasp of the Moor, was run down at length to one corner of the ring, and Molineaux, having got his head under his arm, fibbed away most unmercifully, but his strength not being able to the intent, it otherwise must have proved fatal to Cribb, who fell from exhaustion, and the severe punishment he had received. The best were now decided that Molineaux did not fight a half an hour; that time having expired during this round".

Interestingly enough in Miles' round by round description of the fight he neglects to include the rope incident that occurred in the 19th round. His accounts of the bout were no doubt borrowed from Bill Oxberry, author of *Pancratia*, who was at the fight and was most likely responsible for the reports of the fight found in both *The London Times* and the *Sporting Magazine*, but the details of round 13, 14, 15, 16, 17, 18, 19, 20, 21 or 22 are conspicuous by their absence, in Miles' reiteration. The Oxberry *London Times* report, which gave only round by round descriptions of rounds 1 through 12, did mention the rope incident and the breaking of the outer ring but stated that it had occurred in the 20th round. Therefore, despite Miles' omission of the incident, the breaking of the ring obviously did take place. However, from these reports it is difficult to glean what affect it had on the outcome of the fight. It has to be assumed that the ring was broken by Cribb's supporters, for as Egan mentioned their intent was to free the Champion from Molineaux's grasp. What is unclear is what exactly happened during the incident, how long it lasted and what damage was done to Molineaux in the process? Egan mentions Molineaux's finger being mauled in the fracas, but makes no mention of any other attacks on his person. Molineaux was undoubtedly roughed up during the melee, but it does not appear that it was deemed worthy of mention. Another interesting aspect of the incident is how it may have affected Cribb. He was undoubtedly "in trouble" at that moment of the fight, for earlier in the bout, when he was fresh, he demonstrated his wrestling ability by slipping out of such attempted maneuvers. Did the breaking of the ring save Cribb? It is difficult to say, but there can be no doubt that the incident surely affected the outcome of the fight in some manner. Molineaux's advantage was certainly parlayed into a disadvantage (his injured finger) and Cribb's misfortunes were assisted by the actions of his supporters.

Cribb came up for the 20th round in bad shape. Molineaux, who could hardly be described as being in good condition, was by far the fresher of the two combatants. For the next five rounds, Molineaux controlled the action and beat Cribb severely. All was going Molineaux's way at this point despite the fact that he was noticed to be "now and again having fits of shuddering" caused by the torrents of rain that continued to fall throughout the fight. In the 28th round Cribb feebly attempted to strike Molineaux and "received a leveler in consequence of his distance being incorrect." This punch fairly settled the champion and he fell in an unconscious state. Joe Ward rushed out to drag Cribb back to the corner in the hope of reviving his man in the thirty seconds allowed. Molineaux was probably unaware that he was on the verge of winning the fight, and Bill Richmond needed to lead him back to his own corner. Egan wrote, "Cribb fell in so exhausted a state from the severe fibbing which he had received, that the limited time had expired before he was able to renew the contest, and Sir Thomas Apreece, one of the umpires, cried out, "time, time! but his second Richmond, not noticing the circumstance, Cribb recovered." Miles, again borrowing from Oxberry describes the incident in a bit more detail, "In the 28th round, after the men were carried to their corners, Cribb was so much exhausted that he could hardly rise from his second's knee at the call of time, which was uttered loudly by Sir Thomas Apreece one of the umpires. Joe Ward, his (Cribb's) second, by a little maneuvering occupied the attention of the Black's seconds, and so managed to prolong the period sufficiently to enable the champion to recover a little, thus assisted him to pull through." Ward's maneuvering was later thought to be an accusation pointed at Molineaux and Richmond. Later reports on the fight ascertain that Ward accused Molineaux of fighting with lead bullets in his hands (bullets were used to make the fist stronger and the user's punches more damaging). But although the alleged infraction was refused, as Molineaux supposedly displayed that he had no bullets, the ruse worked to its desired affect. At this point, Tom Molineaux had fairly accomplished what he set out to do: beat Tom Cribb.

What exactly transpired in that time between the 28th and 29th rounds may never be known, for contemporary sources, either by some nationalistic defense or by mere poor reporting, are very vague about the particular details of what took place. It is difficult to say how long the period lasted or how this utter robbery affected Molineaux's constitution. But what is fact is that, by strict interpretation of the rules, Tom Cribb, unable to come to scratch after 30 seconds, was knocked out of time. Tom Molineaux, at that moment should have been declared the winner and champion of England. (NOTE: Some boxing historians have questioned the very existence of any infractions, or unusual incidents during the contest despite glaring contemporary proof. Both Egan and Oxberry, the two most respected boxing writers of their time, clearly mention the incidents in their narratives on the fight. How one could come to the conclusion that these events never transpired, or were invented or vamped up by the pro-Molineaux set after the fight is beyond comprehension).

Unfortunately for Tom Molineaux, he was not the hometown fighter and despite the supposed efforts of all involved to be fair, the fight continued. What transpired next could be considered incredulous, for Cribb, beaten nearly senseless less than a few minutes before, called on his famous "bottom" and regained control of the fight by throwing Molineaux heavily. Egan wrote of this telling round, "the fate of the battle might be said to have been decided by this round". In the 30th frame, Molineaux again surged forward in an apparent attempt to end the battle there and then. Egan stated that, "Molineaux, in spite of every disadvantage, with a courage and ferocity unequalled, rising superior to exhaustion and fatigue, rallied his adversary with as much resolution as at the commencement of the fight, his nob defying all the milling it had received, that punishment appeared to have no decisive effect upon it, and contending nobly with Cribb right and left, knocking him away by his hits, and gallantly concluded the round by closing and throwing the Champion". Although it would seem from Egan's description of the round that Tom Molineaux had again seized control of the bout, Miles' noted a curious incident at the conclusion of the period. He wrote, "Molineaux threw Cribb, but in the struggle fell and pitched upon his head, which so severely affected him that he could hardly stand". Molineaux was led back to his corner by Richmond where Egan noted, "he appeared much distressed on quitting his second." Molineaux was obviously insensible and was surely in no condition to fight anymore. Richmond convinced him that Cribb was as exhausted and beaten as he and the "Black" came to scratch to begin the next round. The bout staggered on for eight more rounds, now merely a battle of attrition and gluttony. In the 39th round when Molineaux fell more from exhaustion than a blow, cries rang out of "foul!"(It was considered a foul for a man to fall without being hit), but were disallowed by the umpires. Molineaux was convinced to try another round, but after again falling without being hit, he cried out "he could fight no more." The match lasted 55 minutes after which Tom Cribb was declared the winner.

"Great events", wrote Pierce Egan, "are often judged by comparison: and however severe the conflict might have been between Johnson and Big Ben—this battle betwixt Cribb and Molineaux was not only more formidable in its nature, but more ferocious and sanguinary. Fifty-five minutes of unprecedented milling, before the Moor thought he had had enough!!" There can be little doubt that Egan was correct in labeling the first Molineaux-Cribb battle as "great". It lived up to all of its advanced billing: but what of the result? Egan undoubtedly felt as though Molineaux had been the victim of foul play as did Oxberry and many other later writers, but was Tom Molineaux truly robbed?

Perhaps Tom Molineaux himself felt that he had been mistreated. A few days after the fight he published a letter, undoubtedly written for the illiterate pugilist by one of his supporters, asking for another chance with the champion. Although careful and calculated in his approach, he and his backers certainly did not want to offend anyone and ruin the chance for a lucrative return match, Molineaux, through a thinly veiled commentary, expressed his feelings on the matter of fair play.

> *Pugilistic Challenge to Mr. Tom Cribb*
> *Sir—My friends think that had the weather on last Tuesday on which I contended with you, not been so unfavorable, I should have won the battle. I therefore challenge you to a second meeting, at any time within two months, for such a sum as those gentlemen who place confidence in me may be pleased to arrange.*
> *As it is possible that this letter may meet the public eye, I cannot omit the opportunity of expressing a confident hope, that the circumstances of my being of a different colour to that of a people amongst whom I have sought protection, will not in any way operate to my prejudice.*
> *I am, sir, Your most obedient humble servant, T. Molineaux.*

Tom's "confident hope" line served as a double-edged sword. In one sense he was expressing his displeasure with the events that transpired in the first fight. Yet he was also making a play for what he hoped would be the English sense of fair play. The letter was phrased in such a manner as to not openly accuse anyone of foul fighting but it certainly placed Molineaux in a position to gain support from the public, while expressing a sentiment that he himself felt that he had been cheated. However, it seems that only in retrospect did the British press in general, and or the boxing writers in specific, seem willing to admit or express their feeling that Tom Molineaux had indeed received a raw deal in his first match with Cribb. Egan, in his third volume of *Boxiana*, written after Molineaux had died and nearly 11 years after the first battle had occurred, wrote, "His first contest with Cribb will long be remembered by the sporting world. It will also not be forgotten, if justice hold the scales, that his colour alone prevented him from becoming the hero of that fight…"

Professor, PHD, and author Randy Roberts notes in his work, *Morals and Maulers: The Ethics of Early Pugilism* that, "Judgment on whether Tom Molineaux was cheated of victory depends as much on what was considered fair in the pugilism of the day as it does upon what actually happened." Indeed, the events that occurred in the Molineaux-Cribb match were not singular to this specific fight. The outer ring being broken, interference from partisan crowds and even delaying tactics were all fairly common at the turn of the 19th century: common, however, hardly legal or accepted, even by 19th century standards. Cribb and his parties had been accused prior to the Molineaux match of using illicit tactics to stall for time, when their man was in trouble. Egan noted that, "our love of impartiality compels us to state, that, notwithstanding the superlative excellence of the Champion of England, he has in more than one instance, been considered indebted to good fortune in being pronounced the victor…in his first contest with Jem Belcher, before the strength of Jem's right hand had left him, the battle was saved for Cribb by the following maneuver of Bill Warr—the odds were five to one on Belcher and while Gully, who seconded Jem, was offering the above odds to Warr, at the conclusion of a round, when Cribb had received so severe a blow the he could not come to time, Warr, on accepting the bet, insisted the money should be posted, and by this stratagem gained more than a minute, sufficient time for such a glutton as Cribb perfectly to recover in". Cribb and his cohorts were not the only ones to have ever bent the rules in order to assist their cause, but as evidenced by the above passage, were not virgin to such tactics prior to the Molineaux contest. Roberts's continues by stating, "the incidents in the fight—entanglement in the ropes, spectators breaking the ring, delaying by seconds, collisions—were all frequent enough in contemporary prize-fighting to not constitute a serious irregularity by the standards of the day." The standards of the day certainly left for some loose interpretation of the rules that, in turn caused confusion as to the legality of certain happenings: such as the rope incident or the breaking of the outer ring. However, there can be little maneuvering or interpretation of a rule as stout and as clear as coming to scratch in the allotted 30 seconds. This rule, while being one of the more ceremonious and important aspects of the sport, was also one of the most fundamental of the games regulations. Violation of this code, if allowed or ignored, could not be interpreted as anything but cheating. It seems then that in the period between the 28th and 29th rounds, when Tom Cribb was clearly given extra time to recover, Tom Molineaux was cheated out of a well-earned victory. The first long count controversy in boxing history had been born.

Tom Molineaux licked his wounds and enjoyed his ever-growing fame. After his ferocious battle with Cribb he was less of a mystery, in terms of his fighting ability, and more of a celebrity. That Cribb had narrowly defeated the black challenger placed the Champion at an all time high in terms of pugilistic reverence, despite the murmurings that not all had been on the level. The fight game itself reveled in a newfound popularity. No matter the rumors that surrounded the bout or the result itself, the interest in the sport generated by the great match brought prizefighting back to the national conscience. Molineaux was paraded around town as if he were a circus attraction. Richmond was even invited to bring his "black" to the Stock Exchange, were Tom was feted and touched like a petting zoo animal and given a 40-guinea gift for his brave effort with Cribb. Again, Tom viewed his celebrity with childlike wonder and recklessness: embracing it as if he were a conquering war hero.

Bill Richmond immediately challenged Tom Cribb to a rematch on behalf of his charge. It was assumed by most, that considering the closeness of the affair, the alleged foul play and the skills and courage shown by Molineaux, that the American black deserved another crack at the Champion. He held no grudge against Cribb and even sparred with Bill Richmond at a benefit for his conqueror at the Fives Court in January of 1811 in front of 3000 spectators. But it was evident, by a speech that Cribb gave on that night that he was in no rush to give Tom a rematch. The Champion explained to a large crowd at the Fives Court that he would accept Molineaux's challenge but only at a stake of 500 guineas or 250 guineas a side. This was a thinly veiled yet effective maneuver, for Cribb and his cronies knew that neither Richmond nor Molineaux could stake that kind of money at the present time. Molineaux and Richmond then took the stage and explained that they could not meet those demands but would agree to leave the match open for twelve months in the hope that they could raise such a sum. Tom then challenged "anybody breathing" to fight for 100 pounds a side. For the time being Cribb was content to rest on his laurels and Tom and Bill to make their money fighting lesser men. But it was inevitable that Cribb and Molineuax would meet again.

The same night that Cribb and Molineaux had appeared at the Fives Court, Bob Gregson introduced a young novice named Heskin "Will" Rimmer from Lancashire to the Fancy. After watching Rimmer spar a few rounds with the likes of Tom Belcher and George Silverthorne, the Fancy declared him a man of great promise. Gregson considered his young pugilist more than just a prospect and when Molineaux had thrown down his gauntlet to fight any man, Gregson accepted on behalf of Rimmer. However, when the two sides met the next day at Gregson Castle Tavern to draw up the articles, Gregson balked at the 100pound stake. He reasoned that he had no desire to put up such a sum for a novice such as Rimmer and that a 50-pound stake would be both more reasonable and appropriate. Richmond was irate and declared that although Rimmer was a novice, "Tom Molineaux is not" and flatly refused to drop the stake below 100 pounds. Negotiations were then broken off.

On April 2, 1811, Tom Molineaux was given a benefit at the Fives Court in which over 1000 spectators attended. Molineaux sparred with Isaac Bittoon, Tom Belcher and Ben Burn all who were, according to the Morning Chronicle, "unable to make an impression on the "Black". Rimmer also appeared at the benefit and showed so well that Gregson then agreed to match him against Molineaux for the desired 100-pound stake. Articles were signed the next day and the fight set to take place on May 21, 1811. Richmond immediately took Tom on an exhibition tour of the North Country where they made substantial amounts of money. But everything was not well.

Molineaux's arrogance, despite his surrender to Cribb, was at an all time high. He traveled, dressed, ate, drank and whored with an excess that appalled even his closest allies. But, there was little if anything that could temper Molineaux's ignominious behavior. Tom even began to turn against those who had supported him when he had arrived nearly helpless little more than a year previous. He defied Richmond on several occasions and considered himself above taking orders. It was not uncommon for him to threaten to "leave" Richmond for another backer when he felt the latter was putting a strain on his extra-curricular activities. Richmond was left with little choice and more often than not he would acquiesce to Molineaux's will fearful he would loose him if he did not. Richmond grew more disdainful of Molineaux every day but needed some sort of return on his investment. Training was nearly non-existent and Molineaux's constitution suffered because of it. Despite all of this, however, a week before the fight, Richmond took Tom up to Kent where he hoped he could convince Molineaux to put in some sort of training for Rimmer. However, according to Henning, a most bizarre and unique event occurred while the duo was in Kent: Tom Molineaux met a woman he wanted to marry! Henning lists the *Morning Chronicle* as his source and states the paper informed the public that, "Molyneaux is to receive the hand of a fair young captivating widow in Kent on Sunday next." Of course, the "marriage" never came off as the bride to be was supposedly carried off "by force" at the hands of two of her brothers. Whether or not the story is true, it is certain that Molineaux had other things on his mind in the weeks leading up to his match with Rimmer other than fighting.

Rimmer was not an experienced man, and in hindsight should never have been matched with such a fighter as Molineaux. Gregson and some of his other backers however, had seen Rimmer prove victorious on several occasions on his own "north country" turf and figured him to be a good man. A win, or even a credible showing against such a famous man, as Molineaux now was, would be good for the future aspirations of their man. Rimmer was a big man but his fighting powers were neither graceful nor scientific. He and Molineaux met at Mousley Hurst on May 21, 1811 in front of an audience estimated to be in the neighborhood of 10,000 strong. The contest would deserve little description if it were not for a striking incident that occurred in the 15th round. By that frame, Molineaux had severely beaten Rimmer in a one-sided contest. In the 15th stanza, the far superior Molineaux knocked Rimmer senseless and few thought the latter would make it to scratch to begin the 16th round.

The crowd had been growing hostile throughout the bout, hurling slurs and taunts at Tom, but when the latter finished Rimmer with a decisive blow in that fateful round all hell broke loose. Egan reported: "A scene now took place which beggared all description: During the time that Rimmer lay prostrate on the ground, the ring was broken, owing it is said, from the antipathy felt against a man of colour proving the conqueror." Miles stated, "Peers and ploughmen, fighting men and chimney sweepers, costermongers, were all in one tumultuous uproar, which continued on for at least twenty minutes. At length, by the exertions of Cribb and others, the ring was restored and the combatants again set-to." Again Molineaux had been the victim of foul play. This time however, because of his absolute dominance over his opponent, he had not been denied a victory. But as Egan noted, the crowd was having a terrible reaction to witnessing the literal beating of white man at the hands of a black. Their emotions ran at such a fervent temper, that they lashed out in order to stop the fight—and in essence stop the beating. Egan, as well as other chroniclers of the melee, made the readers keenly aware of the diverse group that constituted the riot. This was not a rumble involving only low lives and thieves; it was a general riot including men from all classes. The uprising demonstrated that the English, much like their American cousins, were not as comfortable as they may have portrayed with a black man fighting on even terms with a white one. That this feeling took until the Cribb fight to surface, and then subsequently exploded during the Rimmer contest is no surprise. Richmond, who was never large enough to truly have championship aspirations, and Molineaux, were the only prevalent black fighters to have ever competed in England. Their existence, up until Molineaux's first match with Cribb, was generally considered to be a novelty; they up until that time having never truly represented a serious threat to English white dominance. That Tom Molineaux was American certainly put him at a xenophobic disadvantage. That he was a black American made him a monster.

American interest in prizefighting was nearly non-existent during this time. So too was their awareness of Tom Molineaux. His name appeared only twice in contemporary American newspapers. The first instance was in the New York Evening Post, which on February 13, 1811 carried a reprint from *Bell's Weekly Messenger* of London of Tom's aforementioned challenge of Cribb. The second instance was found in the Savannah Republican of July 23, 1811 that carried a short paragraph about the Rimmer match. It read: "Civilization!—A boxing match took place at Mousley Hart, in the neighborhood of London, on the 21st of May, for one hundred guineas. The Champions were Molineaux (the famous black man from New York) and a young Englishman named Rimmer. In the course of fifteen rounds, the black pounded his antagonist most tremendously: when lords, nobles, sweeps, ploughmen, fighting men and assistants from pique or sympathy, crowded into the ring and fought promiscuously about twenty minutes! There were at this brutal exhibition about fifteen thousand spectators of all ranks". Beyond these instances, the American press and public seemed to care little about the fact that one of their own was making a name for himself in England. This was no doubt due in large part to the fact that prizefighting, as a sport, had not yet captured the hearts and imagination of the American public. It is possible also that Tom Molineaux's color prevented him from becoming a true American hero. A black American certainly had less of a chance of gaining any type of national support during that era than would have a white one. However, it seems odd that, on the verge of war with the Mother Country, America would not have taken more of an interest in Molineaux's activities. In later years the press would have undoubtedly played up a match up like Molineaux and Cribb, not only as a battle of racial importance, but one of nationalitic pride as well. Tom's performances against the English champion, as well as those against lesser foes, certainly could have been used to drum up images of the young, strong and important force that America was becoming within the world's political, religious and economical scene. But as it was, America simply was not interested. Thus America's first international, sporting hero was simply ignored.

Molineaux destruction of Rimmer again placed him at the doorstep of dominance. He threw down the gauntlet, challenging any man in the country to fight him for the Championship of England. Cribb, Molineaux and Richmond reasoned, was retired and Tom proclaimed himself as the ex-champion's logical successor. The problem was that after the Rimmer fight, no man dared to face the American. As Tom's claims on the championship grew stronger and stronger with each passing day, pressure was placed on Tom Cribb to fight "The Terrible Black" again. Cribb, who had since settled down to a quiet life as a family man and publican, himself grew weary of Molineaux's constant threats and proclamations. Finally he relented and agreed to meet with Molineaux and Richmond in order to discuss a second meeting.

The interested parties met at Richmond's Horse and Dolphin where John Jackson was elected as the chairperson to oversee the negotiations. Jackson acted as an arbitrator of sorts and was in charge of negotiating the particulars of the bout, drawing up the articles, collecting the stakes and witnessing the signature of both the participants. The men agreed to fight for 300 guineas a side, on September 15, 1811(this date was later changed to September 28th), upon a 25-foot wooden stage, on a spot to be decided at a latter date that was to be no less than 100 miles from London. Captain Barclay laid the stake for Cribb and Richmond (on loan) for Molineaux. Both Cribb and Molineaux attended the meeting but neither spoke to the other with the exception of a greeting and a farewell gesture. Both signed the articles, Cribb with his signature and Molineaux with an "X".

Cribb, who must have been feeling the weight of the world on his shoulders, immediately put himself under the training eye of the famous Scottish pedestrian Aldrice Barclay. "Captain" Barclay was famous as a unique man of fitness and had once won a considerable amount of money by walking 1000 miles in 1000 hours, a feat of tremendous magnitude in his time. He was also known as quite an athlete, considered the finest amateur fighter of his time. He could be found often up at the rooms of John Jackson where he displayed his pugilistic prowess in sparring matches with other amateurs before some of the wealthier and more influential men of London. It is a story of lore that Barclay had once sparred with Molineaux at Jackson's rooms, shortly after Tom had beaten Blake. In fact it was believed that because Tom Molineaux had both broken a few of Barclay's ribs with a body shot and embarrassed him so thoroughly in front of a rather large gathering, that the Captain was eager to gain a measure of revenge by training Tom Cribb. Whether or not Barclay's interest were personally or monetarily motivated, by his taking Cribb "in hand" he virtually assured that the Champion would be in the best shape of his life when he next squared off with "The Terrible Black". Cribb and Barclay left London on July 2 and made their way by stage-coach to Ury, where the Captain had an estate. Cribb was placed under a strict diet and a grueling exercise regime that was novel at the time in its concept.

Tom Molineaux would have no such training. Forced to earn money in order to repay his and Richmond's loan, the men, along with Jem Belcher's brother Tom, took to touring the provinces and giving exhibitions. Molineaux was an attraction almost everywhere he went for nearly everyone wanted to see the famous black American who had so nearly beaten the champion. Some days, Molineaux would exhibit in two to three different shows, owning to the large crowds and small venues where he exhibited. And although Molineaux remained in some semblance of fighting shape, he lushed and whored in almost every town he visited. Richmond, it was asserted, grew so weary of Molineaux's behavior that he simply turned the other way. Tom would become so unruly whenever asked to comply with the most rudimentary of rules, that Richmond finally gave up trying to govern him. The tour was a financial success, and at one point or another, Tom Molineaux turned from a protégé, into a moneymaking machine for Richmond. Bill did stop the tour about two weeks prior to the match and brought Tom to Hayes, near Hillingham Heath, where they accomplished some training. However, Tom Molineaux's dissipations could not be worn off with simply two weeks of work, and although outwardly he appeared fit enough, he was in no shape to be fighting a finely tuned Tom Cribb.

If the first Molineaux Cribb battle had caused a stir, the second match created something of a national phenomenon. Egan noted, "Never was the sporting world so much interested, and for twenty miles within the seat of action not a bed could be obtained on the preceding night: and by six o'clock the next morning, hundreds were in motion to get a good place near the stage, which even at that early period proved a difficult task. It is supposed that near 20,000 persons witnessed this tremendous mill: and that one fourth of them were of the highest mould: including some of the principal Corinthians of the State". The interest in the match however, was not fueled only by sporting curiosity for there was a much larger prize at risk: National Pride. Egan may have summed up England's fears best when he wrote, "whether Old England should still retain her proud characteristic of conquering, or that an American, and a man of colour, should win the honour, wear it, and carry it away from the shores of Britain."

It can read with no surprise then that when Tom Molineaux made his appearance to the crowd at Thiselton Gap, September 28, 1811 he was "greeted with tokens of approbation, though of not so general a nature". Cribb, on the other hand, was met with applause that was "exceeding everything of its kind". Both men looked fit, Molineaux despite the fact that he "underwent anything like a regular training: but on the contrary he indulged himself to excess", and Cribb, because he had prepared for the fight like none before him. Both weighed close to fourteen pounds less than in their prior match; Cribb's reduction in weight obviously due to his Spartan like training and Molineaux's more than likely to have been caused by the initial stages of consumption from which he was probably suffering at the time. John Gulley and Joe Ward seconded Cribb, and Richmond and Bill Gibbons performed the duties for Molineaux. The combatants met at the mark in the middle of the stage at 12:18pm when time was called.

Cribb won the first round when he dropped Molineaux with a right hand to the throat after nearly a full two minutes of sparring. Despite being downed by the champion, the American showed little damage from the blow. In the second round the men rallied heavily during which Cribb landed a tremendous body blow only to be countered by a heavy left hand to the head by Molineaux. The men then closed and "in a trial of strength, Cribb was thrown." Again neither man was much damaged but first blood was awarded to Molineaux as Cribb showed "claret" from his nose. The third round was an interesting one for several reasons. Both men's tactics were born out as it was made clear by the fighting in this session that Cribb wanted to attack and weaken Molineaux's body and the American wanted to attack only the head of the Champion. Cribb landed a tremendous body blow that nearly doubled up Molineaux, but the "Terrible Black", through a series of well landed left hands, "darkened"(closed), the Champion's right eye and damaged his head considerably. The round ended when Molineaux threw Cribb with a cross-buttock maneuver that resulted in a "heavy fall" for the Champion.

Molineaux's superior strength, not only in wrestling, but in punching power as well, was clearly evident. Cribb seemed to be in trouble as he was bleeding from the mouth heavily and his head was so swollen that it was described as being "terrific". However as the fourth round commenced Egan pointed out in his round by round account of the fight, "Molineaux's wind could not be depended upon." The men continued to fight as they had in the three previous sessions with Molineaux punishing Cribb's head and the Champion concentrating his attack to the body of his antagonist. In the fifth round, all of England held their breath as Molineaux punished Cribb severely, knocking him down with a series of dreadful blows. It was at this point in the contest that may be considered the most significant of all for Tom Molineaux, for it was here at the end of the fifth round, where he was again on the verge of taking firm control of the fight that his constitution and condition began to fail him. At the beginning of the sixth round Egan noted, "Molineaux from want of wind, lunged right and left but gained nothing by it", commenting on the lack of endurance that "The Terrible Black" now displayed. Cribb, probably noticing that Molineaux suffered from short wind, again pointed his attack to the body of the American. The Champion then landed a blow to Molineaux's stomach so telling that "it not only appeared to roll him up, but seemed as if it had completely knocked the wind out of him, which issued so strong from his mouth, like smoke from a pipe, that he was literally gasping for breath". This was indeed the end of Tom Molineaux's championship aspirations.

Cribb beat Molineaux unmercifully, knocking him so senseless in the ninth round that Tom could not come to scratch in the allotted time. Cribb, either in an act of defiance or pure redemption, refused to accept the victory that was now his and allowed Molineaux a full minute and a half to recover. Perhaps it was Cribb's own disgust at the accusations that he himself was allowed extra time to recover in the first bout that led him to such an act, but no matter the reason, the bout continued. Upon the fight resuming, Molineaux was dreadfully punished by the Champion and at one point when he was running in wildly the American received a terrible left hand to the mouth that broke his jaw. The tenth round saw more damage to Molineaux as Cribb basically punched him at will. Tom fell now more from weakness than anything else and though insensible was cajoled by Richmond to try another round. Molineaux again did not toe the scratch in the allotted time and again Cribb waived his right to claim victory. "The Terrible Black" was then stood up for the 11th round in such a poor state that the first punch which Cribb threw knocked him completely out. The fight lasted a mere 19 minutes in which eleven rounds were fought.

Tom Molineaux's overconfidence and ignorance had finally caught up with him. He was so blinded by his own arrogance, that according to Egan on the morning of the fight he "bolted a boiled fowl, an apple pie and a tankard of porter for his breakfast". His condition was so detestable that he could not fight at full pace for more than ten minutes. Cribb's body blows, which had bounced off him like rain drops less than eight months before, now had caused him to double up in pain and suck for air like a blubbering porpoise. He had been tamed, not only by Cribb, but also by his own self-indulgence.

And what can be said of Bill Richmond? Undoubtedly he could not be blamed for Molineaux's condition, for even though he was the latter's trainer and chief patron, it has already been shown that he had little influence over Tom's training habits or his personal misadventures. What Richmond can be criticized for is allowing Molineaux to continue fighting after the ninth round when he was clearly a beaten man. Perhaps Richmond sought to teach Molineaux a cruel lesson, but risking the latter's life in such a manner may have been more of a brutal redemption for Bill who by now held a great deal of animosity for his charge. Cribb's grandstanding must too be called into question. His actions in allowing Molineaux to continue, after the latter had clearly been beaten, seem to ring of true maliciousness. The Champion's behavior was hardly magnanimous and possibly he felt that by continuing to beat a helpless man well after he had been defeated erased the contemptuous manner in which he won the first contest. What is clear is that Tom Cribb wanted to punish Tom Molineaux. Whether it was because of Tom's taunts leading up to the fight, the allegations surrounding the first fight, or Cribb's own personal ferocity is unclear. However, the bout was by and large detestable on several levels.

All of England celebrated Tom Cribb's victory as if they themselves had won some great prize. A sweeping sigh of relief rose up across the nation as if a plague had been beaten from its shores. Egan, who was keenly aware of the Nationalistic feelings that surrounded the bout wrote, "The joy experienced by the flash side cannot be described—and considering all the disadvantages under which Molineaux fought this battle, he performed wonders. It is not meant to be urged that Molineaux had not fair play throughout the fight in the ring—it is well known that he had, but the Black had to contend against a prejudiced multitude: the pugilistic honor of the country was at stake, and the attempts of Molineaux were viewed with jealousy, envy and disgust: the national laurels to be borne away by a foreigner—the mere idea to an English breast was afflicting and the reality could not be endured:—that it should seem, the spectators were ready to exclaim—"Forbid it, heaven—forbid it, man!" Molineaux had more to fear than even the mighty prowess of the Champion: in fact, the man of colour received, generally, a very different sort of reception, occasioned, we apprehend, from the extreme anxiety manifested by the friends of Cribb for the safety of his honour and renown." In hindsight, Tom Molineaux never had a chance on that stage with Cribb, and if he had, he may never have had a chance off it.

Molineaux's relationship with Richmond ended shortly after his second bout with Cribb. He made money by touring in several different exhibition tours but without the guidance or friendship of Bill fell deeper and deeper into an abyss of self-abuse and degradation. Miles noted that at this point in his life Molineaux, "quarreled with his best friends, scorned advice and declared himself on all occasions, especially when maddened with liquor, an ill-used man". Tom still had fight left in him as evidenced by a street fight which took place outside of Richmond's Horse and Dolphin in November of 1811. Jack Power, a pugilist of some note, was Tom's adversary and the two fought for 17 minutes before Power's friends intervened to save their companion from a dreadful beating. Molineaux continued to tour, lush and womanize for a full year. He even tried his hand at wrestling, exhibiting at the Exeter fair with a man named Snow, but he was dreadfully out of shape and could barely make a good show of it. In Early 1813 Bill Jay challenged him, but nothing ever materialized. Finally he was matched with Jack Carter, who was backed and trained by Bill Richmond, to fight for 100 guineas on March 31, 1813. However, prior to the match coming off, Bill Richmond had Molineaux arrested, and jailed for failure to pay an old debt. How Molineaux paid the debt nor any of the circumstances surrounding the entire affair have ever been discovered. All that can be assumed is that the matter was cleared up, for Carter and Molineaux finally met at Remington, Gloucstershire on April 2, 1813.

Bill Richmond wanted the Carter-Molineaux match. The feud between the two Americans had come to a place where either man would take any opportunity to harm the other in any way possible. Richmond's anger was understandable. Molineaux had blamed him publicly for his loss to Cribb, sighting that Bill did not take the proper measures to prepare or train him for the fight. Undoubtedly, Richmond had "used" Tom in some capacity as money making machine, and had allowed him to take two rounds of unnecessary punishment from Cribb, but Molineaux had no one to blame for his loss other than himself. Molineaux's ill feelings probably stemmed from some deep-rooted feeling of isolation and abandonment. He could not have truly blamed Richmond for his lack of condition, but maybe for the latter's turncoat behavior after the fight. Tom felt abandoned by Richmond, the one man who he trusted, and the one man who had at least some understanding of his plight.

The Carter-Molineaux affair was a terrible fiasco. Molineaux, true to form, was woefully out of shape, and Carter, by his outward appearance prior to the bout, seemed to be a beaten man before a punch had been thrown. When the bout began Miles noted that, "one was afraid and the other dared not." Carter displayed that he was a fair miller and beat Molineaux easily to the punch. Tom, who took his gruel to the head as he always did, with little or no indication of pain, was lethargic, slow and seemed uninterested in fighting. At different times during the bout he seemed to loose his sense of reality, at one point claiming he had been bitten by Carter and during another crying, "Oh dear! Oh dear! murder!" Molineaux had seemingly gone mad. "Twenty five rounds occurred in which coaxing, persuading, dramming and threatening were resorted to, in order to make the man of colour perform something like fighting", noted Miles. "But to the great astonishment of all the spectators, when Molineaux was deadbeat, Carter fainted, and dropped his head as he sat on the knee of his second." Molineaux had won the fight, more through attrition and gluttony, which is ironic enough, rather than through any modicum of skill or strength. Carter simply wore himself down. The result of the bout was greeted with suspicion and dis-satisfaction and Molineaux's name sank further into ill repute.

The Carter bout proved to be the last time that Tom Molineaux would ever fight on British soil. Shortly after the match, Molineaux, pairing up with his latest conquest Jack Carter, made a tour of Scotland. Tom and Jack would re-enact, with a bit of a revisionist historian's touch, their now infamous battle to sold out crowds throughout Edinburgh and other Scottish communities. They found the Scots to be most gracious hosts and besides making a good deal of money, both Tom and Jack found a certain redemption in the positive reception they received. Molineaux persisted in spending more time carousing, drinking and whoring and his constitution continued to suffer because of it. Although he was still outwardly a physical marvel, his body was beginning to rapidly deteriorate from years of abuse and the full onset of disease.

While in Scotland, Molineaux had yet another chance to settle old scores when Bill Richmond presented another challenge to his old charge. This time it was a young, gifted pugilist by the name of William Fuller. Fuller was not an experienced fighter yet he was exceptional physically and had shown enough to Bill Richmond for the latter to consider him championship material. William auspiciously began his career late in 1812 when he was beaten nearly "off hand" by Bill Jay, the same Jay who had challenged Molineaux, in less than 15 minutes. It was then that Fuller was taken in hand by Richmond and showing what latent talent combined with good teaching could manifest, beat the same Bill Jay in 42 minutes in April of 1813. Richmond then took Fuller on an exhibition tour into Northern England, and eventually up into Scotland. Hearing that two of his old pupils, Molineaux and Carter, were in Edinburgh giving exhibitions, Richmond decided to try and make a match for his latest charge.

Upon hearing of Fuller's challenge, Molineaux, knowing nothing of the former's career or capabilities other than that he was a disciple of Richmond, accepted the challenge and placed his own stake of 100 guineas. The bout was to take place at Paisley, Ayrshire on May 27, 1814 in an unusually large ring of 40 feet. Fuller, who figured with enough room he could use his speed and agility to tire out the more experienced and hard-hitting American, demanded the ring size. Tom, imprudent as always, agreed with no argument: he figured Fuller for easy money.

The men set to at roughly 1pm on a brilliant spring day with Carter serving as Molineaux's second and Joe Ward and George Cooper serving the same capacity for Fuller. Interestingly, Richmond was a mere spectator at the bout: for unknown reasons he chose not to second Fuller. Tom was shorter and stouter than his opponent, weighing close to 182 pounds, however Fuller stood at 5'10" and carried his 170 pounds over a supremely athletic frame. When the bout began, the betting was 5 to 4 in favor of Molineaux. The "Terrible Black" was so sure of victory that he had wagered every ounce of money he had in his possession; not only on victory, but that he would draw first blood and score the first knockdown. The men wasted little time sparring as the Tom took after Fuller immediately. Unable to catch his shifty opponent with any hard blows, Molineaux used his left to fine form, stabbing it through the guard of adversary with impunity. Fuller landed as well, but his blows were described as "being more for show than effect". The men were wagering a fairly tactical battle when after only eight minutes of fighting the local sheriff arrived and stopped the fight. Molineaux supposedly was quite upset with the appearance of the lawman and it was claimed that he stated, "Had I foreseen the stoppage of the fight I would have finished off my opponent before your arrival." The American could find solace in the fact that he had drawn first blood by "tapping the crimson" from Fuller's nose, but no knockdowns were scored. Fuller wanted to continue the bout the next day, but Tom insisted on waiting until, "the following Tuesday". This, the men agreed to and set the date for May 31, having further settled that they would meet within 20 miles of Glasgow.

The second Fuller-Molineaux contest came off as planned and proved to be one of the more interesting contests of its time. Fuller had displayed in their first encounter, that despite Molineaux's rumblings, he would not be beaten easily or "off hand". This was an understatement, and in the first round of their second meeting, Fuller clearly demonstrated that he was indeed a capable boxer. The men were so evenly matched that the first round lasted an amazing 28 minutes. Both men did damage, but Molineaux was far superior in his punching power. However it was noted by Miles that "had Fuller been in the ring with the "Terrible Black" with whom Tom Cribb had contended, and not a frail imposter, he would have been beaten down in less than fifteen minutes." That being said Fuller did some solid work, concentrating his efforts to Tom's body in the hope that he could tire out the American. His face paid a terrible price for his efforts however and his blows lacked serious power. It was Fuller however who ended that tremendous first round by leveling Tom with a magnificent right hand. In the second frame the contest continued to ebb and flow with both men taking and dealing out punishment stoically. The bout finally ended when a tiring Molineaux landed a right hand smash to Fuller's temple that hurt him terribly. Retreating to his own "corner" in order to escape punishment, Fuller was pulled down by his second Joe Ward so that Molineaux could not land another blow. Tom appealed to the umpires, claiming that Ward's maneuver was foul and had cost him his opportunity to "finish off" Fuller. The umpires discussed and agreed that Ward had committed a foul and awarded the bout and the stakes to Molineaux. The bout had lasted an amazing 68 minutes during which only two rounds were fought.

That Tom had won was of little consequence at this point in his career. The fight had clearly demonstrated that he was continuing to deteriorate physically. The length of the rounds was proof that the "Terrible Black" could still take punishment but he could no longer deal it out as he once had. His blows lacked the devastating power that they once carried. Fuller, who although gifted as a boxer, was some 15 pounds lighter and by far the more inexperienced man and should have been an easy mark for Molineaux. Where only a few years before Tom could both break down the guard of Cribb and land his right hand in one powerful movement, he was now reduced to fighting for 68 minutes with a general novice at the game. This would be Tom Molineaux's last victory.

Molineaux continued to roam through Scotland, making money exhibiting in any town he could draw a crowd. But as was his custom, Tom would spend his money as quickly as he earned it, entertaining women, drinking until all hours and buying himself trunks full of clothing and shoes. His appearance began to change as well; for his lifestyle had finally taken its toll on his much talked about physique. His body which was once covered in muscle now bore the fat and loose skin attributed to men who were old or worn out. Disease had also taken its toll on Tom as complications from consumption tinted his skin with a deep yellow tinge, turned his eyes red and sunken, and ate away at his innards. Tom Molineaux was dying.

In 1815 a run in with the arrogant Captain Barclay, who still held some sort of grudge against Tom, resulted in a match with George Cooper. Molineaux however, who was not fit to be fighting his trollops at this point in his life, was easily defeated in 20 minutes by the younger Englishmen outside of Edinburgh. Shortly thereafter Molineaux took his act to Ireland, where he was greeted with curiosity and a tentative acceptance. It was here that he would remain for the rest of his life, roaming the country towns and villages, picking up money wherever he could by giving exhibitions and teaching the art of boxing. Molineaux's physical condition was near decrepit at this stage, and soon he was dependent upon the charity of others in order to keep him in food, clothing and shelter. In 1818 he settled in Galway where he continued to slowly die, eking out a meager existence as a teacher of pugilism. Living under the care of three black soldiers, members of the 77th Regiment of Foot band, Tom Molineaux died on August 4th 1818.

Tom Molineaux's death, much like his life was both tragic and fitting. In the end, he was alone and mostly forgotten. He had been used up, by himself and by others and accordingly discarded. Arriving in England he was first considered a comic sideshow, then a celebrity, a terrible threat and finally a beastly disgrace. He sought friends when he had none and drove them away when he had an entire country at his feet. His one true ally, Bill Richmond, possibly the only man in the world who could have understood his experience, was turned into a bitter enemy. Tom, who had arrived in England alone, left alone as well. And if it had not been for the kindness and charity of a few soldiers, fellow black men far from home, he would have died alone.

Miles wrote that, "Molineaux was illiterate and ostentatious, but good tempered, liberal, and generous to a fault. Fond of the gay life, fine clothes and amorous to the extreme, he deluded himself with the idea that his strength of constitution was proof against excess. He was a brave but reckless and inconsiderate man, on whose straightforwardness and integrity none who knew him ever cast a slur; nevertheless he was the worst of fools, inasmuch as he sacrificed fame, fortune and life; excusing himself by the absurd plea, that "he was a fool but no one but himself." Yes indeed, Tom Molineaux was his own ruin. But, examine for a moment the life that he led and it would seem that he had every excuse to be a victim of such follies.

Tom Molineaux must not take all the blame for the fate from which he suffered. He was used and abused by most of those who he encountered. Even Bill Richmond saw in Tom a mere tool for making money, and neither protected him from society or his own self. Molineaux exposed himself to a world that he did not understand: one that mistook his childlike behavior for boorishness and insolence. Yes Tom was arrogant, but he was also brave and fearless. His courage bordered on insanity, for he literally placed his life in the hands of the unknown by simply traveling to England. Egan noted Molineaux's extreme courage stating that upon his arrival in England, Tom, "peeled with the first rough customer who showed fight." Molineaux was prepared to fight anyone, anywhere at anytime. He did not care for the particulars; his objective was to fight and to win. And in Tom Molineaux's heart he thought, better still, he knew that he would win. But the odds Molineaux rolled against were too great: he really never had a chance to truly win. A black man at the beginning of the 19th century had no business going after the Championship of England. It would not have been allowed, in fact, it was not allowed. Paul Magriel wrote, "he had come too far, from a slave to an within and ace of the championship." The fact was however, that Tom Molineaux had that ace, but it had been taken from him while he wasn't looking. Indeed it had been stolen, while he stood in the middle of that rain soaked ring on Copthall Common, waving in the wind like a black oak tree, covered in blood, nearly insensible. It was then, when Thomas Aprecee shouted "Time!" and Tom Cribb lay unable to come to scratch, that jolly old England stole the black Yank's ace—and never gave it back.

4

In the Shadow of Giants

The rise and fall of Tom Molineaux certainly had its effect on prizefighting. Not only had his emergence brought forth a new interest in the game, but also with it came a new division of fighting men: black prizefighters. They did not come in droves, but rather in drips and drabs. It is a testament to this "next generation" of black fighting men, that in most cases they proved themselves more than worthy to be competing along side their white counterparts. It is also must be noted, that despite the English reaction to Molineaux, most of these men were welcomed into the arena with open arms and treated with fair consideration. Perhaps it was the backlash of the first Cribb-Molineaux contest, or the soul searching that went on afterwards that had the greatest impact on the treatment of the men who followed the "Terrible Black". Or possibly it was truly what the English had always prided themselves on: their sense of fair play. Whatever the reason, England regarded this next wave as they had initially treated Richmond and Molineuax, with an open door policy. And in turn these new black prizefighters demonstrated their right to such policy by showing themselves to be honest, tough and clean fighters. One stood out from the rest as both a fighter and a man of the first class. His name was Henry "Harry" Sutton.

Henry Sutton was born in the Southeastern United States sometime around 1792. He himself claimed to have been a slave but through escape, or some other measure, gained his freedom and made his way to Baltimore, Maryland where he found work as a stevedore and then a seaman. Baltimore was then a thriving seaport, and Sutton, by then a young man in his twenties, evidently found his way to Liverpool through employment as a deck hand. Upon arriving in England, Henry, for one reason or another, decided to stay and settled in Deptford where he found work as a corn porter. His color was certainly a disadvantage and much like Richmond some twenty years before, he was often forced to defend himself against the physical attacks of racists and hate mongers. Sutton was not a small man and his hard life of physical work had left him with an impressive physique. He stood a shade over six feet, with massive shoulders and extremely long arms. He had always known how to fight, but in Deptford, his combative prowess against his attackers brought him notice as a man of supreme fighting abilities. Undoubtedly, Sutton had participated in some sort of an organized prizefight prior to his first recorded ring contest, for he was no novice when he first bowed to the Fancy in 1816. Indeed, Eagan noted that prior to having an "official match", Henry had taken part in "a most desperate fight with a man named Dunn, for an hour and seventeen minutes in the street".

It was by happenstance that Henry Sutton would make his first recorded ring appearance. He had traveled up to Combe Wood on a beautiful spring day in May of 1816 to watch two of his own countrymen fight for a prize of 100 guineas. The fact that both men, Joe Stephenson and Sam Robinson, were black Americans is probably what led Sutton to make such a trip. After the battle between Stephenson and Robinson had ended the Fancy were determined to see another contest. One shouted forth that he should like to see another battle between "blacks". The crowd took up the cheer, and Sutton, who must have looked a likely candidate, was offered up a subscription purse of 25 guineas to take on another African-American from the audience simply referred to as "Cropley's Black ". Henry accepted and the two men immediately stripped for battle, Bill Richmond offering to second Sutton and Cropley and Pad Jones seconding his opponent. After an interruption, (during which Caleb Baldwin, a well respected elder of the prize ring, received a good beating from an unlikely foe), Sutton and "Cropley's Black" squared off. Sutton had all the physical advantages, being heavier, taller and broader than his opponent, and despite the efforts of "Cropley's Black" to turn the bout into a jumping and mugging match, Henry won the battle in three, short, one sided rounds.

Bill Richmond liked what he saw from Harry and offered to bring him back to London. Sutton agreed and Richmond brought him out at the Fives Court the very next week. Henry, who was still primitive in his fighting style, was asked to take the stage in order to exhibit with the powerful and well-polished Tom Oliver. Sutton had little idea what to expect from the entire situation for he had never done anything but "real fighting". Neither could he have known who Tom Oliver was or how well experienced and well respected a "miller" he was. Richmond on the other hand knew Tom Oliver well, and figured a few short rounds with an experienced and skilled man would fully test and exhibit the strengths of his new man. Egan noted, "It seemed a new thing altogether and he seemed rather shy and diffident upon the above occasion. His sparring was far from contemptible: and viewing Sutton as a complete novice, he achieved much more than could reasonably be expected, and put in some heavy body blows. Oliver had very little the best of him: and it was observed, that Tom took the gloves off first." If the night had ended there for Sutton it would have been viewed as a mild success, but George Cooper, who had recently returned from Ireland where had engaged in famous battle with Irish Champion Dan Donnelly, insisted on going a few rounds with Richmond's new black as well. Egan wrote, "Sutton, no way dismayed, stood up well to Cooper, and, in a sharp rally, returned some heavy nobbing hits, and exchanged several blows advantageously. Upon the whole, this new man of colour, received much applause: and it was thought not unlikely, at some future period, that he might be brought forward in a more conspicuous point of view. Cooper, like Oliver, it is also to be remarked, took off the gloves first."

Richmond was thrilled, for Sutton's initial appearance at the Fives was a total success. Not only had he proven himself a worthy competitor, but he was also the talk of the Fancy for weeks after. Bill then decided to take Sutton on an exhibition tour up into Northern England and Scotland along with Jack Carter and Harry Harmer. While on tour, Harry was the least paid, yet the biggest attraction. Black prizefighters were still a rarity and Sutton's impressive physique along with his athletic movements exhilarated the crowds at almost every stop along the way. While on tour Richmond continued to communicate with his friends in London in the hope of matching Henry with some good man upon the group's return. Tom Oliver responded by stating he thought that Sutton would make a fine match for "his black", Sam Robinson. Richmond agreed and the men planned to have the bout take place at the Doncaster Races on September 25, 1816. The touring group returned to London and made their way out to the Races a few days prior to the fight. They set up a booth and continued to exhibit while the crowds filtered through the area en route to and from the race locations. During these exhibitions it was announced that Sutton would face Robinson after the final race of the St. Leger Day in a horse paddock adjoining the race-course. Whenever a crowd gathered in front of the booth, Richmond would urge Sutton to take the stage and "flex his muscles" and demonstrate his style. This brought both a greater interest in the bout and a great deal of attention to the Herculean frame of Sutton.

After the racing had been completed the interested parties moved to the selected paddock area and Robinson and Sutton stripped for battle. Upon ready-ing himself, Robinson announced to Tom Oliver that he had misplaced his fight-ing togs and boots and would have to fight in his dress pants and shoes. Richmond, upon hearing of Robinson's plight agreed to have Sutton fight in his shoes as well. He did not want to give Oliver or Robinson any excuse if Sutton proved the better man. At 5pm, with all outside issues having been settled, Rob-inson and Sutton set to, Tom Oliver serving as Sam's second and Richmond and Harry Harmer sharing the duties for Sutton. When standing across from one another it was difficult to discern who had the physical advantage. Both men weighed close to 195 pounds and both stood a touch over six feet. Robinson seemed thicker in the chest but Sutton's arms were longer and by far the heavier muscled. In the first minute of fighting it was clear that neither man wished to do any type of sparring or "feeling out". They charged at one another and immedi-ately took to exchanging fierce and terrific blows. Sutton drew first blood by landing a long right hand on Robinson's nose, but Sam returned fire and rocked his opponent with several hard counters. Henry saw red and rushed at Robinson with his arms flailing wildly. He landed a tremendous left hand on the temple of Sam but in following up landed a blow so low that cries of "foul" rang up from the crowd. Robinson hit the deck clutching his groin and taking up the call of his supporters. The umpires, realizing that this was a crucial moment, convened and after much wrangling, decided that the blow was incidental and that they would not award the bout to Robinson. However, a duration of seven minutes elapsed before the men again stepped to the scratch to recommence the hostilities. Rob-inson seemingly recovered sufficiently from the blow, but was still complaining about the umpires' verdict. When the bout finally resumed, Sutton again made play for Robinson's body, but this time confined his work to the ribs and stomach. Sam had a great deal of difficulty in getting past Sutton's long arms, and when he did he found that Henry was near impervious to his punishment. By the fifth round, Robinson's apparent lack of conditioning began to tell and Sutton settled in to severely punishing his opponent with long right hands. In the 23 round, Robinson had truly had enough but was convinced by his seconds to try another round. He gamely stood the gaff for two more rounds barely able to stand. In the 25th Sam's state was at such an impasse that Sutton seemed hesitant to hurt him any further. Feeling some sense of pity for his American brethren, Henry appealed to Robinson's seconds to throw in the towel. Upon Tom Oliver's refusal, Harry Harmer shouted to Sutton, "It's no good Harry, he will keep us here all day. You must hit him once full between the eyes." Henry backed away from Robinson as if to measure him and let go with just such a blow. Sam took the blow stoically, but fell face first onto the grass. After 26 rounds and 38 minutes of fighting, Harry Sutton was declared the winner.

Sutton made very little money from his match with Robinson, and it seems that it was his own benefactor, Bill Richmond, who made him the fool of the hour. Showing that he was both ignorant to the ways of negotiation and far too trusting of Richmond, Sutton had agreed to fight for any sum that could be raised. Richmond, Harmer and Oliver, who had set up the match, charged admission to the fight gaining three shillings from every man who entered the paddock. Some twelve hundred spectators were present at the mill and it was estimated that these three men had amassed a sum of close to 180 pounds from admission prices alone. It was rumored that Sutton's cut from this princely sum was barely enough to pay his coach fair back to London. That Bill Richmond was a shrewd businessman has already been displayed. That he would take such cruel advantage of Harry Sutton demonstrated that he could be a cutthroat as well.

Sutton's performance against Robinson raised his stock considerably amongst the Fancy. He was now considered a man of the first quality and one who could be safely matched with any man at near even odds. Richmond entertained several offers but decided on another tour instead. The threesome of Richmond, Jack Carter and Henry Sutton set off for the North Country and ventured up again into Scotland. This was easy money for all involved and although Sutton was again the lowest paid man on the tour, he found the work far easier than hard labor.

Upon his return to London, Sutton was matched with Ned Painter, a prizefighter with serious championship aspirations who had swapped punches with the likes of Tom Oliver and Jack Shaw. Although he had been defeated on both occasions, Painter was still considered a man of the first class. The men agreed to fight for 25 guineas a side on July 23, 1817 at Mousley Hurst. Painter was a tall athletic fellow who stood a hair shorter than Sutton, but "stripped like a fine racing horse" and weighed close to 189 pounds. Sutton, on the day of the contest, weighed 187 pounds and was described as being in the best of physical condition. It was again noticed that Henry's arms were considerably longer than those of his adversary. On the day of the bout, Harry was so confident of victory that when fight time arrived he had to be awakened from a nap, which he took in the chaise which had brought him to the scene of the battle. Sutton may have been a bit over-confident; for as soon as the men began to spar it was evident that Painter was clearly Harry's master in terms of science. The bout itself, which lasted well over 40 minutes, was a contrast in styles, Painter the boxer, and Sutton the puncher. Painter would take the play for a few rounds using his better hand speed and defense to punish and frustrate Sutton and then Harry would turn the tide by either a tremendous blow or fearful throw. Miles observed, "In point of science Painter was far superior than his opponent, but in strength he was materially deficient." What Sutton lacked in science he returned in physical strength. The men fought on nearly even terms for close to half an hour at which point, Sutton's superior strength began to tell. According to Miles, "Sutton's prodigious length of arm was of great advantage and he is pronounced by the best informed on the subject to be the most severe hitter on the present list of boxers." Painter was a brave fellow and stood up to his opponent until, what Miles described as, "Nature refused to move." In the 40th round Harry leveled Painter with a "grasser" and was declared the winner when the latter could not recover and come to the scratch at the call of time.

The Sutton-Painter contest was considered a marvel at the time, for it was thought by Miles that, "Two better men never had a meeting: and a more determined battle could not be witnessed." Egan called the fight a "desperate conflict" and spoke of the ferocity and pluck that each man fought with. Miles also noted that both Sutton and Painter fought a terrific match but also a fair and clean one. He continued by stating that, "no prejudice was shown towards Sutton on account of his colour-impartiality was the order of the day!" (That Miles, again borrowing from Oxberry, felt it necessary to point out that Harry Sutton was not subject to any undue interference from the crowd during his bout with Painter spoke volumes of the still fresh feeling that Tom Molineaux had in some way been cheated. The "pat on the back" comment almost implies a sense of guilt over past wrongdoings and in some ways proves that there was still a general feeling of remorse in regards to the treatment of Molineaux at Copthorn in 1810.)

Sutton was nearly unmarked after his battle with Painter with the exception of a "rainbow appearance" on both of his cheeks; he needed little time to heal. He was again at the height of popularity and continued to appear with Richmond at every benefit or pugilistic gathering in and around London. Richmond however was having difficulty in finding any man who would enter the ranks with his newest black sensation. The fighting men of little or no quality could not find the backing to get a match with Sutton and the major men cared not to risk their ambitions with such a glutton as Henry had proven to be. It would therefore be nearly six months before Sutton would again enter the ring and his antagonist would be the same Ned Painter whom he had beaten in July. Harry was not very interested in again meeting Painter, and actually had hopes of being matched with a man with closer claims to the title, but found that he was in no position financially to be so picky.

The men met at Bungay Common in Suffolk on December 16, 1817. The day was a cold and rainy one, but Sutton entered the ring as a 6 to 4 betting favorite despite the common belief of that time that men of "his race" did not fare well in cold weather. Painter, who was eager to avenge his summer loss, stripped in marvelous form having been under the strict training eye of Tom Belcher for two months, and Sutton although a few pounds heavier than when the two men had met previously, also showed great physical appearance. There was a considerable amount of interest generated by the re-matching of the men and even though the location of the match was kept secret until the last moment, nearly 15,000 spectators were present when the first call of time rang out a 12:15pm. The fight itself was very similar to the first, however this time it was Painter's superior skill that told the story. Sutton, perhaps, because of the rain soaked ground, had considerable trouble with his footing and his blows seemed to lack the devastating force that they had carried in the first match. Painter however, must be credited with both improving his ability to take more punishment and hand it out, by a substantially better physical constitution. Where in the first fight he was being hit and hurt by Sutton's best blows, the second match found him just beyond the long reach of Henry's powerful fists. The battle lasted a full hour and two minutes, during which only 15 rounds were fought. Sutton beaten nearly insensible as early as the 12th round, kept coming to the mark only to be the recipient of more abuse. Again, it was Bill Richmond who, after seeing his man clearly beaten, and having no real chance of turning his fortunes, continued to send his man out to the slaughter. Egan noted in the 13th round that, "Sutton was nothing else but a "good one" or he never could have met his man again. In fact he appeared stupid as to scientific movements: but he nevertheless rushed at his opponent pell mell. The Black was now so dead beat that he resigned the contest to his seconds: when he was requested to try two more rounds, which he gamely did, but it was only to add to his punishment. At the end of the fifteenth round he could barely articulate, "he could fight no more!"

Harry's loss was not a devastating one. In fact his reputation may have improved because of it. Pierce Egan commented, "Sutton, notwithstanding the reverse he experienced with Painter, is a most tremendous boxer; and must be viewed as a truly dangerous opponent for any pugilist, however well versed in the art of milling. Sutton is not destitute of tolerable knowledge of the science—upwards of six feet in height—possessing first-rate weight—longer arms than any pugilist on the list—game of the first quality—great activity—not dissipated in his mode of life—and as a pendulum to all these requisites, prodigious strength. As a man of colour he ranks high indeed." But as with most men who have no championship, but provide stern opposition, Harry Sutton would soon learn that his position was not an enviable one.

Harry took a bit of time away from the ring and settled down, taking a wife and earning his money as a trainer and through exhibition tours. When he decided, either for want of action or money, that he wanted to make a match, he found there were no takers. Like Tom Molineaux, Sutton had a falling out with Richmond, the former no doubt realizing that he had been taken advantage of on more than one occasion, and formed a short lived partnership with another of the ex-Richmond sect, Jack Carter. In late 1818, the two men made a successful tour of Scotland, where Harry met a few willing "customers" in a "take on all comers" format. However, upon again returning to London, Harry was doomed to the fact that he could find no man who would meet him in the ring. Miles chalked up Sutton's negative position to the fact that he presented, "too great an odds for the middle weights and the big ones wanted larger figures than Harry could get backed for." In other words, none of the second tier men wanted to face Sutton and most of the first rate men demanded sums of money, 200 guineas and up, that Harry could not even dream of collecting. That Sutton could not find such a backer spoke more to the times than it did to his discredit. England was in a bit of an economic tailspin in those years due to the strains of war and expansion. Sporting money was not long and the purse strings of the wealthy sports grew tighter and tighter.

In November 1818, Sutton did get a chance to spar with the future heavyweight champion of England, Tom Spring at a benefit for Bob Purcell at Tom Oliver's Peter Street establishment, but it was not a fun night for Harry. Spring was an extremely fast man, who prided himself on his ability to "hit and get away". He was considered a "dandy" of sorts in that his movements and punches were flashy and generally accurate, however his punches lacked any real power and he was thought deficient in the department of taking punishment. Despite these supposed shortcomings, Spring lost only one fight during his career, to Ned Painter and was crowned Champion of England in 1823. Such a man, whose style enabled him to excel at "sparring", presented a most difficult and frustrating opponent for Sutton. Harry was not a man of great science and his abilities could not be properly displayed in a friendly sparring match. However, Sutton knew that an opportunity to show with Spring would increase his chances at gaining a real match. When the men began, the sparring was generally tame and each man tried little to damage the other. The crowd playfully called for more action and Spring, feeling the hero of the moment, accommodated them. Using his superior hand and foot speed he began to slap Sutton with open gloves, laughing at Harry's wild returns and speaking to the crowd. Sutton was normally not a man to be fooled with, however, in the ring with the "mufflers", he stood little chance of retaliating against the superior skills of Spring. The crowd, which was enjoying Spring's mockery of his black opponent began to laugh aloud at Sutton, reverting to racial slurs and other cruel comments to further embarrass and anger Harry. Finally, Sutton tore off his gloves and looking fiercely at Tom Spring shouted, "I am ready to fight you now Tom Spring or any other dammed butcher in London!" At this comment the crowd burst into further laughter and their insults grew so vicious that Sutton jumped into the crowd and began attacking the spectators. Dolly Smith, a prizefighter of minor pretensions who had been standing near the ring and leading the jibbing, was grabbed by Sutton about the neck and thrashed violently. Harry was angered beyond consolation and it took the efforts of Tom Oliver, Tom Owen and Jack Randall to pull him off of Smith. Sutton then turned on Oliver and swung viciously for his head. Oliver ducked the blow and the two men squared off. A short mill ensued, during which both men landed some damaging blows, but was quickly broken up by Tom Cribb, Spring and Tom Owen. After cooling down, Sutton apologized to Oliver and Spring as well as to many of the spectators who he had attacked, but steadfastly refused to apologize to Smith. Lord Brooke, who himself had been ringside when the melee broke out did not blame Sutton for attacking Smith and stated to more than one person, "If a terrier will keep yelping at the Mastiff, why, he must expect to get chewed up!" Harry himself commented that, "the damn little beast got what he deserved." The general feeling was that Sutton had been provoked beyond normal and that Smith had gotten what his actions warranted. As for Tom Oliver, he had little issue with Harry, and in an ironic turn, the two became closer friends because of the incident.

Despite his inability to gain a true match, Harry continued to keep in the public eye by appearing at every benefit and exhibition he could find and by challenging all and sundry without cause or concern. In April of 1819, at a benefit for Bob Gregson at the Fives Court, the main attraction was to be a sparring match between Cribb, who by now was several years retired, and Dan Donnelly, the famous Irish champion. The idea of such an exhibition excited a great general interest among the sports and several thousand turned out to witness the great display. As it turned out, Donnelly had been injured the night before when he had been thrown from his stagecoach and begged out of his exhibition with Cribb. Jack Carter was summoned and took to the stage with the Irish champion, but because of the latter's injured arm, the event generated little interest. Upon Donnelly's exit from the stage Sutton, seeing a chance to make a match for himself took the stage and challenged Donnelly to a fight for 50 pounds a side. Great applause greeted Sutton's challenge. Richmond, who had befriended Donnelly, presented himself and retorted that, "the Irish Champion did not come over to England with any intention of entering the Prize Ring." Jack Carter who still stood on the stage interjected and stated, "Mr. Donnelly meant to insult his friends by fighting Sutton." The crowd erupted with laughter, and Harry fumed with anger. He again mounted the stage and stated that he would fight Donnelly at five minutes notice for 50 pounds, or from 100 to 200 pounds at any given time, in a ring. The crowd again roared their approval but a match was never made.

Sutton luck seemed to turn when a match was proposed with a "raw one" named Harry Larkin. The match was made but then quickly cancelled when Larkin, who was a military man, injured himself during training. Sutton gained some comfort from the 20-pound forfeit he received from Larkin's backers and a greater lift when the latter healed and challenged Henry yet again. A match was once more arranged for a 20 guineas a side stake and was to be settled at a location to be determined by John Jackson on November 4, 1819. Harry was for a second time to be disappointed however, as prior to the match Larkin's superior officer, who hearing of the match, at once sent for aspiring pugilist at his training quarters and ordered him back to headquarters under penalty of desertion. Of course, Larkin acquiesced and Harry had to settle for another forfeiture; this time in the amount of 50 pounds. Sutton would finally get into real action when he was called into duty against another black fighter named Massa Kendrick, when a proposed match between Tom Shelton and Tom Spring was foiled by the pitching of two separate rings in two different locations nearly 20 miles apart. The men who had gathered at Blindlow Heath to witness the Shelton-Spring contest gathered a subscription purse of 25 guineas by which they induced Sutton and Kendrick to have it out. The match was hardly competitive and Sutton beat Kendrick rather easily in less than 20 minutes. It would be Harry Sutton's last prizering performance.

Sutton continued to frequent every prize ring match and exhibition that occurred in the hope of finding some work, but after proposed matches with, Jack Carter and Tom Spring never materialized, Harry resigned himself to the fact that no customers would ever be found. He again took to touring with Jack Carter and Jack Reynolds, but the money was not enough to keep him interested. It was then that Sutton seemingly came unglued, for his lifestyle took a drastic turn from here on in. Now supporting a wife and three children, Sutton gained employment as a valet for a wealthy land baron. However, after being insulted by one of his employer's friends, Harry was fired for beating the man senseless. Sutton took to the bottle heavily and whatever money he made, from his appearances as a second or sparer, was quickly spent in the taverns and carousing with professional women. Late in 1822, Sutton became gravely ill, with what was termed as "the affects of consumption." By as early as February 1823, Harry Sutton was on his deathbed. On February 11 of that year, Tom Oliver took the stage at the Fives Court and appealed to the generosity of the crowd by asking for a subscription to be gathered for the family of Sutton. He stated that, "Harry Sutton is nearly dead. He is in the last stage of consumption. He has not left his bed since he was in the Court when you were pleased to do something for him. He has a wife and three children, without any means of support. I am sure you are too generous to let a brave man want: and I never knew an appeal made here in vain." Oliver's heartfelt speech on behalf of his friend brought a sound round of applause and a subscription collection of nearly 50 guineas. That Harry Sutton was well liked and admired by the sporting fraternity was clear by the sum of money collected. What is not clear is his ultimate fate. No detail or date of his death survives, yet is probable that he expired shortly after Oliver's speech in 1823. What became of his wife and children is also unclear and it can only be assumed that their lot only worsened after Harry's death.

Harry Sutton was never considered as a challenger for the crown of England. His fighting powers were both respected and acknowledged. However, he was never feared in the same sense that Molineaux had been. Perhaps it was the difference in each man's approach. Where Molineaux was brash and outspoken, Sutton was for the most part reserved and quiet. Harry never seemed to aspire to the championship and perhaps that is why the English viewed him with such admiration and muted respect. In a sense they valued the fact that professionally Sutton seemingly new his place—that is to say, he knew that it was not in his best interest to follow in the footsteps of Tom Molineaux. For Harry, prizefighting was about one thing—money. It was a means to an end for him and that end was a better life financially. He was however, a man who would not be trifled with personally, for he clearly demonstrated that when harassed because of his race, he would fight with anyone and everyone. Perhaps Sutton fit his role perfectly—for although he may have stood a chance to gain the championship, all he ever asked for was the opportunity to make a decent amount of money.

5

The First of Its Kind

When Tom Molineaux left England in the spring of 1813, only one other black boxer could be found in Great Britain for the next several years: the venerable Bill Richmond. Although in semi retirement, he was the only black fighter active between the years of 1813 through 1816. However, in the year 1816, either by the fame or relative successes of Molineaux (and in many respects Bill Richmond) or some other divine issue, the African-American would be represented in greater numbers than ever before in the history of the modern ring. Why this phenomenon began in 1816, as opposed to the years immediately following Tom Molineaux's brave stands against Tom Cribb is unknown. However, in one year the prize ring would see its number of black practitioners nearly double as five new black men, Joe Stephenson, Sam Robinson, Harry Sutton, Cropley's Black and Bristow (Young Massa) entered the lists of fighting men.

Sam Robinson was a likely looking specimen, being described as both tall and heavily muscled. His legs were long and thin, his hips narrow and his shoulders tremendous in their breadth. Sam claimed to have been a freeman and a sailor and upon de-boarding in London in late 1815 he sought out Bill Richmond. It is safe to assume that Robinson had heard of the exploits of Molineaux, and considering himself a likely candidate for pugilistic honor, he had hoped to enlist himself among the ranks of fighting men. Bill, as he had done before for Tom Molineaux, took Robinson in and set him up with his first match. Robinson showed better form than Richmond had expected and won his first contest, with a man named Tom Crockery in less than 12 minutes. Three months later, Sam was again returned a winner when he bested Alf Butcher at Coombe Warren in 47 minutes during which 44 rounds were contested.

About this time another black American walked into Bill Richmond's house looking for work. His name was Joe Stephenson and like Robinson he was a fine looking athlete, being tall, nearly six foot in height, deep chested and extremely muscular. However, Stephenson's journey from birth to Richmond's house had been a bit different than that of Sam Robinson. Born a slave in Havre de Grace, Maryland, sometime during his teen years Stephenson escaped his owners by murdering one of his overseers and evaded subsequent search parties by swimming to assorted small islands in the Chesapeake Bay. After several days of remaining hidden he swam to a ship flying a British flag under the cover of night. There he was taken on board and given a job as a steward under which occupation he served for several years during the War of 1812. When the war ended, Stephenson took a similar job with a trading vessel and made his way to Bristol where he de-boarded and left his service. He wandered about in Bristol and worked for a period as an attendant for a wealthy Irishman, who upon seeing Joe thrash a man in a street fight suggested the latter visit Richmond in London. Hearing of the quick wealth that a top-flight fighter could acquire, Stephenson took his employer's suggestion and found his way to the Horse and Dolphin.

Bill Richmond tried Stephenson out himself and felt that although the young black American was strong and could take some heavy punishment, he was not as refined as Robinson. In fact, Richmond decided that Stephenson was such a "novice" and so unprepared for a true match that he confined him to sparring and training. Sam and Joe lived with Bill for a few months, Stephenson helping Robinson prepare for his matches and Richmond attempting to refine both of their fighting styles. Both steadily improved and both benefited from having the other around. Robinson and Stephenson, both being black and foreign, must have enjoyed one another's company, for although Richmond was black and an American by birth, he had become an Englishman for all intents and purposes and probably could no longer relate to the experience of his two new students. But not all was well.

Robinson, after his victory over Butcher had been approached and congratulated by Tom Oliver. Oliver, who took an immediate liking to Sam—as well as an instant fondness for his fighting potential, offered the black American his services as a trainer and sponsor. Tom in an attempt to pry Robinson's devotion away from Bill Richmond also told Sam of Bill's troubles with Molineaux. He stated that it was Bill who had ill prepared the "Terrible Black" for his second match with Cribb and had also been the one guilty of being confused and deceived by Joe Ward in the 28th round of the first battle. Robinson was smitten with Oliver and taken in by his negative talk about Richmond. Later that night when Richmond questioned Sam about his conversation with Tom Oliver, the two had a row and Bill ended the argument by throwing Robinson out into the street. This disagreement would be the catalyst by which a wholly unique and new event would unfold before the eyes of the English Fancy: a prizefight between two black men.

After being tossed from Richmond's establishment, Robinson immediately made his way to Tom Oliver's. The two men came to an agreement and as promised, Oliver agreed to take Sam "under his wing". Richmond was seemingly unfazed when he learned of the new alliance and set his mind to improving Stephenson's chances at ring fame. In Bill's parlor Stephenson showed a great deal of improvement in sparring sessions and Bill eventually felt confident enough to match him with a "good one".

The man who was to be Joe's first opponent was Richmond's old foe and friend, Jack Carter. Carter and Stephenson met at Coombe Warren on Feb 6, 1816 and Carter made a chopping block of the black American. Stephenson, although demonstrating a superior amount of strength, was no match for Carter and defeated with ease in less than one hour.

Robinson was also not having the best of luck, himself being beaten by the same Jack Carter in 18 minutes a few months later. Despite the offerings of Oliver, Sam was hardly fit or prepared when the bout commenced and it seemed to many that he had "taken a step back" from when he was under the watchful eye of Richmond. Whether or not Oliver had truly done his best to prepare his new black charge was a subject for much debate in the weeks following the Carter debacle. Tom quickly grew weary of the subject and angry at the attack on his reputation.

Perhaps seeking to repair his damaged name or better still, possibly only trying to make himself a bit of coin, Oliver, on behalf of Robinson challenged Richmond and Stephenson to fight for 40 guineas. Bill, considering the stake being one that could be easily covered and the opponent one who could be conquered, accepted the challenge without delay. The match was made for May 28, 1816 and was to occur at Coombe Warren. A match between two black men intrigued the Fancy for as the Sporting Magazine noted, "it was a nouvelle exhibition, never before witnessed in this country". Indeed, nothing of the sort had ever been observeed by the sporting public, for up until the time that Stephenson and Robinson had appeared on the scene, the only black men to have ever competed in the modern ring were Lashley, Richmond and Molineaux. If the Fancy were excited to witness something new, or in this case something they considered "exotic", they were not to be disappointed, for by the end of the day, they would behold the skills of five different black fighters in one ring.

Nearly five thousand men were on hand to witness the historic mill between the two American blacks. Stephenson and Robinson entered the ring around 12 noon, and fought for over and hour and ten minutes. Harry Harmer and Bill Richmond seconded Stephenson and Tom Oliver and an assistant looked after Robinson. Joe and Sam fought like they themselves had a grudge to settle. Indeed there had been words exchanged between the two men in which Stephenson chided Robinson for lasting a mere 18 minutes before the same man whom Joe had extended for twice that time. However, there was little else to explain the ferocity of the fight other than both men had a supreme will to win. Robinson was the better boxer by a small margin, but again Stephenson was stronger and showed a seemingly newly acquired aptitude at wrestling maneuvers. The Sporting Magazine described the bout as "lacking in first rate science", but continued by stating "the men of colour made a good battle of it." Stephenson controlled most of the fight by manhandling Robinson who "displayed a great deal of bottom as the falls he took should have defeated him." Sam was not undone by the superior wrestling of Joe and waited for the latter to tire before forcing his own will. In the latter rounds as the pace slowed, Robinson began to take liberties with Stephenson and beat him savagely in exchanges that were marked by their brevity and brutality. In the 68th round, Stephenson, who was noticed to be "done" as early as the 31st round, took a flush hit on his chin and was at length "grassed" for good. And according to the Sporting Magazine, "thus finished the first black mill!"

When the match ended a sea of people broke the outer ring, more out of excitement than any malicious attempt at deviance, and streamed into the inner ring. Robinson helped Stephenson to his feet and walked him to his "corner" where Richmond, who never let go of a grudge, greeted him with an icy return. So pleased were the Fancy with the "battle betwixt the Blacks" that a call went up amongst the crowd for "another black mill". As has been described in another chapter Harry Sutton and Cropley's Black were then chosen to fight for a sub-scription purse gathered by the crowd and stripped immediately to do battle. However, as the men attempted to clear the ring so that the fight could begin, an incident occurred which would bring forward another black pugilist, one who had no intention of ever entering the ring. His name was simply Bristow, but his appellation has been recorded in the annals of the prize ring as Young Massa.

One of the men who were "clearing" the ring was the renowned Caleb Bald-win. Baldwin was a retired man of a fine fighting pedigree. He had drawn with the redoubtable Paddington Jones 1792 and had fought the great Dutch Sam for 37 rounds in 1804. He had figured in over 10 prize ring battles and only the great Sam had beaten him. He was one of the Masters of Ceremony, given the duty of maintaining harmony at the great "black mill", and when order had been called, Caleb drew from his hip a riding whip, which he began to twirl and lash at those who would not clear the inner ring. One of the men that he struck was Young Master Bristow, or Young Massa, a sturdy looking black man who was there in the service of a wealthy sporting patron. Upon being struck by Baldwin, Bristow being, as Miles noted, "new to his freedom and unacquainted with the person and privileges of Caleb as a public functionary" struck the veteran pugilist with two hard blows to the face, knocking him to the turf. Baldwin, both shocked and embarrassed, immediately challenged his assailant to fight it out in the ring. Bris-tow, either full or confidence or truly ignorant to the qualifications of his adver-sary, readily agreed and the men unceremoniously stripped for battle. Bill Richmond, who was still on hand, and was always willing to assist "one of his own", agreed to second Young Massa, and Harry Harmer volunteered to serve in the same capacity for Caleb.

The first round may have summed up the entire contest. Baldwin, who although in his 48 year and still considered a man to be reckoned with, was visi-bly angry and eager to "beat off hand" his presumptuous opponent. He rushed at Bristow and a violent altercation ensued, however, it was Young Massa and not the respected Caleb, who had the better of the exchanges. Further exasperated by his inability to bring down his black foe, Baldwin rushed in furiously only to be "cross-buttocked" and thrown by Bristow.

The second round was a repetition of the first with Baldwin's efforts to reach his opponent wholly unsuccessful, and his "visage' paying the fare in the form of rights and lefts from the young black. In the fourth round, so superior was Bris-tow that Miles reported that the, "young Blackey, full of gayety, pointed his fin-ger at the veteran, by way of derision, and kept moving with great agility." Young Massa's taunting further infuriated Baldwin, but the latter's attempts at physical retaliation fell well short of their mark. In the following rounds, Bristow continued to punish Baldwin at will, and there was a general hush of disbelief that fell over the crowd. Miles noted in the 12th round that, "It was altogether an unfortunate turn up for the veteran; and even the terrors of the ring did not in the least abate the confidence of the young adventurer, who hit out and faced his man more like an experienced man than a raw chance miller!"

In some ways the crowd also began to display their level of discomfort with the fact that the young black stranger was both beating the well-respected Baldwin and taunting him. Miles noted this anxiety and in a tone reminiscent of the first Cribb-Molineaux contest, or better still the Molineaux Rimmer battle, he noted, "Perish the thought; ne'er be it said that Caleb, the renowned Caleb Baldwin, of milling notoriety, ever surrendered his hard earned laurels, into the hands of a mere stripling novice, and that too a black!" There would be no riot, nor any other irregularities, for cooler heads prevailed. At the end of the 13th round some men who seemed overly concerned with what they viewed as the inevitable outcome of the fight, approached Bristow and induced him, by way of a 30 pound offering, to call the fight. Young Massa, who must have at the very least felt vindicated for Baldwin's initial offense, agreed and the fight was stopped. Miles noted that, "Blackey, upon being persuaded to relinquish the contest received his reward for the pluck he manifested in daring to enter the lists with so renowned a punisher as Caleb Ramsbottom Baldwin!" Caleb's reputation was apparently saved by the actions of the men who stopped the bout, for the result of the fight was officially listed as a draw, and in some works it is even referenced as a win for Baldwin.

Caleb Baldwin was taken from the field of battle in bad shape and he would never enter the ring again. However his bout with Bristow demonstrated some of the wonderfully modern, yet wholly contradictory aspects, of English race relations at the time. In 1816 in America, a young black servant would have never dared to strike a white man in public, never mind a man of civic status such as Baldwin. For such an act, a black American could only draw upon himself ridicule, physical harm and in the most severe scenario, death. In England however, such an act was considered within a man's rights, whether he was black or white. Bristow, who was born in America, must have been either living in England for a substantial amount of time, or extremely brave. It seems unlikely that he would have struck Baldwin otherwise. He undoubtedly had little indication prior to punching Baldwin as to how the predominantly white crowd would react to such an action. However, the crowd, including Baldwin, acted as if it were any normal circumstance. As has been discussed, in the early 19th century society of England, arguments or matters of dented honor were most times settled by an organized fistfight. So in essence, Bristow's affront was treated not only by Baldwin, but by the bystanders as well, to be like that of any other man. That Bristow was allowed to defend his honor and personal pride demonstrated that England was light years ahead of her American cousins when it came to race matters. Yet, despite the fair and liberal air of the entire matter, it still seemed that when black Massa began to beat white Caleb senseless, the feeling of uneasiness amongst the crowd again surfaced. Interference, although of a far less intrusive and unfair manner, was again resorted to in order to stop that which made the crowd uncomfortable: a black beating a white. So even though on the surface the English seemed to truly believe in a sense of fair play for all, when the black fighter asserted his dominance a truer feeling of resentment and fear prevailed.

After Bristow and Baldwin had left the ring, Sutton and Cropley's Black settled their contest in just under 15 minutes. Thus in the course in less than 4 hours, 5 black men, 3 who had never before been seen in the ring, competed for fistic honors. The significance of May 28, 1816 then may be seen as two fold. First, it marked the first recorded instance of two black men facing one another in a prize ring battle (this event actually occurred twice, Robinson, Stephenson, Sutton and Cropley's Black all fighting on that day). Secondly, the number of black fighters active in England more than doubled in the course of one afternoon. Before the day had begun, the thought of black men fighting was still considered a novelty. By the day's end it must have seemed to be near commonplace.

Besides Henry Sutton, only Sam Robinson would leave any type of lasting impression on the prize ring. After the Stephenson affair he took part in another six battles in the ring, loosing to Sutton, Jack Carter (again) and to George Cooper, whom Sam nearly knocked out before running out of steam. He also won a few more bouts, defeating the likes of Tom Taylor, Alexander Fangill and a butcher named Dent. Robinson's match with Fangill was a true grudge fight, supposedly induced by the latter's jealousy regarding a certain woman whom both he and Sam loved. Robinson won the fight and the girl, marrying the Scottish seamstress and retiring to a quiet life near Edinburgh where he lived out his days in the service of horse monger. Joe Stephenson dropped from site after his match with Robinson. It is likely that he again took to the sea for employment, probably figuring that despite his ambition he had little chance to gain any real fame or fortune from the ring. His name never again appeared in any contemporary volume regarding the "noble art". Cropley's Black suffered a similar fate for he never again competed in the ring. In fact his true name was never listed in any work. Young Massa Bristow would take part in two more contests, defeating a non-entity named Little Tom in 1817 and loosing on foul to perhaps the even more forgettable Pug McGee in the fall of the same year. After his brief career in the ring, Bristow, like Stephenson, most likely returned to his previous occupation; in his case that of a page or servant.

Despite the less than stellar achievements of the above group of men, they served an important purpose in the development of the black prizefighter. They were the second wave, and in many ways just as important as Molineaux and Richmond. Their accomplishment, although with the exception of Sutton very minor, were the cornerstone on which future generations of black fighters would build. Their skills in the ring as well as their character and comportment, both in and out of the squared circle, demonstrated to the Fancy that they were indeed equal to the task, and in many ways, a group to be both respected and feared.

6

The Not So Roaring 20's

The 1820's were not a specifically vibrant time for the black prizefighter in England. Although the teens had seen a dramatic increase in the number of black men who declared themselves ready to meet the rigors of the ring, only four new black men would fight in the prize ring during the second decade of the nineteenth cetnury. Although all were successful to a certain degree, none would leave a mark similar to Richmond, Molineaux or even Harry Sutton. The first of these men was a tumultuous street ruffian from the West Indies, the second an awe inspiring physical specimen whose career was marred by inconsistency, the third a mere footnote, and the last a confident American sailor who never tasted defeat.

On a crisp May evening in 1819 a group of well known pugilists gathered at the Peter-street watering hole/parlor of Tom Oliver, to share drinks, stories and hopefully make a match between Tom and the Irish Champion Dan Donnelly. The Irishman was present, as were Tom Spring, George Cooper, Jack Turner, Jack Carter, a host of other well known fighting men, and an odd mixture of retired military men, wealthy sports and hangers-on. While the men discussed the proposed match a servant notified Oliver that a likely looking black man had requested Tom's presence outside to discuss an urgent manner.

When Tom Oliver reached his front door he found standing before him a tall, bony yet athletic black man, who stood close to six feet and weighed near 180 pounds. The man presented himself as John Kendrick, and told Oliver that he was a prizefighter. Tom nodded and his visitor continued by stating that he would appreciate the opportunity to be introduced to the gathering and his "challenge" conveyed to all present. Tom asked the black man, "Then what is your challenge?" Kendrick answered that he offered to fight any man present for a subscription purse. Oliver looked Kendrick over and then told him to wait outside.

Upon returning to his guests, Tom announced Kendrick's challenge and immediately Dan Donnelly was asked if he would take on the "black". Donnelly, who had never before fought in England, refused stating, "the initial essay of the Champion of Ireland should not be hidden in a room." Next Carter was offered the assignment, but he was in no condition to even spar having but less than a week prior engaged in a 110-minute contest with Tom Spring. Finally George Cooper was induced to accept the 25-guinea offer to take on Kendrick. John was invited into the parlor, and when told that he would win 21 guineas if he won and 4 if he lost, reportedly replied, "Very well; me win it." After all the furniture and other items had been cleared from the parlor Tom Oliver, in a fit of unnecessary ceremony, stepped forward and introduced George Cooper to the crowd and John as "Massa" Kendrick.

When the men squared off Egan noted that Kendrick looked formidable, but the "knowing ones" were sure that a few short rounds with Cooper would "satisfy the ambitions of Massa". Kendrick surprised most of the men in the room when he won the first round by closing with Cooper, hitting him, and bringing him down. In fact for the first 14 rounds, there was little to choose between the two men, and those who had initially wagered that Kendrick would prove an easy mark for George were heard to mumble, "It's not so safe". By the 26th round, odds, which when the fight began were being given at 10 to 5 on Cooper, where now being given 6 to 5 on Kendrick. John demonstrated that he was no novice at the game of fighting and his technique was considered to be uncanny for a supposed neophyte. "The right hand of Massa", wrote Egan, "was always at work, and he punished Cooper considerably about the head. Cooper could not get his distance to make a hit, the Black bored in so much upon him. The claret was now running down Cooper's face." By the 40th round the fight had lasted well over 50 minutes and Cooper gave no indication that he had the ability to turn the fight in his favor. In the 41st round Kendrick nearly ended the fight when he landed "a tremendous facer on Cooper's nose", which sent the latter down and nearly out. George was a game one however and continued to fight on despite the punishment he received. In the 61st round cries of derision rang up amongst the crowd, for they could not believe that a novice was having his way with such a fine pugilist as Cooper was considered. But George had something left and as Kendrick began to tire, and Cooper began to sober himself to the task before him, the tide of the battle slowly changed. By the 63rd round, nearly an hour into the fight, Massa Kendrick was running out of gas, and Cooper was taking advantage. In the 65th Kendrick was exhausted and claimed to his second that he had "had enough", but was urged to continue. George forced the pace and knocked Kendrick about for 4 more rounds until latter, through sheer exhaustion, was forced to concede defeat. What was supposed to have been a turn-up lasted one hour and five minutes.

John "Massa" Kendrick was born in St. Kitts on May 11, 1798. It was his 21st birthday on the evening of his encounter with George Cooper. He had come to England much like every other fighter who would appear in the prize ring: as a sailor on board a trade vessel. He had earned himself a reputation as a fighter on board his ship, and in several of the minor ports where he had traveled. His decision to stay in England was probably based more on monetary gain than any championship aspirations. His skills were considerable, yet his methods were unusual and, in many cases, abrasive. A month before his initial appearance at Tom Oliver's, Kendrick had created somewhat of a sensation by purposefully insulting Bill Richmond outside of the Fives Court. Kendrick, who had hoped to induce a fight for a purse with Bill, must have truly angered Richmond for the latter, who was noted for his calm demeanor, responded to the jibe with slap to John's face. The two men immediately began to fight, and had quite a turn up until separated by several sporting men. John challenged Richmond to a fight for 50 pounds but when asked to produce the money he could neither foot the bill himself nor find a backer. His initial plan to make a fight foiled, Kendrick then made his way to Tom Oliver's.

Even though Kendrick had lost his bout with Cooper, he must have considered the night a success. For as Egan noted after the fight, "The black although defeated gained a few friends." The "friends" that Egan spoke of where the wealthy men who could back Kendrick for future fights and thus guarantee him at least the opportunity to make some good money. In fact, a week after Kendrick's initial turn up, these "friends" offered Cooper a fight with John for a 50-pound purse. George refused however stating that, "defeating Kendrick would not add to his reputation". Hearing the above response many of the Fancy criticized Cooper for turning the bout down figuring that it was an easy 50 pounds for George to make. However, only Cooper could truly know how "easy" it was to fight John Kendrick, and judging by the near hour of punishment he had taken from the latter, Cooper was well within his rights to turn the bout down.

Kendrick was seemingly out of luck as most of his challenges fell on deaf ears. His predicament was a familiar one in boxing: he was a high-risk opponent who offered little reward. But he remained undaunted. Two weeks after fighting Cooper, John walked from London to the Epsom Races where he was told by some of the men who had offered to back him, that an impromptu match with some good man could be made. Sure enough, upon arriving, Kendrick was offered a match with his former host, Tom Oliver, for a 50-pound purse.

The fight was slated to begin at 6pm after the last of the races had begun. This was a very late starting time for a prizefight, and an indication that the men who had made the match figured it to be a walkover for the accomplished Oliver. Kendrick was again much better than had been expected and gave the skilled Oliver life and death for over 30 rounds before giving in. Miles noted, "The battle was not won with the ease which had been anticipated, and it was asserted that if Massa had been in better condition, and had possessed the advantages of patronage, he might have proved a troublesome customer. As it was the battle lasted over an hour." Kendrick again displayed both a good knowledge of fighting and a very potent right hand. His stamina again betrayed him, but considering his circumstances he had neither the resources nor the sponsorship to adequately train. The 15 mile walk from London to Epsom probably also served to further drain his physical ability. Thus it seems that Kendrick, although a fighter of quality was never truly prepared to fight Oliver or anyone else for that matter. That he had fought on somewhat equal terms with Tom was a testament to his natural skill.

The spontaneous nature of Kendrick's fights with both Cooper and Oliver would define his career, for never was he truly prepared for a fight in the traditional sense. However, he was always ready to fight. His battle on the street with Richmond was only the first in many incidents, outside the ring, during which Kendrick would exchange blows. In 1825 he was brought before a magistrate twice for allegedly committing a violent assault on the driver of a hackney coach in Westminster named Thomas Feethy. In 1826, he had a barroom brawl with none other than Tom Cribb himself. The row ensued after Cribb attempted to toss a drunk and disorderly Kendrick from his pub by kicking him in the backside. Kendrick was jailed and both men were brought before the magistrate. When questioned about the incident Cribb stated, "If I was not to take such a step as this, now and then, I could not carry on my own business or even live in my own house, for these swaggering black guards!" Kendrick, when asked by the magistrate if he intended on posting bail, replied, "Massa Cribb is the most quarrelsome man in all of England. He is a fighting man and I am a fighting man, an if I gives him a punch on the head and he gives me another, what's that to anyone else? And so what's the use of talkin' about bail?" Both the men were released, Cribb with no fine and Kendrick with a stern warning. They also agreed to stay clear of one another.

Kendrick continued to roam London and the vicinity looking for any willing customers but his challenges were generally scoffed at. He ended his initial year in the prize ring by taking a fearful beating from Harry Sutton at Blindlow Heath, another match in which John engaged in while hardly trained or prepared. But as was his custom, John never showed lack of fight and hoped in the very least that as Egan noted, "If he did not win the purse he might experience the liberality of the amateurs". Egan in fact felt that because of his destitute circumstance, Kendrick took the bout with no real feeling that he could win, but rather because he thought he might be able to pocket a little bit of well needed coin if he showed pluck enough during the fight. Kendrick had again walked from London to Blindlow Heath and was described as being, "thin and with a grubbery as empty and hollow as a drum." Egan riding in a carriage on his way to the fight spotted Kendrick on the road to Blindlow, "without a single brown, trotting along the road, bearing up against the wind and rain, anxious to get down to see the fight between Oliver and Shelton ". As has been described in another chapter, the Sutton Kendrick mill was an unplanned fight, which occurred on account of Oliver and Shelton showing up at different locations for their fight. Kendrick looked sickly and small next to Sutton, who when stripped showed the magnificent physique of a well trained, and suitably fed, athlete. The fight was a mismatch and lasted barely 17 minutes, but John took the worst beating of his career. So superior in strength was Sutton that at one point during the fight he literally lifted Kendrick over his head and threw him to the ground. Henry then fell upon him with the entire weight of his body, a maneuver that was perfectly legal in the prize ring. Kendrick's injuries were of such a serious manner that he had to be carried from the field of battle. He was placed in a coach, and by the generosity of a noble sport driven back to London in comfort and placed under the care of a physician. The sympathy the crowd felt for Kendrick was manifested in a rather substantial subscription purse that was gathered and presented to him in London.

It did not go unnoticed by the Fancy that John Kendrick had now fought three different battles under supreme handicaps. In fact, it was stated by several men who had seen him fight that with a sufficient amount of training and proper living standards (food and nutrition), Massa Kendrick might make a tough day for any good man. So sure were some of these men that they attempted to match Kendrick with Thomas Hickman "The Gas-Light Man" who had defeated among others, George Cooper and Peter Crawley. John's supporters also offered to place their man under a careful trainer and put him up with a "proper place to reside and all the bare essentials". However, Hickman had other ideas and politely declined the 25 guineas a side offer. Mass Kendrick was again out of luck.

Kendrick did get a chance to finally show what he could do with proper training and a bit of time to prepare when he fought Dick Acton in December of 1821. In this contest Kendrick mastered his man throughout and instead of tiring as the bout grew longer, John strengthened until finally finishing Acton in the 17th round after 25 minutes of fighting. It was a solid win for Kendrick and one that gained him a new respect and new accolades from the Fancy. He was not allowed to rest on his laurels for long however and he and Acton were re-matched the following February. On this occasion Acton turned the tables on John. After again dominating the fight for close to 20 rounds, Kendrick had his jaw broken in the 21st round and never recovered. He fought on gamely for another 11 rounds but ultimately gave in after 35 minutes of fighting.

John Kendrick never again appeared in the prize ring. He continued to make his money as a fighter, training others, and touring with several different exhibition troupes but he never truly made the big money for which he so desperately tried. For several years he worked for John Hunt at the Tennis Courts as an "exhibitor of the manly art", for which he was paid 2 pounds per week, but even this excursion gained him little fame or riches. His fortunes would continue to spiral in a downward path until he became no more than a street beggar and he ultimately died of consumption in 1844. He was buried in a pauper's grave.

James "Jemmy" Johnson could not have posed a more stark contrast to John Kendrick. He was quiet, unassuming and generally well liked by all who met him. Not much is known about Johnson prior to entrance into the fistic world other than that he was a 20 year old American when he arrived at Bill Richmond's doorstep in 1820. His first essay in the ring was a 3 round destruction of a man named Smith who as Egan noted, "was so frightened that he bolted out of the ring". Johnson was by all accounts an extremely intimidating physical specimen, standing a shade over six feet, weighing close to 185 pounds and possessing what Egan called, "the most tremendous arms and shoulders ever witnessed for doing execution". His arms were long, well over six feet in measurement and covered in extensive, rock hard muscle. But size and strength don't always win fights and after Johnson's initial fight even Egan was cautious in his praise stating, "Johnson has yet to be tried."

Egan would seem to be prophetic for in his next bout, Johnson was defeated in 86 rounds by the serviceable Jem Carroll. The bout was not a total loss however as Carroll, who was well seasoned, had never been defeated (and never would be), and Johnson did his share of damage. In fact, for most of the bout he was giving as much as he was taking and if not for want of experience the result of the bout may have been different.

After working with Richmond for a year, Johnson returned to the ring in the summer of 1822 and took the measure of a second rater named Nixon in 9 rounds. It was a good exhibition of power and Jemmy displayed some of the new tricks that Richmond had taught him, the foremost being the use of his superior reach to keep his opponents at bay. It was an effective strategy, and one that would serve Johnson well throughout his career. In fact Egan took notice of this technique and stated that when Johnson used this tactic, "it is impossible to get at him without encountering the most dangerous punishment."

While Jemmy Johnson was in the midst of getting his career in high gear in 1822, another black man appeared briefly on the pugilistic map. He was simply referred to as Daniels the Black. Like Johnson, little if anything was known of his antecedents, other than that he was an American, when he appeared on the turf at Weybridge Fields on October 7, 1822 to face off with George Croft. The fight itself received very little attention, no full report of the bout appearing in any contemporary journals, but Daniels must have been nothing more than a novice, for he fell before the fists of Croft in less than 22 minutes. Daniels seemingly never fought again, for his name does not appear anywhere thereafter.

After his victory over Nixon, which was well attended by the Fancy, Johnson had difficulty in finding a customer. He at last was matched in January of 1823 to fight Harry Fowler for 20 pounds at Wycomb. Fowler was nothing more than a second rate fighter but he was able to absorb tremendous amounts of punishment. He took what Johnson had to give and then returned with his own heavy artillery. The result was that after two hours, Johnson wore out and gave in. It was a devastating loss and one that had the Fancy commenting of the "white feather" character of the black American. Johnson was not finished however, and

Bill Richmond stuck by his side. They quickly got themselves another match and this time Johnson proved his mettle by beating Tod Harris in 15 brutal rounds.

Jemmy won two more fights in 1823 against decent opposition and was then matched with one of the best men in England at the time, future Champion Jem Ward. Ward was still two years away from winning the Championship from Tom Cannon, but even at this stage was thought of as a man earmarked for championship honors. Johnson and Ward had one common opponent, Rickers, who the former had beaten in 40 minutes and the latter in 15, but this gave little indication as to how a match between the two would unfold. The two Jems met at Southampton, and Ward was the master from start to finish. He handled his larger opponent with ease and knocked him about as he pleased. The Fancy remarked that it was an easy payday for Ward and even the future champion himself stated that he wished all of his bouts could have been as soft a mark as Johnson. It was a demoralizing loss and one that all but erased any hopes that Johnson ever had for fighting for big money. After such a setback, one in which Johnson never stood a chance, he and Richmond would never be able to find the backing for any kind of a match over 50 pounds.

In Johnson's next bout with Harry Griffen, nearly three months after his loss to Ward, he showed signs of unwillingness and reluctance. During the fight Richmond repeatedly scolded his seemingly uninterested charge, "to fight, fight!" Jemmy shook his head at Bill's verbal assault but did little to heed the advice. After the tenth round ended, Johnson told Richmond that he no longer wanted to fight. Bill, seeing that his man was in no shape mentally to continue, threw in the towel and conceded defeat. Bill was disgusted with Johnson, but stuck by him nonetheless. Jemmy would reward his mentor's loyalty by winning his next fight with Phil Crossley in 25 rounds. Johnson weathered an early storm, one during which he was beaten nearly senseless, showed pluck which he had never before demonstrated, and used his physical advantages to perfect form. In fact, the manner in which Johnson won the fight seemingly erased his woeful performances from the collective memory of the Fancy and he was again tagged with the designation of a "good un".

Johnson began the new year of 1824 much in the same fashion as he had ended the previous year: with a victory. His victim this time was a serviceable fighter named Bishop Harris who Jemmy ravaged over the course of 57 rounds lasting 70 minutes on a cold January morning at Oxford. The Fancy was in exaltation over Johnson's performance, during which Jemmy again demonstrated his resolve and strength. In his next contest he proved victorious yet again, defeating a man calling himself Jewin the Navigator in just over a half an hour during which 27 rounds were contested. Jemmy was so dominant that the *Morning Chronicle* noted, "Johnson had nary a mark as he left the field of battle while his opponent was senseless and some thought in danger of suffering internal damages of some serious proportion".

Seemingly hitting the full stride of his career and with the embarrassing losses to Ward and Griffin well behind him, it would seem that Johnson was now on the right path toward prize ring prominence. However, he would never fight again. With no explanation or hoopla, Jemmy Johnson disappeared from the boxing world. He never again appeared in a prizefight nor did he work as a second, trainer or as a sparrer. He simply vanished from the scene. Whether or not Johnson was struck down by disease or some other misfortune, decided to return to a former occupation, or disappeared for some other, darker reason may never be known. His exit from the pages of prizefighting history was as inglorious and ambiguous as his entrance.

Jemmy Johnson was never considered a first rate pugilist. The men he faced were, for the most part, second raters. With the exception of Jem Ward, the list of his opponents and more importantly their relative merit as fighters could not be considered impressive. Johnson lacked consistency and at times seemed to suffer from fits of haphazard interest in the game. However, when "right", he was in the least a very durable and damaging fighter. It must also be noted that Johnson was an extremely active fighter, taking part in 12 prize ring battles in just under five years. In 1823 alone he had 7 contests, which considering the duration of some of the battles and the brutality of the sport in those times, was an amazing figure in its own right. Some of the prize ring's greatest heroes did not have as many fights in a career. That Jemmy had mixed results during that year, winning 4 and loosing 3, could in part be contributed to the fact that he never properly recovered from some of the injuries he incurred during those battles. Consider that after fighting for two hours with Harry Fowler on January 1, 1823, Jemmy fought just 27 days later for 2 hours and 20 minutes with Tod Harris. With the ferocity of these types of battles, one month could hardly be considered sufficient time for a human body to heal from such punishment. But, for all of the ups and downs Johnson endured during his brief yet spectacularly vigorous career, he up until that time fought more ring battles than any other black fighter in history. For that alone, Jemmy Johnson must be considered an impressive and important figure.

From the disappearance of Jemmy Johnson in early 1824 until the emergence of another black American, Thomas Morgan, in the summer of 1827, no black fighter appeared in the English Prize Ring. Again, the fact that three years would pass without a single man of color appearing in the ring, further illustrates the fact that the black pugilist's entrance into the game, as a large and equal faction, was a slow and non-singular occurrence.

Morgan, much like many of his predecessors, was a sailor by trade, and a very good one by most accounts. Egan noted that Morgan "stood well in the opinions of the owners of the vessel he belonged to and was always sure to obtain a ship". That Thomas would find any kind of lure in the ring was summed up best by Egan when he stated, "that by a hit Morgan might fill his pockets with more blunt in less than an hour than he could procure in six months by pulling rope". Indeed it was undoubtedly the money that Morgan eyed, but Egan declared, "Massa, who had heard of the great pugilistic fame gained by his countryman, Molineaux, was also determined to have a shy in the prize ring, or, in other words, try his luck". It had been assumed long before Morgan that most of the black men, who had appeared on the scene after Tom Molineaux's great ascent and downfall, had been influenced by the "Terrible Black". However, in Morgan's story, as told to us by Egan, we find the first written affirmation that a black man had indeed heard of Molineaux, and at least in part had been inspired to try his hand at fighting due to the legend of the "first tremendous man of color".

Morgan claimed he was an experienced fighting man when he arrived in London in May of 1827. He declared to have taken part in more than 50 "turn ups", while at sea and abroad. It was a captain on board his latest vessel who, when hearing of Morgan's aspirations to enter the prize ring in England, and seeing first hand his apparent talent with his "mauley's", instructed the would-be fighter to seek out Josh Hudson, "the original John Bull fighter" at his public house in the Leadville Market section of London. There Josh kept the Half Moon tavern, where he both whetted the appetites of the sporting fraternity with drink and discussion, and taught young men the finer points of the game. Morgan, using a letter of introduction, presented himself to Hudson, and upon impressing the latter in a short sparring session, was given room and board by his new host.

Hudson introduced Morgan to the Fancy at a benefit for Jonathan Bissell, a.k.a. "Young Gas", at the Tennis Courts on June 21, 1827. There, Thomas, who was presented to the crowd as "Molineaux the Second" and "Massa Morgan" by Hudson, offered to spar with any man present for the benefit of the crowd. The first man to step forward was Fischer, who was known as an amateur of some distinction and Champion of Oxford. Morgan, who stood 5'11" and weighed close to 180 pounds, was much the bigger man and surprised many in attendance with his apparent familiarity with "the science". He toyed with Fischer, who although a very good sparrer, was not a true test for the new man. After two minutes of fighting, Thomas landed a tremendous "facer" to his opponent's nose, which drew a small trickle of blood. Recognizing that he stood nary a chance with this "new black", Fischer promptly rose, removed his gloves and after shaking Morgan's hand, left the stage.

Young Gas, along with the rest of the crowd, was somewhat displeased with Morgan's behavior. It was generally considered bad manners for a man to deliberately hurt his foe during an exhibition, and Gas decided that he would take it upon himself to teach Thomas some discrimination. Taking the stage and lacing up his "mufflers" quickly, Young Gas glared at Morgan and stated, "You have served out an amateur, let us see what you do with a real fighting man!" Morgan, obviously unaware of his affront, turned to Hudson with a confused look. Josh neatly nodded his head, signaling Morgan to ignore Bissell's statement and fight. Thomas did just that and with his first telling blow, knocked the surprised Bissell to the stage. Gas, was both shocked and embarrassed, as the crowd roared with approval. He straightened himself and moved forward again, this time with a bit more discretion. Gas landed a left hand to Thomas' chin and a right to the stomach, but was again dropped on the seat of his pants by a straight right counter from Morgan. At this point Hudson jumped up onto the stage and began to pull the gloves from Morgan's hands. Young Gas was furious and demanded that Massa, "stay and take what's coming to him!" However, Josh knew that the night was already a success and that the Fancy had seen enough of Morgan's prowess to make him the "talk of the town". Bissell stole some of the play back from Josh by taking the stage again and challenging "Massa Morgan" to fight for 100 pounds, but Hudson politely refused and acquiesced that his man could not find such backing. He did promise to match his new man with any opponent who could be found for 25 pounds per side within the next two months.

Hudson and Morgan found no takers for their challenge and continued to exhibit at the Tennis Courts regularly. Finally, in the aftermath of White-Headed Bob's victory over Jem Burn at Ranscombe Range, near Twyford Berks on July 3, 1827, a man named Abbinet agreed to fight Morgan for a subscription purse of 10 pounds. Thomas, who was still very new to the game, was told of the arrangements and immediately stripped for the battle. According to Pierce Egan he promptly stated, "I am satisfied and I am sure that the "gemmen" will give me fair play".

When the men stripped and set-to Egan noted that Morgan, "appeared a precious strong-made fellow, and capable of "tipping it" in fine style, to any glutton. He laughed, and nothing ill-natured, or any thing like ferocity marked his front piece." Abbinet was lighter than Morgan, maybe by five pounds or so, but showed his own confidence and "entered the ring quite cheerful and confident against the man of colour." Upon time being called, Abbinet rushed Thomas and seemingly surprised the latter with his sudden attack. Morgan took two blows to the chin, and in turn looked around to Hudson, seemingly in desperation. "Don't look at me!" shouted Josh, imploring his charge to focus on the battle. Abbinet, sensing the confusion that gripped his foe, again rushed Morgan, but was this time met with a different reception. Grasping Abbinet around the waste, Thomas lifted his rival up in his arms and as Egan observed, "laid him down as tenderly as if is adversary had been a lady." In doing so, Thomas split his trunks straight down the seam of his backside, which brought tremendous roars of laughter from the crowd. Morgan himself was seemingly embarrassed by the situation but was again steadied by his mentor Hudson who calmly stated, "Never mind, worse things happen at sea."

Morgan, his initial jitters now gone, dominated the next several rounds and even staggered Abbinet so badly in the fourth stanza that Hudson shouted, "D'ye see what you have done? You have made Abbinet quite drunk!" Thomas was in such complete control by the sixth that he chose to add a bit of showmanship to the event by waving his left hand like "a flag in the wind, before striking out with it." Josh, who was nearly overcome with the joy of seeing his protégée perform in such a dominant manner, shouted to Thomas at length, "I lay 100 pounds to a shilling that you will not go to sea anymore!" Morgan punished Abbinet severely for the next several rounds and a number of the onlookers began to ask if the bout deserved to go any further. Egan noted that shouts of "disapprobriation" began to arise from the crowd until the well-respected Hudson silenced them by shouting, "if he were a white one it would be alright." Thomas, after being repeatedly told by Hudson to "draw it mild", settled down to business and finished the outgunned Abbinet in the eleventh round. The fight lasted a mere 11 minutes.

"The Black possesses powers likely to do mischief", wrote Egan in his remarks on the fight. "He hits well with his left hand: and his temper also appears to be good. With a little more practice, he will prove a very troublesome customer in the hands of a good boxer. It will take heavy blows to stop his rush: he is not to be disposed of as a matter of course; and it must be a big one, and a strong one into the bargain, to tackle him with success." Egan as well as many of the other members of the Fancy who watched "Massa Morgan" toy with Abbinet, were very impressed by his strength and his ability to punch. Some questioned his "bottom", pointing to his confusion and lack of confidence when the fight began, but most saw little to support such statements.

Hudson attempted to match his man again immediately, but was unsuccessful. Morgan, being "industrious" in nature decided to again return to the sea. He promised to again try his hand in the prize ring upon his return to London, but even his most ardent supporters figured they had seen the last of "Molineaux the Second". However, after a nearly two-year stint at sea, Morgan reappeared on the scene, and again presented himself to Josh Hudson as ready for action.

Josh wasted little time and immediately threw out a challenge to all and sundry for a fight with his "black" for a 50 pound purse. Surprisingly a customer was found in Bill Flemming, a novice of some reputation, and the match was scheduled to take place at Market Deeping on March 24, 1829. Morgan had little time to train but was "physically hard" due to his long and arduous time at sea. Flemming was a big man, 187 pounds, and showed himself to be "worked to the minute" when stripped to the waist. At the call of time the men readied themselves and then proceeded to spar for an opening. Thomas worked his left through the guard of his foe and was then countered lightly by a punch to his chest. The men broke ground and moved away from one another, seemingly to size up the situation. Morgan "snorted like a bull" and rushed at his opponent behind his right hand. An exchange ensued and the men both landed fairly upon the upper-works of their rival. But just as they seemed to be drawing back, Morgan let fly with a tremendous right hand, which caught his opponent full upon the temple. Flemming dropped like felled tree, face first, onto the ground. His seconds dragged him to his corner and attempted to revive him, but Bill was unconscious. After just two minutes of fighting, the contest was over and Thomas Morgan was declared the winner.

After his brutal and alarmingly quick victory over Flemming, Thomas Morgan again returned to the sea. Whether he departed because Hudson could not find him another match, or because he truly loved the life of a sailor, is unclear. He never again appeared in the prize ring and no record survives of his life thereafter.

Morgan undoubtedly was a fighter of supreme power. His skills, although not fully refined, also seemed to be, at the very least, serviceable. That his opponents were not of the highest level, and his inability to obtain a match against a higher caliber man, leaves us only to deal with speculation on his true capabilities. But it seems that "Massa Morgan" was deemed by his fate not to leave any lasting impression on the prizefighting world, for although his record was sterling, his body of work was by far too incomplete to truly judge whether or not he could have handled championship level men. Nonetheless, in many ways his story encapsulates both the lure and the frustrations that the prize ring held for men of color in the early part of the 19th century. What drew Morgan was the temptation to make more money than he could ever hope to procure as a sailor. What evidently forced him away was his inability to find the matches that would have, in the least, afforded him the opportunity to make such sums.

7

The Black Prince of Pugilists

James Wharton was born in Tangiers, Morocco in 1813, his father an African trader/sailor and his mother a local peasant. When just a young boy of 12 years he found employment as a cabin boy with an East Indiaman vessel called the Hopewell, which specialized in the three month long voyages between Cairo and London. Wharton was a well-liked boy who serviced his employers well, and showed a certain athletic ability in both swimming and running. Young James served on the Hopewell for over seven years and seemingly would have spent the rest of his adult life at sea if not for a curious incident, which prompted his course to change.

It was a row with the cook on board the Hopewell that would stamp James Wharton as a lad with a future in the fighting profession. After being accused by the cook of stealing supplies from the galley, Wharton attacked his accuser and a furious mill ensued. The two men were separated quickly and ordered to report to the captain's quarters. The captain must have been a sport for after hearing each man's side of the story, he promptly ordered the men to fight according to the rules of the English prize ring, on the main deck in front of the entire crew. Wharton was not a large boy, standing 5'9" and weighing close to 150 pounds, and was considered to be at a great disadvantage for his foe was a large specimen of humanity, standing close to six feet and weighing 180 pounds. However, James proved to be the master of the situation, avoiding the clumsy blows of the cook with the coolness and dexterity that he would later make famous during his ring career, and knocked his adversary about until the larger man gave in. His defeat of the cook seemed to have swelled Wharton's head in the estimation of the other crew members on board the Hopewell, and he was thereafter constantly challenged by sailors who thought they could tame the fighting cabin boy. But Wharton had an answer for them all and met each challenge with the same skill and speed with which he had defeated his first opponent. James' fighting prowess did not go unnoticed and a certain passenger on board, Major Broadfoot, urged the young fighter to make himself available to the Fancy upon the ships' arrival in London. It took little persuading from the Major to convince Wharton that the prize ring could hold greater rewards than life at sea.

Upon reaching London in the January 1833, Broadfoot brought Wharton to the Queen's Head Tavern that was run by a retired, heavyweight pugilist of note named Jem Burn. Burn took Wharton in and personally "tried him out" in his back room. After a brief time of sparring Burn told the Major that he shared the opinion that the colored cabin boy had a unique gift with his fists. Burn agreed to take Wharton under his wing, refine his fighting technique and match him as soon as possible. As promised, not more than two months later, Burn matched his new man with Tom McKeevor for 10 pounds a side. McKeevor, who hailed from Whetstone, was no light touch having scored two prior victories in the prize ring with no defeats. The fact that the match was scheduled to take place in Tom's own town further illustrated that Burn took no pains to match Wharton with a soft touch for his first foray into the ring. As Jem expected however, James, who had been dubbed, "Jemmy the Black" by his mentor, was more than equal to the task and although the bout had its rough moments, Wharton proved victorious in 51 minutes during which 38 rounds were fought.

Wharton would continue to impress the Fancy taking the measure of two trial horses, Evans "The Herefordshire Pippin" in 14 minutes in October of 1834 and Jack Wilsden "The Hammersmith Cowboy" in 22 minutes in January of 1835.

Despite these victories, James was still considered a fighter of only minor importance for his opponents were not of the world-beating mold. Compounding this fact was Wharton's weight. Being only a 150-pound man, James was too big for the lightweights and too small for the heavyweights. He was in essence, lost in the purgatory of prizefighting. During that era it was these two classes, lightweight and heavyweight, which garnered the greatest attention and respect, and were generally considered the weights at which the best fighters fought. In due time however, James Wharton would change that notion.

It took some time for Jemmy to find any willing customers. So few were willing to share the ring with him that he accepted an offer to meet Nick Ward, a 175 pound heavyweight of note for 15 pounds a side. The bout, which was to have taken place at Mousley Hurst on May 12, 1835, never occurred. Ward was arrested the night before the contest by the local magistrates at Norwood, where he had done his training for the match, and was detained for a week under orders of "keeping the public peace". Wharton escaped any such imprisonment but was both frustrated and disappointed by the events. There were those who claimed that Ward, despite his pedigree (he was the brother of Champion Jem Ward and would himself become Champion in 1840), had instigated his own arrest. It was asserted by some of those close to the matter that Ward did not think he could defeat Jemmy and therefore had himself detained so that neither he nor his backers would loose face or forfeit any of the stake money. It would be difficult to prove such a story but no matter the reason, Jemmy the Black had to find another customer.

As Jemmy waited for another match to materialize, he accepted an offer from future Champion of England Deaf Burke and his partner Bob Cootes to work with their traveling show. Wharton took on all comers in a boxing booth atmosphere, and sparred with Burke and Cootes at an assortment of fairs, races and provincial shows. It was during this time that he earned the second of his great nicknames being dubbed the "Moroccan Prince" by Caunt himself. Wharton also gained a great deal of experience and technique working with Ben and the other men on the tour. Surprisingly when the group reached Liverpool, the Prince learned that Jem Burn had induced a trio of wealthy backers to put up a 25-pound stake on behalf of Jemmy in acceptance of a challenge from Liverpudian William Fischer. Wharton was thrilled at the prospect of another prize ring contest and immediately went into training.

Wharton, seemingly like Richmond, was a student of the sport, and understood the importance training when preparing for a ring contest. He was a tireless worker and often times "ran" his own camp, needing little or no persuasion to tend to his daily routine of walking, sparring and exercise. He also liked to scout his opponents, learning what he could of their styles, tendencies and weaknesses. Jemmy wanted every advantage, both physically and tactically, and prepared for his fights as if every one was a championship affair.

The Prince had good reason to prepare for Fischer, for even though he had not entered the ring in nearly two years, Bill was a seasoned fighter with several impressive wins on his resume. He had been defeated on two occasions prior to his meeting with Wharton, but even in those contests, which lasted 70 and 193 minutes respectively, Fischer had proven to be a tough nut to crack. Bill was a thick, stocky man who seemingly carried the majority of his 154 pounds in his neck, legs and chest. He and Wharton presented a stark physical contrast when they stripped and faced one another in a field behind a tavern known as the Horse and Jockey near Staffordshire on November 24, 1835.

The fight itself was fairly settled in the first round. Fischer, who figured himself to hold a distinct advantage over his opponent in wrestling technique, closed with Wharton and attempted to throw him. To his surprise however, he was greeted with a fearful left hand, which stunned him beyond description, and left him waving before his opponent. Jemmy seized his opportunity by grasping Fischer around the waist and throwing him to the ground with such force that he nearly knocked him clean out. A splash of cold water and some steady work from his seconds enabled Bill to make it up to scratch for the second stanza, but he would never get the opportunity to fully recover from Wharton's first devastating blow. Fischer was as tough as nails however, and despite repeated cries of "Take him away", from the partisan crowd, he refused to surrender. According to *Bell's Life* by the 40th round, Wharton himself was asking Fischer's seconds, "Do you want me to kill your man?" They in turn attempted to concede defeat, but Fischer would not hear of it. Jemmy continued to punish Bill until the latter was so dreadfully beaten that Wharton, fearing that he would indeed kill his opponent, refused to punch him anymore. From the 45 round until the 49th and last, Wharton did not strike Fischer, instead choosing to throw him in the hope of ending the battle in a more humane manner. Finally, after his backers had entered the ring and threatened to have him removed by force, Bill Fischer conceded defeat. The battle had lasted 70 minutes.

Jem Wharton's defeat of Bill Fischer, and more so the manner in which he secured the victory, led many of the Fancy to comment fervently on his fine fighting skill and his gentlemanly behavior during the contest. Josh Hudson, who had been ringside for the fight, and who on more than one occasion could be heard shouting, "bravo to the Prince", decided that he saw in Wharton the specter of another great man of color, Thomas Molineaux. He therefore tagged Wharton with perhaps his most famous and appropriate soubriquet, "Young Molineaux".

Liverpool was not so enthusiastic about Jemmy's fine victory however. Their provincial pride dented they determined to find another Liverpool man to take the measure of Wharton. They chose the tough and ready Tom Britton to be their man, and immediately presented the Young Molineaux faction with a challenge to fight for 50 pounds per side. Wharton readily agreed, now considering himself one of the best 11 stone men in England.

For Jemmy, Britton presented a similar challenge to that of Bill Fischer in that he was not a fancy boxer, but durable beyond description. His toughness was fully displayed in 1831 during his first prize fight when he lasted over two hours with Bob Hampson, a heavyweight who neared 176 pounds in weight, and counted Deaf Burke as one of his opponents. Britton would follow up this magnificent battle with a victory over the previously undefeated heavyweight, Jem Corbett, who Tom simply out lasted in a contest lasting 50 minutes. But unbeknownst to Jemmy, there were other forces at work and he would have more to contend with than just his opponent.

Jem Wharton and Tom Britton met on a brisk winter day in a field at Chesire on February 9, 1836. The crowd which had come in droves from London, Manchester and Liverpool, was laden with the rougher elements of society, the most conspicuous being 300 or so of the Liverpool thugs known as the "Hard-Ups" who had come in mass force to root for their man Britton. The ring was pitched by 9a.m. but the fighters would not enter the scene of combat until near noon. The outer ring was hastily set up and it was noticed that many of the "Hard-Ups" had placed themselves, by force and intimidation, in positions along the outskirts of the ring where they could be nearest to the battle.

Jemmy was the first to make himself known to the crowd, strolling into the ring and flipping his cap casually to the ground. A ripple of laughter rolled though the mob when Wharton opened his coat to reveal a dandy display of colorful fighting togs. He casually pulled from his belt a bright orange handkerchief which he waved in the air lightly to the crowd (Wharton had a particular fondness for oranges and therefore adopted the dye of the fruit for his fighting colors). Britton entered the ring not a few moments afterwards and was greeted with an uproarious cheer from his partisan backers. Several of the "Hard-Ups" broke the outer ring and saluted their man with back slaps and hand shakes. Tom seemed stoic and resolute, passing them off as he would a stranger. After another 10 minutes of light pre fight ceremony, Britton and Wharton shook hands and readied themselves at the scratch.

The real story of the fight was Jemmy's left hand. Britton could not find a way around it nor could he find a way to stop it. It wreaked havoc wherever and whenever it landed and as early as the fifth round, Britton's face was chopped to pieces. Tom tried in vein to wrestle with the Prince, but no maneuver was successful in obtaining a good grasp on the slippery black. Each time Britton attempted to close, he would be met by Jemmy's left fist. As early as the twelfth it was apparent that Tom's only chance was to bide his time and hope that he could wear down Young Molineaux. However, as the bout progressed into a one sided beating, the "Hard-Ups" began to get anxious, realizing that even a dour man like Tom Britton could only stand such punishment for so long. *Bell's Life* stated that, "all the while a storm was brewing, and with each punch landed by the black, the unsavory faction moved closer to the brink of riot." Disaster was seemingly avoided when in the 22nd round, Britton finally broke through and grassed Wharton with a clean right hand punch to the throat. His dominance was short lived however, and by the time the men came again to scratch, Young Molineaux seemed steady and ready to re-assert his supremacy. And so he did, and by the end of the round, the pattern, which, up until the time of Britton's right-hander, had defined the bout, began again. Jemmy's left hand was back to work like a piston, shooting straight from his shoulder, and seemingly unable to miss some part of Britton's anatomy. By the 56th round there seemed to be little hope for Britton. He stood firm but on his haunches as if any slight movement might cause him to lose his balance. However, Wharton's blows were no longer coming in swift violent movements and his left hand was terribly swollen from his knuckles to his wrists. He had landed so many blows upon his adversary's difficult skull that his hands were no longer the damaging weapons they were when the fight began. Nevertheless, the "Hard-Ups" were now pressing their way into the ring, leaning over the ropes and hurling insults at Jemmy and his seconds.

In the 145th round, Dick Curtis "The Pet of the Fancy", Wharton's trainer and second, was literally attacked by the Liverpool gang, and chased from the ring and away from the general location of the bout. The Prince fought for 23 rounds with no second to attend to him. By the 187th round the ring had been completely broken and the "Hard-Ups", and other rough elements, were actually in the ring surrounding the combatants. All hell had broken loose and there seemed to be no way that anyone could restore order to the occasion. A call went up amongst the more civilized members of the crowd that Wharton should be allowed the dignity of a second, but after Jem Burn had volunteered to take the place of Curtis, he too was accosted by the Liverpool roughs and forced from the scene.

Amidst all of this Britton and Wharton fought on, literally enclosed in a small circle of humanity. The crowd was now so close to the fighters that according to *Bell's Life*, "they barely had a few yards square in which to operate." Tom was battered beyond recognition, and Jemmy was both exhausted and frightened for his own life. It was truly a desperate and ugly scene. Finally, after 200 rounds the bout was humanely brought to an end. *Bell's Life* reported, "The battle was protracted for four hours. It was a cruel and shameful spectacle, and at last the backers of both heroes resolved to put a stop to it and ordered the men to make a draw of it. But the men refused and another few rounds were fought. It was a mockery of fighting and it was feared that fatal consequences might ensue if the men were allowed to go on further. The combatants were forced to shake hands and consent to a draw, which they reluctantly did after fighting for four hours and seven minutes."

Wharton left the scene of the battle under his own power and made his way to the Horse and Jockey at Woore where he found a beaten and scared Dick Curtis awaiting him. *Bell's Life* reported that Jemmy, "was very little marked, his eye being closed and his lips swollen and that was all. His left hand too, was completely knocked up with the awful hammering he had given Britton's head." Britton was taken back to the Green Man and Still in nearby Buerton, where he remained in bed for close to a week.

The battle was a dreadful experience for Young Molineaux, not due to his performance but rather because of the treatment he and his faction had received from the crowd. Interestingly, the Liverpool roughs seemed to take no issue with Jemmy's color, but more so with the fact that he was representing London. Their fierce territorial pride overrode any sense of fair play, and the fact that a "Londoner" was getting the best of their man was more than they cared to see. However, despite their hope of spoiling the victory for Jemmy, and more specifically London, *Bell's Life* clearly noted that, "Molineaux, without the slightest doubt, would have won had he received anything like fair play".

Jemmy would have to wait nearly a year for his next contest. He traveled with his own exhibition troupe, which included Tommy Roundhead, who had at one time been the trainer for Deaf Burke. Young Molineaux's name was now a familiar one amongst the masses and wherever he and Roundhead traveled they seemed to draw large crowds and larger gates. It was a tremendously successful tour and Wharton was almost sorry when he had to break off from the circuit when he found out by letter that he had been matched to fight Harry Preston of Birmingham.

Preston was by far the best fighter who Jemmy had yet to be matched with. His unblemished record included names like Sambo Sutton, Birmingham Davis and Tass Parker and it was said that Young Dutch Sam had once had himself arrested on the eve of fighting Preston rather than face the "Brum" in fistic combat. Harry was naturally a bigger man than Jemmy, normally weighing 165 pounds, which during that era would have classified him as a heavyweight. Tall, broad shouldered and athletic, Preston was thought by his backers to have a championship in his future.

The arrangements for the bout were made at Albion Hotel at Newcastle on January 21, 1837. The articles for the bout stipulated that the fight would take place on April 16th at Woore at a stake of 100 pounds a side. The Prince was not to weigh more than 154 pounds and Preston not more than 161. The reason for the lengthy delay between the signing of the bout and it's planned occurrence was said to be an ankle injury suffered by Preston in his bout with Sambo Sutton the previous January. A more likely reason was that Harry, who had recently become a publican, was doing far more drinking than training, and had ballooned up in weight to close to 170 pounds. He and his backers, more than likely, felt that he needed those three months to work himself back into shape and shed some unwanted flesh.

On the morning of April 16, 1837 by all outward appearance the three months of training had indeed procured their desired affect on Harry Preston. When he stripped for battle in a field behind a horse paddock at Woore, he demonstrated the physique of a well-tuned fighting man. Preston titled the scales at a rock hard 159 pounds, which although a full five pounds below his normal fighting weight, showcased to all his determined preparation for battle with the "Black Prince". Wharton for his part was also in fine condition weighing in below his prescribed weight at 153 pounds. Both men were confident of victory, Preston making a private wager of 20 pounds to 10 pounds with Wharton that he would defeat the latter. The crowd was for the most part orderly and quiet and there was but only a small faction of the rough element who plagued Jemmy's last bout with Britton.

The fight was a savage affair with both men doing substantial damage over the course of the first ten rounds. The combatants seemed to be evenly matched in the striking department, both showing rare form in both stopping and hitting straight from the shoulder, but it was Wharton who demonstrated a superior strength and ability to wrestle. Most rounds ended with Jemmy throwing or cross-buttocking Preston to the ground after some fierce exchanges. Coming up for the sixteenth round both men were punished and tired. Preston attempted to hit Wharton with a left lead, but in the same moment, Jemmy closed with his foe and with an astonishing display of strength, hoisted Preston into the air and threw him heavily to the ground. Harry landed on his head, twisting his neck and body in a grotesque series of movements. When his body came to a halt, there was no movement from the fallen man. His seconds, Bold Bendigo and Peter Taylor rushed to where their man lay prostrate and tried to revive him by pouring brandy and hot rum down his throat and nose. Preston was unconscious however, and none of his seconds' efforts to arouse his senses proved successful. It was feared that his neck was broken and word quickly spread amongst the onlookers that Harry Preston was dead. Harry was not dead but seemed to be in dire straits. Jemmy was concerned with his fallen opponents' state and assisted in hoisting him into a chaise where he could be transported back into Woore and examined by a physician. Preston was brought to the Falcon Inn where a doctor, tipped off by a forward messenger of the fighter's state, awaited his arrival. After several anxious moments the doctor pronounced that Preston had not broken his neck, and despite suffering from some facial bruising and a few broken ribs, was in fine health.

Wharton's defeat of the previously unbeaten Preston brought his fame to unprecedented levels. Rumors that Jemmy had broken Harry's neck, and in some stories his back, circulated widely, and gave even greater motion to the hysteria that was now surrounding the Moroccan Prince. Wharton returned to London briefly where the "great metropolis'" Corinthian Fancy treated him like a conquering hero. He was feted on by the richer patron's of the ring, and offered financial backing for a wide assortment of endeavors, ranging from opening his own tavern to buying a horse farm. Jemmy turned downed his well-intentioned admirers, and again set out on an exhibition tour with Tommy Roundhead. The duo traveled far into Northern England and then over into Scotland. The pair worked out a show which consisted mainly of sparring between the two pugilists, re-enactments of Wharton's now famous battle with Preston, and a running monologue by Jemmy where he would entertain the crowd by signing, dancing and telling jokes. By all accounts, Wharton was quite an entertainer and his fame only grew during the tour.

In the latter stages of the excursion, while the men where exhibiting in Scotland, Molineaux was challenged by a large Scot, named Sandy McNeish, who fancied himself a true fighter. During one of Wharton's monologues, McNeish rose from his seat and outwardly challenged the black pugilist to "fight for real". Jemmy was offended by what he deemed as insolence and offered to pay ten shillings to the Scottish brawler if he could stay five minutes on the stage with him.

McNeish gladly accepted and took the stage amidst thunderous applause. When the men squared off it looked like a mismatch as the burly Scot towered over the somewhat slight looking Wharton. The bout was a farce but it was McNeish who was overmatched. With a quick feint and a tremendous right hand, Jemmy floored and bloodied his bewildered antagonist. Sandy was dazed and made no attempt to rise. Wharton stood menacingly over his beaten foe and shouted, "Come on and get up, you've only had a shillingsworth, you got another nine shillingsworth yet!" Needless to say that McNeish, embarrassed and still a bit dazed, quietly left the stage.

Wharton had visited Newcastle-on-Tyne during his trip through England, and it was from this locale that he would receive his next challenge in the form of Will Renwick "The Tynside Hero". Renwick was not an experienced prize-fighter, but was a champion wrestler who had taken part in some "country battles" against other local men, and proven himself the best of the lot. On these merits alone, Renwick could hardly have been looked upon as a worthy challenger for the now fame Young Molineaux. However, what Will may have lacked in skill and polish in comparison to Wharton, he certainly made up for in physicality. Will Renwick was a true heavyweight by even modern standards, standing an even six feet and weighing anywhere between 185 and 190 pounds. His body was a study in sturdiness, his legs thick and stout and his chest deep and powerful. The sporting men of Tyneside, who had seen Jemmy spar, and found his gaudy clothes and lofty attitude a bit to their disliking, thought Wharton was "too pretty" to handle a rough, large man like Renwick, and therefore placed their money behind their "hero".

The match was scheduled to take place at Cambo, which was not more than twenty miles from Newcastle, on October 31, 1837. Interference from the local magistrate chased the bout from Cambo to Middleton Ridge, where a ring was hastily put together and the men forced to set to with little ceremony. Wharton was once again in supreme condition having weighed in at Cambo at an even 156 pounds. Renwick looked a bit drawn and surprisingly weighed in at a extremely low 177 pounds, leading some to state that he had "trained off".

The fight was a simple case of great skill overcoming superior strength and size. Jemmy was brilliant, and found that despite taking some fearful body blows, of which he later stated where the hardest he had ever tasted, he had little trouble in beating his man to the punch. Most of Renwick's blows aimed for the face and head of Wharton were easily stopped by the latter and Will could never close quite fast enough to catch his smaller opponent in a good hold. All the while Jemmy punished "The Tynside Hero" with fast and damaging combinations of punches, raising hideous red welts on his foe's face and body. To the Prince went first blood, first knockdown blow and first throw. It was all Jemmy Wharton and by the 84th round, Renwick was a sad sight to behold. At the beginning of the 85th round Jemmy approached Will's brother Joe, who was his sibling's second, and asked him to concede the battle stating, "Look here this is your brother, if you have any love for him you better take him away." Both Renwicks refused to surrender and two more rounds were fought before Young Molineaux finished off his game opponent with a knockout blow between the eyes in the 86th round.

Wharton had again proven that he was indeed one of the best pugilists in the British Isles, and for a long period of time there were no fighters at or near his weight to challenge his supremacy. It was surmised by many that he would have stood an equal chance with the Heavyweight Champion William Thompson, and many of Wharton's supporters urged him to challenge "Bold Bendigo", as Thompson was known. Jemmy, who felt he had the ability to beat any man on equal terms decide that he would indeed challenge the Champion. Placing a stipulation that Bendigo could weigh no more than 162 pounds, Wharton presented his challenge to the Heavyweight Title Holder. Thompson, who normally weighed between 164 and 168 pounds surely could have made the weight had he desired the match, but there were extenuating circumstances that further complicated the matter. Bendigo shortly after winning the title from Deaf Burke in February of 1839, had injured his knee while doing somersaults during an exhibition. The injury severally limited his mobility and his punching power. Thompson refused Wharton's challenged with the excuse that he was no longer able to fight because of this injury. True to his word, Bendigo did not appear again in the ring for close to five years, when he again claimed the championship with a victory over Ben Caunt. Jemmy tried to make a match with Tass Parker with similar weight considerations but the latter had no desire to enter the ring with the Black Prince.

Jemmy returned to the lucrative business of touring in the late summer of 1839, this time joining an exhibition troupe that consisted of Joe Birchall, Bob Hampson and Charely Langan. Their tour, which traveled by slow coach, made its way up through Northern England, through several stops in Scotland, and over into Ireland. Everywhere the group traveled, the Moroccan Prince was the main attraction, his skin color and flashy costumes creating a stir in the small towns and provinces where such things were a rarity.

Jemmy did not fight again for nearly two years. Upon his return to the ring, his old nemesis Will Renwick was again his opponent. It is unclear as to why this match was again made, for The Prince clearly demonstrated his superiority in the first contest. However, for some reason the Newcastle sports again rallied behind their man this time to the tune of a 100-pound stake. The match took place at Shap Fell, Westmorland, which was about halfway between Liverpool and Carlisle on June 18, 1839. This bout was the first fought by Wharton under the London Prize Ring rules which had been instituted in 1838 by the Pugilistic Club in order to replace Broughton's Rules which had been in use for close to 100 years(see Appendix B).

Renwick showed himself to be a bit improved, but was still no match for the famous Moroccan Prince. Jemmy again dominated his larger opponent with speed and skill and despite some brave stands by Renwick, there was little to keep Wharton from punishing his opponent. The bout lasted just over an hour during which 14 rounds were fought. The match ended with Jemmy knocking his man fully unconscious with a thunderous right hand punch behind the ear. Will Rencwick never fought in the prize ring again.

By early 1840, there seemed to be no mountains left to climb for Jem Wharton. With the exception of a match with James "Deaf" Burke, who had claimed the Championship after Thompson had retired with his knee injury, there seemed to be little hope of finding a worthy foe. It was then that Molineaux received a welcome but wholly unexpected challenge from John "Hammer" Lane.

Lane was like Wharton in many ways, clever, strong and most importantly, undefeated. He had beaten every man who had ever dared step into the ring with him, seven victims in all. His most impressive victory may have been his defeat of the famous Owen Swift, who the Hammer beat in 2 hours during which 104 rounds were fought. By 1840, Lane was thought to be invincible, but plagued by the same problem that had seemingly halted Young Molineaux's career; there were no men left at his weight to fight.

Lane's challenge of Wharton stipulated that the men weigh no more than 150 pounds. This was an unfortunate circumstance for Jemmy, for he knew that he could not reduce himself to that weight and still be the same fighter. Fearing that at such a weight he would be easy prey for the accomplished Hammer, Wharton returned a challenge to Lane with the following stipulation: the men would weight no more than 155 pounds. Hammer balked at this offer, and for a long while both men refused to budge from their position. A simple matter of five pounds either way was what kept the men apart. The Fancy was dismayed by the fact that the most attractive match of their generation was not to be made because of such a trivial matter. Five pounds they deemed was little for each man to acquiesce. The supporters on each side publicly backed their man, but behind the scenes each faction implored their fighter to accept the match on the other man's terms. The problem remained that both Wharton and Lane were fairly satisfied that their own demands were within reason and neither felt the need to bend to the other's will. Thusly the match did not materialize.

Jemmy Wharton announced his retirement from the ring in February 1840. Finding that he could not make a match with lucrative enough stakes to excite him, he simply walked away from the game. His announcement was greeted with an outpouring of disappointment, for it was well known that any battle that Young Molineaux engaged in was sure to be a good one. The game was loosing one of its great stars and would suffer because of it. However, his retirement would be short lived when on April 9th, 1840 the following challenge appeared in *Bell's Life*, "Sir—you will oblige me by informing Molineaux that I am prepared to fight him according to his own terms, viz., neither man to exceed 11st 1pound(155pounds), for 100 pounds a side, providing the distance be 100 miles from Liverpool and Birmingham. As a proof that I mean fighting, my money is ready at T. Horton's, King's Head, Digbeth, Birmingham, or by paying my expenses I will meet him at any house he may appoint. John Lane"

Hammer Lane blinked first and threw down the gauntlet, stipulating that he would fight Jemmy at 155 pounds. When the news of this challenge reached Wharton, who was on an exhibition tour with Dick Cain, he immediately returned to London. He made his way to Jem Burn's establishment, and assured the London Fancy that he would make his way to Birmingham to seal the match with Lane. Jemmy was in no rush however, and while on his way to Birmingham continued to stop at each town and hamlet on the way where he and Dick Cain persisted in their touring schedule. By the time they reached Birmingham, a good month later, Hammer Lane was incensed and threatened to back out of the match. Jemmy was confident that Lane had no such intentions and squabbled over every detail of the match during the drawing of the articles. Several times during the negotiations, Wharton and Hammer came near to blows, but were finally induced by their backers to shake hands and conclude the conference amicably. The result was that the match was confirmed to take place on June 9, 1840 for 100 pounds per side at a location not less than 100 miles from Liverpool and Birmingham under the regulations of the London Prize Ring Rules.

Both men went into serious training after the signing of the articles, Lane under the watchful eye of his brother Bill and Dave Davis at the Angel Inn near Birmingham, and Wharton, with Joe Birchall and Tommy Roundhead, at The Hare and Hounds at West Derby near Liverpool. Training was not an issue for either man and both were assured to be in the best of physical preparedness the day of the fight, although Young Molineaux did not make it through his training period without incident.

Jemmy had chosen the Hare and Hounds because he was evidently enamored with the landlord's wife. While there he had an affair with the woman and in consequence was nearly clubbed to death by her husband. Tommy Roundhead notified Mr. Besant, one of Jemmy's backers, of the trouble, and the latter immediately called a meeting with the scorned husband. Besant smoothed the entire incident over by producing a 10-pound note and offering it to the landlord in payment for his troubles. The landlord agreed to allow Wharton to continue to stay at the Hare and Horse but only after sending his wife to stay with relatives in nearby Liverpool.

Interest in the bout was paramount. Both Lane and Wharton drew large crowds to their training quarters where admirers could talk to the fighters, and perhaps, more importantly, the betting men could see for themselves the condition of each man. The match was considered at the time to be of greater interest and intrigue than the Championship match between Bendigo and Deaf Burke over a year and a half before. Betting was brisk albeit, neither faction was willing to give great odds that their man would prove victorious further illustrating the equality of the match.

A fortnight prior to the contest both sides agreed that the fight should take place at Linderick Common near Worksop with both men to enter the ring by 9 am. Jemmy made his way to Worksop where he stayed overnight at the private residence of a supporter. Feeling confident and ready when he went to sleep at sundown, Wharton woke in the middle of the night with terrible cramps in his stomach. An attack of diarrhea followed and Jemmy was unable to rest peacefully. At eight the next morning he sent word to the Lane camp that he would not be able to enter the ring at 9a.m. as prescribed and asked if the time of entrance could be pushed forward to 11a.m. Hammer agreed. Jemmy felt better by 9:30 and made his way to the corn chandler's farm where the men had agreed to weigh in. They did so at 10 am and to almost every onlooker's surprise, Hammer Lane tipped the scales at 154 pounds, two pound heavier than Molineaux. Lane's outward appearance, lean and hard, stopped any talk of him being out of shape and his added weight was immediately attributed to increased muscle. Wharton was a bit light, which led some to believe that he may have "trained off", but with his bout of diarrhea the night before it was assumed "normal" that he would weigh in a few pounds under his normal 154-156 pound range.

The men both appeared on the scene of battle near 10:30. It was an intensely warm day and the sun sat in the sky without the hint of a cloud. The crowd was a mixture of fighting men, wealthy "Corinthians", sports, and some lower lights. Famous fighters such as Jem Burn, Jem Ward, Dick Curtis, Mat Robinson, Jack Adams, Bill Looney, Peter Taylor and Jack Langam were on hand. So too were Byng Stocks and Owen Swift, two men who had been beaten by Hammer Lane and were probably there to witness what they had hoped would be his downfall. Swift, it was reported, had laid his house and tavern on Young Molineaux to win. The Marquis of Queensbury and Waterford was also on hand as well as, what *Bell's Life* reported as, "the most respected and distinguished company to be present ringside since the days of Cribb."

Jemmy entered the area first, seemingly recovered from his overnight sickness, where he offered his colors to anyone who cared to pay, "a guinea if I win and nothing if I loose." He handed out over two hundred bright orange handker-chiefs to the crowd, most of whom were Londoners that had made the journey to see their man do battle. Lane entered shortly thereafter and met the crowd with a similar offer to buy his deep crimson handkerchiefs for the same price. By the time the men and their representatives met at the center of the 24ft, it was near noon, the heat was excessive and both combatants seemed ready to get to milling. Wharton won the toss for corners and strategically picked the one with his back to the sun, where he tied his colors to the ring post. Jemmy was seconded by Joe Birchall and Nick Ward, Lane by his brother and Dave Davis. After a brief dis-agreement over the selection of the referee, a Mr. Bainbridge being finally selected, the men readied themselves for battle.

The first minute of the first round between Lane and Wharton was spent in light sparring and then as *Bell's Life* reported, "a complete stand, both earnestly looking at each other, and keeping their arms in the same position as when they met. At this moment the elegant mien of both was universally admired. It was a perfect picture and was well worthy of being immortalized by the pencil of Rubens." Molineaux got the fighting started in earnest when he stuck out with his famed left hand and caught Lane square on the side of the head. Hammer tried to counter, but was parried. He attempted the same punch again but was for a second time blocked by Wharton. Lane's third attempt proved successful, after which a short exchange ensued before the "Brum" threw the Prince with a spec-tacular wrestling maneuver. The first round had lasted just four minutes, most of which was spent sparring and neither man seemed to display any type of superi-ority.

The second round was similar to the first with the exception that Young Molineaux closed the round by throwing Lane with a perfectly executed cross buttock. The third through eighth rounds were similar in that neither man was dishing out more than he was receiving. It was noticed however that Jemmy was sweating profusely; due it was surmised to the extensive heat, and a possible relapse of his previous night's sickness. In the ninth round Lane took control and punished a visibly weakened Wharton with lefts and rights to the body and head. According to *Bell's Life* Hammer then, "got Molineaux to the ropes and clasped his arms around the black's neck, which he held very tight upon the ropes. Lane grasped harder, squeezed with all his force and held gigantically firm. The black appeared in great agony." Lane held Wharton in this chokehold for sometime before Jemmy was finally able to extricate himself by "drawing his body into the smallest compass imaginable and getting to the turf". Molineaux, the air extinguished from his body, was in bad shape. He had nearly lost consciousness and was visibly weak when he met Lane at the scratch to begin the tenth round.

The Brum took advantage of Jemmy's weakened state and punished him severely over the course of the next few rounds. At the end of the twelfth frame, Hammer stunned Jemmy with a fearful smash behind his left ear and then threw him to the turf. *Bell's Life* reported that "Molineaux layed upon his face until time was called." The supporters of Jemmy were outwardly concerned as their man was now seemingly in dire straits. But Wharton responded to the call of time for the thirteenth round with what was described as, "an alarming amount of alacrity considering his condition." The next few rounds found Molineaux working himself back into the fight while slowly recovering his wind. His face took on a new demeanor as he glared at Lane with ferocity and purpose. Hammer still had the advantage, but Jemmy was now countering his adversaries punches with a "coolness and calculating eye". In the seventeenth Wharton landed his best punch of the fight in the form of a right hand that, "hit out with such force that it brought the claret from Lane's cork." In the eighteenth stanza Lane again attempted to place a chokehold on his foe but was unsuccessful as Wharton "seized his right hand in a firm grasp so as to prevent a repetition of the ninth round." Despite Jemmy's small comeback Hammer Lane was still confident that the battle was his to be won. During the 30 second rest between the nineteenth and twentieth rounds he could be seen, "laughing out loud and smiling out right". The smile did not leave Hammer's face as he came to scratch, and he again took control of the bout by landing a left hand, and then placing Wharton in a headlock. With his left arm firmly in place around Wharton's neck, Hammer Lane hit his prone enemy twenty or thirty times with his right hand, finishing the round by throwing the weakened Prince to the ground. The next round was marked by similar punishment for Molineaux, who despite matching Lane blow for blow, appeared the more damaged and more exhausted of the two combatants.

Jemmy looked a fully beaten man when he answered the call for the twenty-second round. Lane smashed him with a right hand on the throat that made Wharton wince and retreat. Thinking that the finish was near, Hammer closed with his opponent in the hope that he could end the match with one or two more decisive blows. But Young Molineaux was not done. Bell's Life described the incredible turn of events that then transpired. "Desperation gleaned in the eye of Molineaux. He suddenly dropped his arms caught Lane instantaneously round the waist, lifted him up and flung him with terrible force upon the ground; his heels flourished in the air and his nob first to the earth." The Hammer was nearly insensible, as he lay motionless on the ground. His seconds rushed out to their man while the Wharton crowd cheered. Like in his bout with Preston, Jemmy used his tremendous strength to dramatically alter the complexion of the fight.

Lane never recovered from Jemmy's tremendous throw. In the next ten rounds, Molineaux slowly gained back his strength and punished Hammer severely. In the forty-first round *Bell's* reported that, "Molineaux was cool, determined and went to work with great effect, cut Lane's eye, and gave him a tremendous right hand knockdown blow, being the first given during the fight." Jemmy, a consummate professional, never allowed Lane to take back control of the fight. He systematically beat him to a pulp with a mixture of heavy throws and damaging punches. In the forty-eighth round, The Prince threw Hammer so heavily that *Bell's* stated, "the ground was almost shaking with the violence of the throw." Hammer Lane was a beaten man, and by the fiftieth round he was a pitiful site standing at the scratch awaiting the inevitable. Jemmy, ever the sport, asked Lane to concede defeat but the latter refused. Molineaux knocked his man to the turf with a light blow, hoping that Lane would not make it to the mark again, and thus avoid a more savage ending. But Hammer Lane was a warrior and refused to go out on anything but his shield. He came to the line for the fifty-first stanza, "his eyes vacant his arms refusing their office." Molineaux stepped forward, and drove a right hand straight at Lane's forehead, which landed with an awful thud and ended the fight. The battle lasted one hour and twelve minutes.

"Molineaux", wrote *Bell's Life* in its remarks on the fight, "once more stands in the proud position of a conqueror. This, his last, or so he vows, and most celebrated contest has raised him higher than ever. He never before met such an opponent as Lane, and his defeat of him is the greatest gem in his pugilistic diadem. His science is beautiful and his foresight and generalship is pre-eminent. His tactics in reserving himself, his manner of attack, and his great superiority in having "a few rounds in him", fox like, when wanted and knowing when they would be serviceable, is a trait of no ordinary character, and when prudently practiced, will always be found advantageous to the operator." Through his defeat of Lane, Wharton cemented his already firm position among the great men of the prize ring. In his match with the undefeated Hammer, he displayed everything that made him the greatest fighter of his time: generalship, amazing strength, unrivaled science, and the ability to think and adjust in the ring. More importantly, Jemmy demonstrated a fierce will to win and the ability to turn a loosing situation, one where the odds were long for recovery, into a winning circumstance. James Wharton was now considered the best fighter on the planet.

Both Lane and Wharton had announced prior to the bout that the contest between them would be the last for each man. Hammer Lane did not keep his promise and returned to the prize ring a few years later, even fighting with the famed Yankee Sullivan the following year. Jemmy, however, was done with prizefighting forever. The men would form a unique friendship, one that had been born out of mutual respect, and both accepted invitations to a benefit at the Queen's Theater Liverpool in their honor just a month after their now famous battle a Worksop. The benefit was a wild success and when the two beneficiaries took the stage to wind up the proceedings with a mock presentation of their battle, the applause was deafening. The pair decided to take their act on the road and set out on a tour of England that brought them through Sheffield, Leeds, Bradford, Nottingham, Leicester and London. Everywhere they appeared huge crowds turned out to see the heroes of the hour. It was the most successful endeavor of Jemmy Wharton's career, and put him in such a stable financial state that he decided to open a tavern with the proceeds.

Jemmy hung his shingle in Manchester taking over the ownership of the St. Paul's Tavern. He married a local girl and began a family, eventually fathering three children. After several years, Wharton picked up his stakes and removed to Liverpool where took control of Jem Ward's old tavern the Star in Williamson Square. Jemmy, during this time, was still working in the sport of boxing although not as an active fighter. His reputation as a man of science and condition led to his selection as both a trainer and second for such well known men as Champions Bendigo Thompson and Ben Caunt as well as some other lesser known luminaries of the ring. However, Wharton also began to drink heavily and before his fortieth year began to show the effects of consumption. In the April 6, 1856 addition of *Bell's Life* it was reported that, "Jemmy the Black lies in a very dangerous and precarious state, having been confined to his room for the past twelve months; in fact little or no hope is entertained for his recovery."

James Wharton died less than three weeks later, on April 25, 1856 at his home in Liverpool of what was reported as the affects of consumption.

James Wharton was the most complete black prizefighter who ever entered the "lists" in England. His career, unmarred by defeat, was the finest of any who had come before, or would emerge after him. Where Tom Molineaux, Bill Richmond and Harry Sutton had failed in their biggest fights, Jemmy The Black proved victorious in his. His resume, both then and now, is impressive, and despite never receiving a title in name, he was generally considered a champion. His story was not unique in its adventurous beginning, or its sad end, but what lay in between was special.

Perhaps overshadowed by the fabulous career of the Moroccan Prince was another black fighter named Sambo Sutton. Little if anything is known of Sutton's life prior to his entrance into the fistic world other than that he came under the tutelage of Jem Burn sometime in 1835. Sambo was a good sparrer and considered one of the better exhibition performers of his time. A well-proportioned man standing 5'10" and weighing around 165 pounds, he was well liked by the male students of Cambridge University where he taught the many art, and counted among his students the famous moral author Charles Kingsley. Sambo's first essay in the prize ring was against the aforementioned future Champion of England, Nick Ward on May 27, 1836 near Finchley. The bout was an impromptu event having transpired after Jem Burn and Nick's brother Jem Ward had an argument at a cockfight. Ward and Sutton set to in field and fought for 12 rounds. Ward showed himself to be a clever man but when pressed and punished by Sambo in the twelfth stanza, he simply turned away and quit.

Sutton reveled in his newfound fame and became one of the more popular men on the scene. He displayed many other talents besides his boxing skill, the most unique being his ability to stand on his head and sing, eat, drink and even dance while in that awkward position. Sutton again entered the ring December of 1836, loosing a tough contest to Harry Preston in a 53 round battle lasting well over an hour and a half.

After this match Sutton would not fight in the prize ring again for close to six years. He was again matched with Nick Ward in the spring of 1838, but this match was prevented by the arresting of both parties by a local magistrate who had caught wind that a battle between the two was to take place in his jurisdiction. Sutton remained active however, traveling with different boxing troupes and engaging in many different theatrical endeavors. In 1839 he gained a modicum of fame in London with his signing performances at the London Theatre, where Sambo performed number such as "Such a Getting Up Stairs" and "Jump

Jim Crow" to sold out houses. He also toured with Deaf Burke in an odd show which featured sparring advertised as representing the Shakespearean tragedy "Othello". Sutton played the lead and Burke starred as Iago. The show also featured Sutton performing what was billed as "his astonishing feat of dancing a hornpipe on his head and sparring with his feet while in that position." Evidently, Sambo's true calling, or perhaps more accurately his background, was in show business.

Sutton did not return to the prize ring until October 25,1842 when he met Austalian John Gorrick, more commonly known as the Bungaree, at Milbourne Heath. Gorrick defeated Sambo in a grueling 72 round contest that lasted over one hour and ten minutes. There was ill feeling between the men and they met again the following January, this time Sutton returning the winner in just under 50 minutes. That was the end of Sambo's career as a fighter. He again returned to the theatre and continued to travel the country sparring and exhibiting wherever he could find customers. He died in London in 1852.

8

Uneasy is the Head that Wears the Crown

As the 19th century rolled into its fourth decade, the black fighter found himself represented in greater numbers than ever before. The quality of these men was first rate, many of them leaving the ring without a blemish on their records, one with a championship. However, it seems that although successful, this group of black pugilists also suffered some cruel and unusual fates: one being imprisoned, one dying from disease while at the pinnacle of his career and one loosing his eye. But the 1840's also represented the first time that men of color would partake in prizefights outside the boundaries of the British Isles. And perhaps more point-edly, the decade would see the first instance of black men involved in an organized prizefight in the United States. Yet England still remained at the forefront of involvement and continued to spawn a small sum of excellent black pugilists. Perhaps the best and most enigmatic of all these men was a black sailor named John Perry.

Perry's early life is somewhat of a mystery. He himself varied the story of his origins at different times during his career. He once had stated that he was born in Annapolis, Nova Scotia sometime around 1824 to a white mother and a black British sailor. However on most occasions he claimed that he had been born in Dublin, Ireland in 1819, the son of a black American drummer in the 3rd Regiment of Foot and a Jamaican woman. According to Perry his father was known as "Black Charley" and stood six feet in height and weighed a muscular 180 pounds. John claimed that his father later became a sailor on a British Man of War where he earned a reputation as a fighting man of the first class. Due to his father's travels, Perry was not well kneaded in home life and he took to the sea at a young age. He settled for a time in St. George, New Brunswick while still a teenager, and then became an apprentice to a ship's carpenter aboard a trade vessel that frequented several different English ports. In 1841 he docked at Liverpool where John left the service of his ship. Perry never mentioned doing any type of fighting while at sea, but it seems almost a certainty that he did, for upon his de-boarding in Liverpool, he was determined to make a living with his fists.

Initially, John Perry met with little success and despite taking part in a few "scraps", he found that making a living as a fighter was more difficult than he had imagined. He wandered up to Bristol where he took on odd jobs to support himself, and seemingly gave up on the idea of a career as a prizefighter. He stayed on in Bristol for a short time and then took a job in Bradford as a valet for a wealthy publican. One night at one of the taverns of his employer, Perry took part in a subscription match against a big Yorkshireman and won handily. His boss, noticing the easy manner in which he had dispatched of his foe, asked John if he had ever fought before. Perry replied that he had, and it was then that his employer again put the idea of fighting for living into John's head.

Armed with a letter of introduction from his kind employer, John Perry set out for London to find Johnny Broome. Broome was a retired prizefighter of great note that at one time had been considered the champion lightweight of England. He ran a tavern called the Rising Sun in Piccadilly, and it was there that Perry introduced himself to his future mentor. Broome was impressed with John's physical stature, for like his father, Perry was a large man for his day, standing 6'1" tall and carrying a solid 190 pounds across broad shoulders. But Broom was keen enough to realize that stature alone did not automatically translate to success in the prize ring. He called on his younger brother Harry, who in 1851 would defeat William Perry "The Tipton Slasher" for the Heavyweight Championship of England, to have a spar with the new man. Harry, who at that time was considered the Welterweight Champion of England, was only a few inches shorter than his opponent, but severely out weighed. The men set to with the mufflers and Johnny Broome was astonished at what he witnessed. Not only was Perry skilled, parrying most of Harry's initial attacks, but he was fast as well. Despite his best efforts, the younger Broome could not reach his man with a solid punch. John, on the other hand, was fully successful in moving his smaller opponent where he pleased and punching him into retreat. John Perry was not a stupid man however, and knowing that his future lay in the hands of the brother of the man he was fighting, he took care not to hurt his adversary. At one point, Perry stopped and looked at Johnny Broome exclaiming, "Sir, I do not want to offend you by hitting you brother." Broome smiled and agreed that he had seen enough.

Johnny Broome was so impressed by what he saw of John Perry the fighter that he immediately published a challenge in *Bell's Life*. It read: "Johnny Broome will back his Black Novice against any man in England for 100 pounds a side, and will produce his man and money on Wednesday evening next at his house in Air Street, when he trusts some of the would be champions will come and try to redeem the character of the Ring." Ben Caunt, who at the time was claiming the Championship, despite being beaten by Bold Bendigo the previous year, (this decision was disputed the fight being awarded to Bendigo on a foul after Caunt had allegedly fallen without a blow. Caunt denied this accusation and continued to claim the championship), took offense to Broome's challenge and replied shortly thereafter in *Bell's Life*. His reply read, "Ben Caunt in his reply to Johnny Broome, begs to say that Broome and his black know where he lives and Caunt will find a man to fight any man, black or white, Broome can produce 300 pounds or 500 pounds a-side." Needless to say that neither Broome nor Perry had any such money and were in essence looking for a lower level stake type match.

It was Jem Burn who finally answered the challenge presenting his newest protégé, Bill Burton of Leicester as the man to take the shine off of Perry's black skin. The men agreed to fight for 15 pounds per side on January 20, 1846 at Erith, London. When the men entered the ring and stripped, Burton, who although standing 5'10" and weighing 180 pounds, looked like a mere child next to Perry. John strode to the center of the 24ft ring and produced an open hand to Bill. Burton took the hand and Perry offered to lay 10 pounds to 5 pounds on the contest, but his foe declined. Overhearing the declined offer, Ben Caunt stepped from the crowd and himself took Perry's bet. John smiled at Caunt and questioned, "Ha, Massa Caunt, me and you have a turn up for the Championship?" Ben, who could not hide his outrage replied, "You got to lick Burton yet and a few more before I take you in hand!"

The men set to at 12:20 pm. When they came to the scratch, Perry was superbly confident, placing his hands on his hips in an almost defiant attitude. John, seemingly justified in his confidence, leveled Burton with the first punch he threw, winning both first knockdown and first blood honors. Burton came up for the second round and attempted to punch his black foe to the body. Perry blocked the punch nimbly and in the same motion again knocked Bill down with his long right hand. The bout followed a similar pattern for most of the fight, Burton boring in only to have his efforts repaid with stiff counters. Perry was well in control of the bout by the middle rounds and so confident was he of victory that he began to taunt Burton and his supporters. Using his long arms to ward off the feeble attacks of his foe, John began to mock Burton by mimicking his thwarted efforts and sticking his tongue out in a contemptuous manner. The crowd did not take kindly to this behavior and soon they voiced a strong dislike for the new black. But Perry regained some favor by helping Burton to his feet and patting him on the shoulder after knocking the latter down with another right hand. The bout dragged on with John seemingly trying to punish his opponent without finishing him off. The crowd began to grow uneasy with the spectacle and Perry's corner immediately instructed him to stop the pantomime and finish his game opponent. This John did by driving Burton to the ropes and landing a terrible straight right hand between his opponent's eyes.

John's debut in the English prize ring was interesting if not solely for his behavior before and during the fight. Challenging Caunt was both a brave social act and an ingenious display of self-promotion. Perry it seems was an extremely confident man, and there is little doubt that he himself felt that he could have beaten Caunt and any other man who cared to try his wares. John also demonstrated what may be considered a general wish to both punish and embarrass Burton, a man who he had never known socially, and for all intents and purposes, had no reason to dislike. Perhaps it was John Perry's way of lashing out. Similar to Jack Johnson, some 60 years later, Perry seemingly was laughing at both the inferiority of his opponent and playing on the inherent fears of the crowd. He chose, like Johnson, to taunt and batter his foe, a man who was clearly no threat to him as a fighter, as opposed to beating him outright. What John Perry had hoped to accomplish with such antics is unclear, but whatever his reasons, his performance certainly earned him a reputation.

The physical performance of John Perry also left an indelible mark upon all those who had seen his fight with Burton. *Bell's Life* quoted several old time members of the Fancy as stating that, "the new man is the best big black since Molineaux." Perry, like most fighters after a popular ring victory, accepted an offer to tour with an exhibition troupe. Among the men traveling with John was, William "The Tipton Slasher" Perry, Charley Jones and Bill Tranter. The group spent a good six months on the road, and when they returned to London John Perry took his earnings and opened the Wheatsheaf Hotel in Covent Garden. Business was brisk for the black entrepreneur, and he even found a wealthy patron, in the person of the Marquis of Downshire, to support his ever-growing business. John enjoyed his newfound prosperity, and despite always essaying his willingness to meet any man in the ring, seemed in no great rush to return to active combat. Johnny Broome was a bit more anxious for Perry to appear again and repeatedly tried to match his fighter with Ben Caunt or William Perry but neither cared to tackle Broome's black. For the time being Perry was content to make his living as a publican and continued to operate his business with great success. However, a terrible accusation would soon appear and change John's life forever.

In the spring of 1847, John Perry was convicted of forgery and sentenced to fourteen years transportation—a sentence that meant that the accused would be deported to Australia. The particulars surrounding Perry's arrest and conviction are a bit sketchy and it is not clear as to whether he was truly guilty of the said offense, unwittingly involved in some larger crime ring, or simply framed. It was reported by *Bell's Life* that Tom Oliver was the person who upon receiving a 20-pound bank note from Perry for an old debt, realized at some length that the note was indeed a forgery. He in turn notified the authorities and had John arrested by a local magistrate. Perry was given a trial, where his defense argued that he could neither read nor write and therefore could not have known that the note was a forgery. However, the prosecution pointed to the fact that John ran his own business for which daily he handled money. They also told of Perry's fraternization with an "illicit gang" of known criminals, who he often entertained and shared business with. The jury believed the prosecution and Perry was shipped off to Australia shortly thereafter.

John landed in Van Diem's Land, now known as Tasmania, in the summer of 1847. After two years of hard labor, Perry was allowed to go into private service and traveled to Sydney where he became a valet for a Major Hamilton. Hamilton was a sport and knowing of John's reputation in London, immediately attempted to match him with some good man. The sports in Sydney, after watching Perry in an exhibition, immediately dubbed him as worthy of meeting the Champion of Australia, George Hough.

George Hough was a stand up fighter, weighing 200 pounds and standing at a solid six feet. He began fighting in 1843 when he defeated a man by the name of Bayley for a 20-pound stake and followed up this victory the following year by pummeling Jim Hadgeway in seven rounds lasting barely 8 minutes for 50 pounds. George, who relied on a quick and devastating straight right hand to do most of his damage, continued to win until finally being matched with William Chalker for the Australian Heavyweight Championship. Chalker had been the champion for close to three years when he and George met at Sydney Harbor on February 18, 1846, but was no match for the gigantic Hough who beat his opponent with ease in just under an hour. It took Hough a full year and a half to find another customer but finally induce Ike Reid to fight him for 100 pounds at Sydney Harbor on April 6, 1847. Hough punished Reid dreadfully but lost the bout on a foul when he was accused of falling without being struck in the 67th round. George and his backers were irate and demanded a rematch but no amount of wrangling could convince Reid, who suffered permanent damage to his nose and eye socket as a result of his first battle with Hough, to enter the ring again with the Champion. Hough reclaimed the championship and could not find a man to meet him until the supporters of John Perry approached him with an offer to fight for 100 pounds a side at Cummings Point on December 10, 1849.

John Perry was still a physical specimen when he stripped to do battle with Hough on that bright but cool day. His opponent wore a sullen and grave face as he entered the ring, but as was his custom, Perry simply smiled confidently. The fight was an absolute mismatch. Hough had told his friends and admirers before the match that one of his mighty right hand swings would do the trick, but he was never able to land his favorite blow. Perry opened the bout by attempting to feint George into throwing his vaunted right hand smash, but the latter, after two attempts could not be tempted. A third feint brought the desired affect and as Hough attempted to deliver his punch, John stepped in and according to *Bell's Life*, "landed his own blow with a crashing effectiveness that was audible to all around the ring". Hough dropped as if shot and some of the crowd could be heard to shout, "good heaven's it is over!" George dragged himself to the line at the call of time and John resorted to the mocking antics that he had displayed in his bout with Burton, rolling his eyes about maniacally and sticking his tongue out at his bewildered foe. Hough, visibly angered by Perry's taunts, lunged at his adversary only to be clipped with a left hand on the eye, which brought an immediate flow of blood, and a superior right hand, which grassed him. George made a mini rally in the third stanza when he managed to land his right hand on Perry's lip, drawing from it a trickle of blood. John shook off the blow and, according to *Bell's*, pointed to his mouth and stated, "Oh! You're coming for me are you?" John then set upon Hough with a ferocious barrage of punches that when completed again left the Australian Champion in a heap on the ground. Most of the spectators knew that the end was now near. In the fourth, Perry braced himself and let go of a frightening right hand that caught George flush and sent him sprawling. John, confident that he had just ended the fight, did not bother to return to his corner and instead stood over George with his arms folded and a look of both contempt and satisfaction covering his face. The bout lasted four rounds during which time a mere five minutes had elapsed. John Perry was now the Champion of Australia.

Perry's winning of the Australian Heavyweight Championship marked the first instance in history of a black man winning a nationally recognized pugilistic title. Tom Molineaux claimed the Championship of America in 1809, but there was no discernable lineage to that title, and little fact to back his claim. The Australian title however, was nearly 30 years old when Perry captured it and had a clear and traceable history. That Perry was allowed to fight for such a title further illustrates the fact that organized fighting, at least in Australia and England, maintained a policy of inclusion when dealing with black fighters. That is not to say that John never faced any discrimination because of his color. Quite to the contrary in fact, as his actions outside the ring were often times scrutinized closely and in most cases he was held to a much higher standard of behavior than his white counterparts. Even prior to winning the title, Perry was given little room for error. In the weeks leading up to the fight with Hough it was written by *Bell's Life* that, "If Perry forfeits this chance he will find considerable difficulty in gaining another." In essence the paper meant that John would not be denied his chance, but he had proven unsuccessful he surely would not have received a second turn.

After winning the title, Perry became a well-known character on the Sydney sporting scene, taking part in several exhibition programs and delighting theatre crowds with what he called his "boxing pantomime". There was however an ever-growing faction of the Australian Fancy who found both his person and his act less than appealing. The press also was not very fond of Perry and in the spirit and language of the time spoke of him as a physical marvel, a dandy and a braggart. Despite a great deal of popularity not all of Australia was comfortable with the flamboyant John Perry who both knew and acted like he was the best fighter in the land. One contemporary paper described their view of John after seeing him at an exhibition as "parading around town got up in a broad-brimmed white beaver hat, immense white muslin cravat, with a jeweled pin to correspond, green Newmarket cut coat with large steel buttons, white knee cords and top boots surmounted by white stain ribbons, and as he came down the street with his heavy hunting whip under his arm he certainly looked a magnificent specimen of the human animal." Hidden within this description of John's splendid dress is a caveat of the growing fear and loathing regarding the black pugilist. His displays of arrogance, represented by his clothing and gait, were an uncommon and threatening sight to the white male writer. The typically subordinate and meek black image exhibited by the aboriginal blacks in Sydney at this time were what was expected of any colored man, whether a foreigner or not. John's behavior, neither submissive nor humble, was the antithesis of what was anticipated of black men and generally perceived as the "correct behavior" of the "lower race". Perry, however, was not an ordinary man, and though undoubtedly aware of the stir he was causing, refused to change his attitude or behavior.

After a tour of New South Wales, during which *Bell's* noted that those who had seen Perry display his boxing techniques in exhibition matches were noticed to be "opening their mouths tolerably wide", John returned to Sydney determined to get back to the business of fighting. There was one problem; no man could be found to challenge "Black Perry" as John was now known. Several matches were purposed and often times talk would surface about an "unknown" who was making his way to Australia to take the measure of the Champion, but nothing ever materialized. Perry's reputation, along with his complete annihilation of Hough, had undoubtedly scared off most worthy fighters from taking a crack at his title. But Perry himself did not help matters by continually demanding purses that in many cases were far too great for any man to accept. It seems that John was not keen to the fact that most of the Fancy agreed that there was at that time no fighting man in Australia who stood even a slight chance at beating the champion and that such a high stake would simply be "lost money".

John, frustrated by his inability to gain a match, turned to training other fighters and making the exhibition rounds as a means of keeping himself in good money. The Champion also began to drink heavily and on more than one occasion found himself fighting in the street as a result of his binges. One of his students, an aboriginal boxer named "Perry's Pet", proved victorious in his first fight in 1850, but after a subsequent disagreement and eventual break with John, was never heard from again. Perry turned back to the hotel business for his next venture and opened an establishment in Windsor which was quite successful for a number of years until Perry's drinking and gambling woes led to its closing two years thereafter. John returned to Sydney and again challenged the world to fight for his title, but again no takers could be found. He continued to make his money where he could and even appeared in a production of Othello in 1857, but his heavy drinking persisted and his constitution and physical appearance began to dissipate.

In 1858, a challenger was finally found in the person of Bob McLaren who came to Australia claiming the Heavyweight Championship of California. At a meeting of the Australian Fancy at the Sydney Hotel during June of that year, a match was made between Perry and McLaren for 300 pounds. However, when the two men met in an exhibition match later that month, John's physical appearance and display against the American was so pitiful that his backers immediately pulled out their stake money and the match was canceled. It was later discovered that not only was Perry woefully out of shape when he showed up for the exhibition but he was fully inebriated as well.

John Perry's star had set. Thirteen years had passed since his triumph over Hough and he was no longer the seemingly invincible prizefighter that he had appeared to be on that day. But Perry's contribution to the sport would not end. He continued to train fighters and even opened a boxing academy in Glebe, which remained in operation through most of the 1860's. Perry still had his troubles with the bottle however and was more times drunk than sober. Despite all his shortcomings, and his rather scant ring performances, "Perry the Black" was still respected as fighting man. As late as 1871 his reputation was still so formidable that the famed Larry Foley sought out the now ex-champion for fistic tutoring when the former was preparing to fight Sandy Ross. Foley won the fight and would later become one of Australia's greatest champions, eventually bridging the gap between the bare-knuckle and gloved eras. Perry's fate would not be so kind.

There is a bit of mystery surrounding the ultimate providence of "Black Perry". One version of his demise states that he ultimately drank himself to death and was found dead in a storefront doorway with a bottle in hand. Another, more likely version, is that sometime in the late 1870's, John was committed to an asylum in New South Wales where he died both disillusioned and disenfranchised. Neither story gives any indication that Perry died with any dignity and surely, by whichever method he met his maker, it was a sad end.

John Perry's career was strange at best. It is difficult to gauge his true ability as a fighter for although impressive, two fights could not be considered adequate proof of greatness. However, his reputation and his short and complete decimation of the sturdy George Hough, lead us to believe that John Perry was certainly a man of considerable fistic talent. His winning of a championship also lends credence to the argument that perhaps he was the most important black fighter of his generation. His title winning effort, and subsequent reign as a champion, albeit a non-fighting one, was a standard bearing achievement, and one that should be considered important purely for the age and context during which it was achieved. However, John Perry must also be looked at as a revolutionary character. Up until his appearance in England, no black pugilist dared to display the kind of arrogance and pride that marked every facet of John Perry's personality and ring craft. His attitude was one of superiority, and he seemingly took every opportunity to ensure that the white masses understood that. He was a predecessor of Jack Johnson, a man so fully confident in his fistic abilities that he treated most of his white opponents with contempt and a smug condescension. Perry was not afraid to display that he was "the better man", and as he exhibited in his bouts with both Hough and Burton, he actually went to lengths to ensure that all who witnessed his domination were aware of it. His taunting and mocking of opponents was thought to be both in bad taste and a discredit to the ring. Any fighter, white or black, who displayed such an ugly disregard for their opponent was considered a poor sport. But Perry's actions were not rooted in bad taste, but rather in defiance. His displays of arrogance were done with purpose, meant to evidence to any onlooker, that he was not inferior and would not stand to be considered as such. John's dress and attitude outside the ring served a similar purpose. Like Johnson, Perry would not be refined by the racial mores of his society, and in contrast flaunted his wealth and physical prowess whenever he was given the opportunity. These actions certainly led, in some way, to the downfall of Perry, for it is without doubt that he found more detractors than sympathizers through his choice of behavior. It must also be assumed that his heavy drinking was in at least some way the consequence of his behavior and the outflow of negative public opinion it brought with it. But to John's credit, this neither moved him from his position nor did it change his outlook or conduct. Perry remained absolute and even into his later years continued to be a confident and unyielding man.

While Perry made his way through the world, other black pugilists were springing up in England. Among the seven black men beside Perry who would make their entrance in the fistic world in 1840's England, two were of particular note; James Robinson, "The Ebony Phenomenon" and Thomas Welsh "Young Sambo ".

James "Jemmy" Robinson first appeared in Liverpool in 1846. He claimed to have come from Virginia, where at the age of 12 he was hired on as a cabin boy aboard a trader then docked at Norfolk. He worked in such a capacity for over four and a half years before taking leave of his ship in Liverpool to look for work in that metropolis. A street fight gained him the attention of a sporting man who took him to the Fighting Cocks, a tavern kept by a pugilist of note named Young Norely, in Salford. Robinson, still only a boy of seventeen, stood a smidge over five feet three inches and weighed a mere 120 pounds, but was lightning quick and displayed an extensive knowledge of fighting with his fists. Dubbed, "Young Norley's Black", he was given a trial bout with Jem Millwood, an amateur of some note, at the Fighting Cocks, where he so impressed the crowd that he was immediately matched with Jem Evans, a Welshman who had been tutored by Hammer Lane. Norley's Black was the master from the start and after nearly and hour had elapsed Lane himself conceded the defeat of his protégé'.

Jemmy Robinson's victory over Evans created no small stir among the Fancy who began calling him by the flattering moniker of "The Ebony Phenomenon". Robinson demonstrated that such a nickname was just when in his next bout he out-punched, out-lasted and out-gutted the tough 130 pound Johnny Peach on a bitterly cold March day at Buxom, England for a purse of 30 pounds a side. Three months later, Jemmy again proved victorious when on June 15, 1847 he bludgeoned London favorite Charley Mullet to defeat in 73 minutes. After this victory, Robinson was considered by many to be the best man at or near his weight in all of England. The few who did not share that opinion were the backers of the famed Enoch Horridge "The Pocket Hercules" of Manchester.

In 1849, Enoch Horridge was a veteran of 10 prize ring battles. He had tasted defeat on two occasions, one a suspected cross(fix), and the other a confusing occurrence where Horridge was accused of using a foul blow to down his opponent. Enoch had also spent some time in jail, serving two separate six months sentences for his part in three different prizefights broken up by local magistrates. When Jemmy Robinson's supporters began making noise about their man being the best in the land, Horridge took it as a personal offense.

After much wrangling between both sides, Horridge and Robinson were finally matched to meet for 60 pounds per side at Manchester on June 13, 1848. When Enoch stripped for battle his brawny, yet squat figure, aptly fit his given moniker. He stood a mere 5'3" inches but was heavily muscled with legs described by *Bell's Life* as "the finest set of pegs ever developed." Jemmy himself cut an impressive figure when he de-frocked. As *Bell's* noted, "His condition was perfect, whilst his beautifully symmetrical frame elicited general admiration, and though good judges thought that his legs were too light, there could be no doubt that his limbs, chest, and back were every inch clothed with muscle." The fight itself was a fierce and determined encounter. Both men saw their fortunes change with the rounds, and both received a tremendous amount of punishment. It was a contest that called on all of their skill, courage and determination. Enoch was good, but Jemmy Robinson was a step better. As *Bell's Life* stated in its remarks on the fight, "The Pocket Hercules could see by the 22nd round that he could not hope to win against a man who was superior in science, in reach, in freshness and in strength." The bout ended as few did in that era: with Horridge, who still seemed to have some fight left in him, extending his hand to Robinson and conceding defeat.

Jemmy Robinson, who was only nineteen when he defeated Horridge, seemed destined for a long and prosperous career in the prize ring. However, he would be the victim of a far crueler fate. On June 8, 1849 the Ebony Phenomenon, a picture of youth and health, contracted cholera and died three days later at Bird in Hand Hostelry in Salford. He was buried the same day at the Rusholme Road Cemetery. He was 20 years old.

About the same time that Robinson was dominating the featherweights, Thomas Welsh, alias Young Sambo, was busy making a similar record among the lightweights. No record exists of Welsh's life prior to his fighting career, but he did claim to be an American by birth. Thomas began his fistic life in 1839 when he took part in a turn-up fight with Jem Shaw for the benefit of some sports, and a subscription purse, in the loft of Reuben Martin's Rat Pit in London. Both men were mere novices but the bout was contested at breakneck speed until stopped in the 40th round due to insufficient light. Welsh was pronounced the loser of the contest but his reputation as a fighter of note was dually recognized. It seemed that Thomas was well equipped to handle the rigors of the ring, and a bright future was predicted for the young pugilist. However, sometime in early 1840 Welsh was involved in street altercation during which he was stabbed in the left eye with a knife, blinding that optical permanently. Despite this unfortunate handicap, Young Sambo was still eager to fight, and insisted to his would be backers that he was a better fighter with one eye than most of the two-eyed men in London. However, the moneymen did not share Welsh's enthusiasm.

Finally, in January 1843, after nearly two years spent earning the reputation as the "best sparrer within 10 miles of London", Welsh had proven his ability to fight despite his bum eye, and was matched for a real prizefight. Brighton Jack Sears was the opponent and proved to be a tough customer, fighting Sambo for three quarters of an hour before conceding defeat. Welsh would follow this victory with two more impressive wins against Bill Jones and Tom Verdun before being matched with the famous Billy Jordan of Manchester.

Jordan, who would later immigrate to the United States where he would enjoy a fabulous career as a ring announcer, was a crack lightweight and thought to be the best of the crop by his North Country supporters. He and Young Sambo fought for a 100 pound purse near Purfleet on January 21, 1845. The battle was characterized by skillful displays of boxing by both men, but ended in general chaos. The referee first awarded the fight to Welsh on a foul in the 48th round, when Jordan fell without a blow being landed, and then amid pressure from Jordan's supporters reversed his call, and ordered the men to fight on. However, Young Sambo had already left the ring, and refused to fight on, claiming that he had already won the bout. The referee then reversed his verdict yet again, and proclaimed Welsh the winner. The bout had lasted a total of 105 minutes.

Due to the unsatisfactory ending of the first fight, the men agreed to meet again on March 11 of the same year. This time they settled on Norley as the location, and both men agreed to weigh in under 131 pounds. Unfortunately for Jordan, on the day of the fight he was two pounds over weight, and Welsh insisted that he fight without his shoes so as to comply with the weight agreement. This Jordan did. The bout was again characterized by its science, and the men fought on fairly equal terms for most of the match. In the later rounds however, Welsh's blows seemed to carry a bit more power, and eventually wore his opponent down. In the 113th round, after fighting for just under four hours, Jordan collapsed, and Young Sambo was declared the victor.

After his stirring victory over Jordan, Thomas Welsh was not seen in the ring for over three years. He, like all before and after him, confined himself to the exhibition circuit, and even developed his own boxing troupe, which visited all of the fairs and festivals in England, Scotland and Ireland. On June 20, 1848, Young Sambo was induced to enter the ring again against a tough 140 pound man named Alec Keene. Sambo was not fit for the bout and only lasted a mere 15 minutes against the aggressive Keene. Another two-year hiatus from ring activity would be ended in December of 1810 when Welsh fought a two and half hour draw with the great Jem Cross at Long Reach for a purse of 100 pounds. Two years later the men would again meet at Long Reach, this time Young Sambo taking the measure of Cross in 29 rounds.

After his victory over Cross, Thomas Welsh never fought in the prize ring again. For years he was a respected trainer, second and teacher. He was also an integral part of the ring fraternity in London, which had a hand in every facet of the game in that area.

At a glance, Welsh's career could be considered very successful. He lost only one contest in the prize ring, for which he was not properly prepared, and fought some of the best men of his generation. However, the fact that he accomplished all of this with the severe disadvantage of being blind in only one eye is truly remarkable.

9

They're Coming to America

The prize ring in America had a slower and far more deliberate maturing process than it had experienced in England. The sport, although practiced in a far more liberal and relaxed manner, had been followed in the United States since before the country won its liberty from England. However, its evolution into a sport of the masses, with observed rules, rituals and practices, did not manifest itself until the early 1850's. Boxing in America prior to that time had been more incidental and sporadic, contests often following makeshift rules, and men often times fighting for "the sport of it" as opposed to an agreed sum. English stars, such as Deaf Burke, had come and fought on American soil as early as the 1830's, but even the influence of such fighters was minimal in terms of the effect it had on the sport's growth.

It was not until 1841 that Tom Hyer would be recognized as the first, true American champion, by those close to the sport, and another eight before the press, and more importantly, the general public, would take a zealous interest. Hyer's 1849 battle with the famed Yankee Sullivan may have been the first prize ring contest in America, where anything close to a national interest could be considered evident. Hindering this growth was the 1842 battle between Christopher Lilly and Thomas McCoy at Hastings, New York, which resulted in the death of the latter: the first notable death in the American ring. The outcry was considerable, and prizefighting itself came under great scrutiny, being considered by most to represent the decaying character of American cities. Without the patronage of rich or powerful men, prizefighting was associated with saloon culture, gambling, and political corruption; less a sport than a means to settle a grudge. Furthermore, prize fighting, which was illegal in most states, was closely monitored by the authorities, making it difficult for fights to even occur in most areas. However, boxing remained alive and continued to grow in popularity despite the reluctance of the general public to embrace the sport.

Coinciding with the expansion and growth of prizefighting as an organized American sport was the maturation of sparring, as both an exhibitive activity and as a method of learned defense. William Fuller, who had fought Tom Molineaux in 1814, was the first to successfully introduce the refined art of "sparring" to the American public. After running successful schools in England and France, Fuller came to the United States during the 1820's and toured extensively, giving lessons and exhibiting on stage. He eventually opened a gymnasium in New York, where he taught the "noble art" to a wealthy patronage. Fuller's attempts to separate prize fighting from its cousin "sparring" and his "arts of self defense" were amply demonstrated by the clientele that he sought. Playing on the fears of the upper class, urban socialites, who were more and more threatened by the growing lower "masses" in all American metropolises, Fuller lured his cash heavy students to his "rooms" by promising to provide them with a means of protecting themselves. Fuller's work was generally thought to be noble, and his crafty use of boxing's more artful aspects appealed to the refined tastes of the educated and cultured men to whom he taught.

This mingling of sparring and the upper class would eventually spawn the American Fancy. This was in essence the transformation of wealthy men who would ultimately replace the rather tepid and sanguine practice of sparring with gloves to with the far more visceral and exciting experience of bare knuckle fighting. Therefore, by the early 1840's, with the lower classes occupying their positions as the fighters, trainers and seconds, and the upper crust fulfilling the role of financial backers, prizefighting in the United States reached a more mature level and therefore began to take a firmer hold on the American pysche.

The story of the black prizefighter in America followed a much different path than it did in England. From the sport's beginnings in the United States, there was a distinct sense of exclusion. In England and Australia, black men, if deemed pugilistically worthy, were allowed to fight white men—in some cases even champions—without regard to their skin color. America, however, had a very different set of rules for her black participants. The first recorded instance of black men fighting in an organized boxing event in the United States fully illustrates these variations.

On June 1, 1842, Dan Knox and Sam Briggs, both African Americans, fought under the revised London Prize Ring Rules at Hoboken, NJ for 18 minutes during which 7 rounds were fought. Knox won the bout and was thereafter called the "Colored Champion of New York". That such an appellation even existed speaks volumes of the way in which black athletes were already being treated in the United States. By that time black men had been fighting in England for over 40 years, and never once had they been reduced to fighting for a "colored title". Knox fought again the next year, defeating another African-American fighter simply called Butcher Mack, but was never heard from again. He and his "colored title" simply disappeared.

There were certainly black prizefighters active in the US, before and after Knox and Briggs fought their contest, but their battle holds a certain significance, for it was the first ever recorded in the American Press. Whether or not there was a sub culture of black prizefighters is not known, however, it is clear that no African-American fought any white fighter of any note during these years. And after Knox's disappearance from the fighting scene, it would take another decade for the deeds and fights of another black man to make their appearance in the press of the day. His name was Aaron "Molineaux" Hewlett.

Next to nothing is recorded of Aaron Hewlett's life prior to his entrance into the sporting world in 1850, other than the fact that he was born in Brooklyn, to a black father and a Native American mother. Hewlett evidently grew up in Brooklyn where he learned how to handle himself in street fights and other test of strength, but where his pugilistic aptitude came from is a mystery. He first appeared in the ring on June 11, 1851, when he fought and defeated another black man named Timmons Black Boy in a tenement lot in Brooklyn. Hewlett, who stood around 5'8" and weighed 160 pounds, thrashed his larger opponent with ease, taking less than 21 minutes to settle the matter of superiority while earning 5 dollars in the process. Armed with a small reputation he ventured into

Manhattan and visited several sporting men who he had been told would be happy to match him with some willing customer. After several setbacks he was matched with William Hastings, a white Englishman who went by the colorful sobriquet of "Dublin Tricks", for 50 dollars. Hastings, who had earned himself somewhat of a reputation by defeating the popular New York pugilist Awful Gardner, was a well-schooled fighter, and was known to use any means necessary to procure a victory.

Hewlett and Hastings fought under a bridge near the Harlem River on Aug 13, 1852. About five hundred spectators witnessed a battle that was savagely contested for over one hour and ten minutes. The backers of the event, who carefully handed out small bribes to the necessary "coppers", had neatly averted any police interference by their artful handling of the New York authorities and the fight concluded without interference. In the 36th round, Hewlett threw Hastings to the ground and pounced down upon him with such force that the latter was knocked completely unconscious. Aaron, who was badly marked about the body but remarkably injury free around his face and neck, was declared the winner and given the purse of 50 dollars. Hewlett had not only won the fight but also became the first professional black fighter to defeat a white opponent in a boxing match on American soil.

After this victory, Hewlett opened a small sparring academy in Brooklyn where he taught boxing and wrestling. Molineaux also became known as somewhat of a strong man and athlete, performing feats of strength and endurance in both burlesque type exhibitions and organized "dares" or bets. Once in 1852 he won $50 dollars for running around a ½ mile park ten times in under forty minutes. On another occasion he won $25 dollars for carrying two men, said to weigh 150 pounds each 100 yards in less 40 seconds. These types of exhibitions along with his well-known background in fighting brought Hewlett a certain amount of fame around town and better still, a great number of students to his gymnasium.

Molineaux's clientele was not typical for a sparring teacher, and his parlor drew more roughs than he cared to handle. One such man was named Mingo, a black stevedore who had won some fame as a wrestler. After visiting Hewlett's gym for a few lessons, he figured himself ready to master his teacher and challenged Molineaux to a fight. Hewlett, his reputation on the line, duly accepted the challenge with the condition that the men fight for a $100 dollar purse. It took the challenger a bit of time to raise the necessary funds but finally on June 23, 1853, in an open park, Mingo and Molineaux set to. The fight was a farce and after ten minutes Mingo was a badly battered man. In the fifth round Molineaux asked his student, "have you had enough" and through swollen lips Mingo apologetically answered, "yes sir."

Hewlett admired Mingo's pluck and determination and was magnanimous in victory. After sending his pupil away from the scene, with an invitation to return to the gym at any time with no hard feelings, Molineaux, displaying a bit of his musical talent, danced for the spectators and played a few tunes on his mouth harp. Mingo did return to Hewlett who subsequently took him under his wing and matched him for several wrestling engagements. Mingo proved to be a far better wrestler than pugilist and won several matches before being defeated by a Native American wrestler by the name of Caesar Coit.

Caesar Coit was an interesting character in his own right, standing a mere 5' tall and weighing a speck over 150 pounds, he was considered at that time to be the best wrestler in New York. Not only were his athletic abilities held in high regard but he was also a reputed "man for hire" being available for "rent" to any gang who might need an extra pair of experienced hands when going into combat with rivals. Coit it was said, had once fended off a group of 10 Irish thugs who had attacked a respectable woman in Brooklyn, saving the girl from certain peril. Coit defeated Mingo in November of 1853, in three straight falls after a bitter but short struggle.

Noticing that the famed Molineaux was visually upset by the loss of his prized student, Caesar challenged him to wrestle for $300 dollars. Hewlett accepted and the two men met less than a week later. Molineaux was a good wrestler but was no match for Coit. Despite outweighing Caesar by 10 pounds and carrying an 8 inch height advantage, Hewlett could not match the speed or skill of his adversary. The match dragged on for over an hour at which time, despite being felled 15 or 20 times, Molineaux declared the match a draw and left the scene of battle. Enraged by the fact that Hewlett would not admit defeat, nor pay the bet off, Coit took his complaints public through the medium of the press. *The New York Clipper* published a derogatory letter by Caesar stating that Molineaux was both a cheat and a sore loser. Hewlett responded a week later with a similar letter, decrying the unfairness of the match and the supposed trickery and deception used by Coit's backers to goad him into a match that he deemed "unwinnable". The banter continued on until the two sides agreed to fight it out, "rough and tumble" for $150 a side. This, determined Hewlett, would settle once and for all who was the better fighting man. With little ceremony, the men and their backers met on February 24, 1854 at the corner of Park Avenue and proceeded on to a vacant lot on Cumberland Street. There they stripped and set-to with fewer than 25 spectators watching. From the beginning of the fight it was apparent that each man wanted to stick to what they felt were their strengths. Hewlett wanted a stand up fight where he could use his superior height, reach and boxing ability and Coit wanted to take the fight to the ground. Both were successful to a point but it was Molineaux who did more damage. Even though he was thrown heavily on several occasion, Hewlett made Caesar pay dearly for every attempted rush with heavy punching. By the time 30 minutes had elapsed the matter of superiority was all but settled by Hewlett who during this round, with one frighteningly accurate delivery of punches, opened a nasty cut over the right eye of his opponent while also dislodging several teeth. Coit was knocked unconscious a few minutes later and Molineaux declared the victor and awarded the stake money.

Despite his matches with Mingo and Coit, Aaron Molineaux Hewlett did not particularly care for prizefighting. He preferred more artful displays of his craft, and despite the money and fame he had acquired in his native neighborhood, he deplored the brand of people he was attracting to his gymnasium. Despite several more challenges, Hewlett confined himself to pugilistic teaching and exhibition sparring. At a benefit for Old Bill Tovar, he had the opportunity to show his wares and rub elbows with such respected fighters as Harry Gribben and Tom Davis. Gribben was impressed with Hewlett's skill and invited him to spar with him at an upcoming event in Manahttan. Hewlett's showing against Gribben two weeks later impressed many of the New York Fancy and he was immediately labeled with the nome de Plume of Professor Molineaux. The new Professor was then given a benefit at his own gym in Brooklyn where an audience member named Tom Davis, who had acquired a certain amount of fame as a prizefighter, challenged him to fight with bare knuckles on the stage. Hewlett, who only accepted the challenge when Davis produced a $50 dollar stake, made a fool of his antagonist and knocked him off the stage in less than five minutes.

Tiring of the constant challenges that his reputation in Brooklyn brought, Hewlett pulled up stakes and moved to Hoboken, NJ. While living there he continued to appear at an assortment of benefits and exhibitions. Hewlett was perceived by the press to be one of the best "men of fistic science" in New York, but was also gaining attention for his gentlemanly behavior. Once while sparring with Harry Gribben in an exhibition, Molineaux landed a flush right hand which hurt and dropped his adversary to the stage floor. The audience applauded loudly for what they viewed as a decisive and well timed punch. Hewlett, after assisting Gribben to his feet, silenced the crowd and according to the *New York Clipper*, "immediately came forward to the footlights, saying to the audience that the blow was not a square one and that he begged Mr. Gribben's pardon for giving it." The crowd responded even more voraciously to this short speech and Molineaux gained even more respect for the gentlemanly way in which he handled the situation. It was considered unsportsmanlike for a man to purposefully hurt another man during an exhibition match. Hewlett certainly did not mean to hurt Gribben, but because he had, he immediately admitted his error and asked for the forgiveness of both his adversary and the audience. That Molineaux reacted in such a manner, during such a delicate impasse, demonstrates that he had both a keen knowledge of the "rules of culture" and that he was, despite his rather rough background, somewhat refined. This quality, along with his superb athletic and pugilistic ability, combined to offer Hewlett an inroad into a part of American society that few African-Americans had access to: upper class society. Molineaux's new identity as a "professor of pugilistic arts" and his disassociation with the rougher elements that surrounded prizefighting afforded him a status that brought him a white socialite following and a new clientele. However, despite this newfound respect Hewlett was still, at times, called upon to revert to what was termed by the *New York Clipper*, "the calling of his race", when he was constantly asked to perform his song and dance routine after many exhibitions. These acts mainly involved Molineaux signing "darkey tunes" to the accompaniment of his own mouth harp, and the dancing of "nigger jigs" with bottle caps tied to his shoes. (Interestingly, Hewlett also performed some rather athletic feats while being called to the stage to perform his "minstrel show". One of his stunts involved balancing two glasses of water on his head while he picked up coins with his mouth. Others included hoisting audience members on his shoulders and jumping over ropes tied to a set of chairs at a height of one and two feet.) These acts were not denigrating in themselves, although they could hardly be considered respectable in the context that they were performed, however the symbolism they involved demonstrated one salient point; that despite Aaron Hewlett's success he was still, in the eyes of many, simply a black man.

Sometime in 1855, Hewlett again pulled up stakes and moved to Worcester, Massachusetts. There he opened the "Professor Molineaux Sparring and Athletic Academy" where he taught boxing and physical training. Hewlett's new operation attracted a mostly white, upper class clientele, through which he developed several important friendships that would eventually bond him to some of the more principal citizens in both Worcester and Boston. It was these connections, as well as his reputation, which eventually landed Hewlett the position of "Director of Physical Education and Culture" at Harvard University in October of 1859.

The appointment was the first of its kind in the United States, and groundbreaking not only because an African American had landed the post but also for the reason that many colleges and universities had not yet discovered the importance of physical education and training. (Most schools would not follow Harvard's lead until after the first few years of the Civil War, when the poor performance of the young Union army prompted several of the countries' leaders to denounce the physical condition of America's young men). Hewlett's appointment was well received by most of the Harvard community and his work there would be considered revolutionary. Devising an easily taught and practiced system of gymnastic exercise as well as teaching the "future leaders of America" the art of self defense, Molineaux stressed the importance of physical fitness. Using a "sound body-sound mind" philosophy, Hewlett taught his arts at Harvard for over 12 years. His employment with Harvard turned out to be the last job he would ever hold, Hewlett faithfully serving until his death in 1871.

From rough and tumble bouts in vacant lots, on to the austere surroundings of New York's theatre's and exhibition halls, to the hallowed and cultured setting of Harvard University, Aaron Molineaux Hewlett was a unique, powerful and talented man. For a black man to move through and flourish in mid nineteenth century America as Hewlett certainly had, was an amazing achievement and one to be studied with amazement. His story was the American story—the individual rising from humble beginnings by his own wit, intelligence and talent to a level of success thought impossible.

It is difficult to say what impact Molineaux's success had on the black community of his time, for his accomplishments received little attention. His impact on Harvard was certainly profound for even after his death, one of his students, African American John Bailey, as well as Bailey's son George, both held posts as boxing instructors at the school well after Hewlett's death. Furthermore, during the 1890's, black middleweight Andy Watson would also be hired to teach boxing to the Crimson's student body. But unfortunately it would seem that Professor Molineaux's accomplishments had little effect on the sport of prizefighting. Unlike Tom Molineaux and Bill Richmond, whose performances in the ring against white opponents paved the way for generations of future black fighters in England, Hewlett's ring record and subsequent successes did little to further the integration of the sport in America. His career, it would seem, meant little to the sporting public outside of its singular importance. Besides their respect for his skill and demeanor, the white men who made up the American Fancy, took no stock in Hewlett's accomplishments as a sign of race equality. In fact, as time moved on, and the sport became more organized, the color line would become far more defined. Men of color would then be judged, not on their individual merits as fighters and gentlemen, but as a group—one that would be forced to fight amongst themselves in Jim Crow type competition.

This policy would again be well illustrated during the career of the next prominent black prizefighter to make a name in America, George Brown. Brown was born a free man in Boston sometime around 1825. At the age of 10 he found work as a horse trotter and groomer, where he developed a small reputation as a "fighting jockey", winning several impromptu fights against his brethren stable workers. At the age of 15, he was working as a coal heavier when he began visiting the sparring rooms of the well known John Bailey. Bailey, who was a close friend of Aaron Hewlett and would later gain fame as the teacher and backer of George Godfrey, was considered one of the finest instructors of the pugilistic arts in Boston. He groomed the 5'10", 168 pound Brown, from a rough and tumble fighter, into a scientific pugilistic who displayed a superior array of speed and strength. Bailey ensured that George had ample opportunity to both display and refine his art by making certain that he was on any and every exhibition card that took place in the Boston area during the years of 1852 and 1853. Brown impressed all who saw him, but was not satisfied by simply exhibiting his skills. He wanted to make some real money and he knew that the only way to accomplish such a goal was to take part in real prizefights. Bailey, who had never been a participant in a true prizefight and did not particularly care for that form of the sport, tried his best to find a match for his man, but was unsuccessful.

In 1854, the famous sparrer, John Davis of New York put on a show at the Hall Theatre in Boston with Bailey and Brown in attendance. George was impressed with Davis' display but felt confident that given a chance he could beat Davis in a real fight. Buying space in the *Boston Herald*, Brown published a challenge to Davis to fight him in Boston for the sum of $60 a side. When notified of the challenge, Tom, who had by that time returned to New York, immediately replied that he would be happy to accommodate Brown for any sum he found suitable. George, showing himself to have a certain knack for publicity, immediately rented out the plush National Theatre and had advertisement sheets printed and posted all over town announcing his "exhibition" with Davis. It was known to all however, that the listed exhibition would actually be a prizefight. Brown, with the assistance of Bailey, filled out the program with an assortment of musical, theatre and sparring attractions, which would be capped off by the "match" between Davis and Brown.

When Davis reached Boston he was a bit shocked to learn that he had unwittingly agreed to "fight" Brown. John's forte was not prizefighting but rather sparring. When he had received the challenge he had understood it to mean that the men would, "spar for scientific points" with the winner of the stakes to be chosen by a judge or referee. John and his entourage visited Brown at Bailey's and Davis expressed his unwillingness to take part in a contest that would require him to "fight to a finish". George was irate and both accused Davis of cowardice and threatened to sue him for the cost of putting the program together. Brown reasoned that he had sold the public a real fight and anything short of such a contest would ruin his name in town. John, knowing that he had little ground to stand on, finally acquiesced to meeting George in a mixed contest, which would observe specially designed rules. Davis stipulated that the men would not be allowed to wrestle or throw and only "stand up fighting" would be deemed appropriate. Additionally he demanded that the fight would last a maximum of 30 minutes with rounds to be determined by a man falling of being knocked to the stage. A felled man would be given a full minute to return to scratch if hit to the stage and 90 seconds if knocked completely from it. Brown, seeing that he had little other opportunity, reluctantly agreed to Davis' rules.

Due to Brown's advertising and the reputation of Davis, the National Theatre was packed with over 1000 men on the night of Dec 15, 1854. After the two hour preliminary show, Davis and Brown took the stage. The special rules of their contest were announced to the crowd and received with some derision, but as soon as the men set to, there little doubt that a skilled contest would be witnessed. In stand up fighting, John Davis was the master. He constantly beat Brown to the punch and for the most part landed at will against his charging antagonist. George, when he did manage to hit his opponent, showed himself to be a damaging puncher, but the clever Davis did not allow himself to be caught too frequently. The manner in which John fought made it clear to all who witnessed the bout that he would have had a far more difficult time fighting Brown according to the London Prize Ring Rules. The rules as they were in this bout however, played to Davis' advantages and he and his backers were vigilant that Brown follow them. According to the *New York Clipper*, in the 10th minute of the bout, George attempted to close and grab Davis so that he could strike him, when the latter yelled, "foul"! George, frustrated by the tactics of his adversary, ignored Davis' charge and with one hand grasped the belt of John and with his other punched freely. Davis sunk to the canvas where he again claimed foul, yelling that he would not continue unless Brown adhered to the predetermined rules. The *Clipper* reported that George motioned to Davis and then the crowd repling, "then stand and fight. That is what these people came to see." The crowd shouted support for Brown, but Davis could not be persuaded to fight on. He left the stage to a chorus of catcalls and George was declared the winner of the fight.

Somehow, days after the contest, Davis convinced Brown to call the fight a draw and return half of the stake. George consented but there is little indication as to why. *The Clipper* later reported that their initial report on the fight was in error and that it was Brown and not Davis who had refused to continue. In this second report on the fight the paper claimed that after Davis had thrown George to the ring and then fell upon him with a body slam, the latter was in fact the one who could not and would not continue. What further confuses the matter is that supposedly Davis stipulated that there would be no wrestling during the fight and his reported win with such a maneuver would seem highly irregular. Despite the confusion regarding what really happened during the fight, the men eventually split the money and decided that the bout would be considered a draw. Future attempts by Brown to goad Davis into a legitimate prizefight proved unsuccessful.

George Brown now saw his fortunes wane even further, as the better men started turning him down at exhibitions. He could not find a man who would spar with him at any benefit. For what reason this apparent conspiracy transpired is unclear. Perhaps scorned by Brown's attempt to "trick" him into a prizefight led the well known and well connected Davis into "black balling" George on the circuit. He certainly had the influence and friendships in New York and Boston to pull off such a stunt, but no firm evidence suggests that such a scheme truly took place. The fact remained however, that in Boston, Brown was a man without an opponent.

Brown spent the next two and a half years training with John Bailey and trying his best to find a match. With his finances depleted he went back to work, first as a stevedore and then returning to the coal heaving business. In the spring of 1857, he had a stroke of good fortune when the well known John Mackey of Chicago wrote to Bailey looking for a black fighter to take on the former's new "Black Star" Richard Plume. Bailey, immediately contacted Brown who agreed to take the fight for expenses and a $50 dollar side bet. When George arrived in Chicago, he learned that Plume had injured himself and would not be able to fight. Mackey then added insult to injury by informing the Boston man that he would not pay his expenses because the fight had been canceled. Brown, with no money, was in essence stranded. Mackey offered him a place to stay and promised that he would find a spot for him at his next sparring exhibition.

George lived like a pauper for the next few weeks until he was finally given a chance to show his wares at Mackey's Sporting Club on the evening of June 10, 1857. Brown boxed a three minute exhibition with another black fighter named Young Sambo and was cheered loudly. Mackey put George on again a few weeks later, and again he pleased the crowd with his displays of science. In his next exhibition, Brown sparred with Mackey himself and gave such a fine performance that he was immediately re-matched with Richard Plume, who by this time had pronounced himself "healed" from his previous injury. Brown and Plume met on the outskirts of Chicago before a small audience of about 100 men. They fought for 20 minutes during which only 11 rounds were fought. George Brown won every one of them. After George finished Plume with a cross buttock in the final frame and had been declared the victor, Mackey, impressed by Brown's performance, announced that he had found a new champion and dubbed George "Young Molineaux".(That Tom Molineaux's name was still held in such high regard by the American Fancy illustrates that his impact on American prizefighting was far more influential in later days than it had been during his time. That nearly every black fighter who was deemed a "good one" by the Fancy was in some way compared with Tom, speaks to what a lasting legacy he had left.)

Convinced by Mackey that he could make real money in the "Windy City" Young Molineaux stayed in Chicago where he continued to work at as an exhibitor. He evidently took part in a few minor prize ring contests, (which are referenced but never detailed by the *New York Clipper*), and built on his ever growing reputation as a fighter of the first rate. On Independence Day 1859, he and Mackey visited Cleveland where Brown fought "The Black Strap" Andy Foster for 45 punishing rounds. In the last round, George earned a victory by smashing Foster in the ear with a right hand that the *Clipper* reported, "could have felled three men." The duo stayed in Cleveland where Brown attempted to induce several different white prizefighters to try his game but nothing materialized. Mackey stayed on in Cleveland where he opened his own club called Mackey's Clipper Shades, but Brown returned to Chicago. George again sparred for his living and further increased his reputation by having the better of several good men, including the brother of Tom Heenan, then the Heavyweight Champion of America, Tim Heenan. In February of 1860, Brown revisited Cleveland where he was matched to fight Fred Adams, another black boxer, for $50 dollars at Mackey's club, but the latter did not show. Johnny then offered George a lower purse to fight Andy Foster again and the latter agreed, winning on a foul in the 33 round. After his victory, Mackey insisted that George stay in Cleveland but Brown again returned to Chicago where he felt he had better opportunities. As it would turn out Young Molineaux could not have been more correct as his decision afforded him the opportunity to meet the famous Lazarus Brother's of England.

Harry and Johnny Lazarus immigrated to the United States from England in 1852. The sons of the famous Izzy Lazarus, who had once fought Owne Swift for close to two hours, the boys spent most of their early lives traveling throughout England giving exhibitions under the advertised moniker of the"The Infant Wonders." Because boxing had fallen under great scrutiny in England and had been banned outright in many English cities and towns, the teenage boys brought their act to America. Traveling to most of the major cities in the United States, Harry and Johnny became well known and helped to build interest in boxing by giving lessons and putting on exhibitions throughout the country. Mostly they sparred with one another, but both were more than willing to mix it when asked to perform with a local hero. Neither boy was large, Harry the elder brother being slightly heavier built than the younger Johnny, but both were highly skilled boxers and more than capable of handling larger men. Izzy lazarus along with his wife followed his boys to the United States the following year and despite settling in New York City, toured with the boys extensively. In 1857 Izzy moved to Buffalo, New York. There he opened a saloon, where along with the daily activity of running his business, he actively promoted sparring exhibitions and organized prizefights.

George Brown met the Lazarus clan in Chicago when the trio was passing through the city on an exhibition tour. Brown sparred with Harry and so impressed the latter that Lazarus convinced George to come to New York, where he promised there were real fights to be had. Young Molineaux traveled with the Lazarus' for six months and then returned to New York with them in February of 1861. With the Civil War now imminent, the Lazarus's confined their operations to New York City and Buffalo. George found New York to be a much different town than Chicago and without the benefit of his reputation to assist him in his attempts to find sparring work or a fight, he remained inactive for several months.

Brown also found the racial climate to be somewhat hostile, as the war had certainly raised some delicate issues among the white citizens of New York. The upper class feared a break with the South, their lucrative trading partner, would cripple the city's economy and felt that defending the freedom of a supposedly inferior race was not worth such a risk. Many working class and poor New Yorkers, were also anti-abolitionist and outright racist. They feared that the war would free the slaves, who would then take away their jobs. Raising racial tensions in New York was the fact that black men were not allowed to join the Union Army, nor were they drafted—allowing them in essence to flourish in a society with an ever dwindling, white male workforce. In the early stages of the war and even into the latter stages black men in New York were finding the job market full of opportunity and many black businessmen were thriving. It was a tinderbox that ultimately exploded during the New York draft riots of 1863 which saw hundreds of African-Americans beaten, lynched and killed. Targeting the black population, and New York's wealthy elite, the poorer masses of New York's immigrant and native lower classes rioted against the Conscription Act passed by Congress to swell the ranks of the Union armies. There was little mercy shown to the upper classes, who were allowed to buy their way out of the draft, and the black population, who by this time had been deemed the cause of the war by white Americans. The riot reached such a vicious peak that the Colored Orphanage Asylum, which housed some 300 black children, was burned to the ground.

George was finding it difficult to make a living with his fists, but his relationship with the well respected Harry Lazarus kept him from starving. Eventually, Lazarus was successful in finding George an opponent in the form of a well-backed black New Yorker named Ed Heddy. Heddy was a middleweight like Brown and was reported to be the owner of an unblemished record in the ring. The *Clipper* reported that he had won several "private mills" and had even once killed one his opponents by breaking his adversaries back. Despite the sensationalized history of Heddy's fighting career, he was deemed to be a good man, who may have been short on experience but extremely strong and durable. Brown took the fight despite his dissatisfaction with the measly purse offered, and went into training with Lazarus.

On April 24, 1861, three days after the Union Army under Gen. Irvin McDowell suffered a defeat at Bull Run 25 miles southwest of Washington, Young Molineaux met Ed Heddy at a secluded lot in Manhattan for a $25 dollar purse. Brown was seconded by Johnny Lazarus and Heddy by John Woods and Kit Burns. The *Clipper* reported that both men were in poor condition and that the early rounds were marred by Brown's illegal use of the tactic of hitting and getting down; a strategy that meant George would strike Heddy and then fall to the ground before the latter could retaliate. Lazarus scolded Brown from using such procedures and in the 10th round the referee warned that another infraction of such a manner would lead to a disqualification. Heeding the official's advice, George got down to fighting in the 11th frame. His work was mainly to the head of his opponent, while Heddy confined his punches to Brown's body. The *Clipper* noted that, "Heddy's blows while well directed left only but slight marks, while Brown's hits told a dreadful tale." In the 22nd round, Molineaux broke Heddy's arm with a hammer like blow that landed while the men were closing. Somehow, the game New Yorker came out for the twenty-third round but was almost defenseless and immediately thrown by George and knocked out of time. The entire match lasted 51 minutes.

Brown's performance against Heddy earned him a benefit less than two weeks later at Kerrigan's Hall in Manhattan. However, the event, which was considered at the time to be a compliment, turned into an ugly spectacle instead. On the night the Hall was packed with over 500 spectators eager to see "the new black champion" as well a host prestigious fighting men like Johnny Lazarus, Dan Kerrigan, Jerry Concklin, Young Hollaway and Johnny Monaghan. The card was well received by the crowd and there was a general feeling of excitement when Brown and Heddy took the stage to round out the evening. However, when the men set to, Heddy, whose broken left arm was still heavily bandaged and obviously useless, begged the crowd to excuse his inability to perform. George took it easy on his injured foe and the men basically walked around the stage in a mock exhibit of sparring. The *Clipper* reported that when the crowd voiced their displeasure with the match, Brown stepped to the front of the stage and addressed the assembly. "It is not possible for me and Mr. Heddy to properly perform because of his injury. I ask the crowd to select any man present and I will exhibit with him now on this stage." The crowd began chanting Kerrigan's name, but he politely declined. They then began to call on Johnny Monaghan but he too stated that he wished not to show with Brown. It was apparent after Concklin and Hollaway also declined that not one of the fighters present wished to spar with Brown. The *Clipper* was clear when it noted, "it was not Molineaux's ability that was feared but rather his color." After a delay of nearly twenty minutes, Johnny Lazarus, who was suffering from a terrible cold, finally took the stage and sparred for 10 minutes with Brown.

Brown's benefit was both the first and last time that he was seen in action by the general public in New York. After this event he seemingly disappeared. It is possible that he returned to Chicago or Cleveland and continued to fight and exhibit, but no reference of his activities was ever mentioned by the press after his brief stay in New York. George Brown, like many before and after him, simply fell off the pugilistic map.

Brown was the most prominent black prizefighter of his time in America. That he was forced to fight under unwritten, Jim Crow type conditions is not surprising considering the racial climate in United States at the time. He was both a victim of bad timing and circumstance. While only a few years prior to George's rise Aaron Hewlett had fought with white men in New York, Brown was forced to make his living fighting only those of his race. That the attitudes of the American Fancy(and the white public in general) had taken more of a hard line attitude with Brown than they had Hewlett, illustrates the changing racial attitudes of Northern whites in the years leading up to and during the Civil War. Where Hewlitt was viewed with a certain amount of respect because of his skill as a pugilist, Brown was seemingly feared because of his. In many ways, George Brown's career set a precedent for African-American boxers, as well as other athletes, in the United States: a model of segregation and frustration.

What is also interesting about the career of George Brown was that it seemed to have little influence or impact on future generations of black athletes. After his disappearance in 1861, no other prominent black boxer could be found in the United States for close to 20 years. There were undoubtedly black fighters active in the years between 1861 and 1879, however, due to either some editorial conspiracy or mere indifference, the press of the day, with the exception of some sporadic reports of fights involving black participants, did not detail any such careers. It is also possible that no black prizefighter made a record impressive enough to deserve repeated mentions in the press. However, no matter the reason, it seems evident that the decades between the beginning of the Civil War and 1880 were an abyss for the African American fighter in the United States.

10

Nat Langham's Black

While Hewlitt and Brown struggled to make their way in America, the black prizefighter was thriving in England. Represented in greater numbers than had ever been seen before, a score of "colored" pugilists were making a living with their fists, and leaving their mark on history. Colorful characters like John Augustus Edward Plantagenet Green, a crafty lightweight with more skill than courage, Kendrick the Black, an Adonis like heavyweight who had never tasted defeat, George Robinson, the brother of the ill fated "Ebony Phenomenon" Jemmy Robinson, and Joe White, who was playfully nicknamed "Black Joe", were all active in England during the 50's and 60's. However, the best of the lot was Robert Travers, a.k.a. "Nat Langham's Black".

By his own account Travers was born in America on June 21, 1832 and brought to England as an infant by his parents. Oddly, some contemporary chroniclers of the ring claimed that Bob had been born in England, at Falmouth, and raised in nearby Truro. Why such a debate would even be considered is beyond comprehension, for Travers must be considered the best source for his own history. He never claimed to be anything but American born and why some disputed this fact remains a mystery. What is clear is that Bob was raised in Truro, where he spent his youth assisting his father as a vendor of crockery.

Travers introduction to the sport of boxing was through a pair of black fighters, named Young Congou, a lightweight veteran of the prize ring, and Young Kendrick (not John Kendrick), who in the early 1840's had been a very good heavyweight prizefighter. The two met Bob at an exhibition while touring England in 1853, and induced young Travers to travel with them as an assistant. Bob agreed, and spent the next six months with the tandem moving from town to town, all the while learning the tricks of the pugilistic trade from his new mentors. When the trio reached Manchester, Congou introduced his new student to veteran pugs Charley Jones and Jemmy Massey. Jones, who had taken part in over 25 ring battles, and Massey, himself an accomplished fighter, took Bob under their wing for a short time and gave him further tutelage, refining the young black's guard and punching techniques. When Kendrick came back through Manchester a few months later, Jones suggested that Travers was ready to be "tried" out in live action and should be taken to London. Kendrick offered to accompany Bob on his journey and promised to ensure that he was left in good hands.

Once in London, the pair immediately went to Nat Langham's Cambrian Stores located on Castle Street in Leicester Square. Langham, the retired Middleweight Champion of England, was noted as a man who knew two things extremely well: fighting and fighters. He was the only man to have ever beaten Tom Sayers, one of England's most beloved champions, and was renowned for his ability to spot talent in aspiring pugilists. So when Travers put on the gloves and sparred in front of Nat for a brief spell, the latter instantly recognized that he had a true and talented fighter in his midst.

Langham wasted little time in putting his new charge to work, matching him with George Baker, a 135-pounder from Chatham, for 25 pounds a side. The men met on a rainy day at Tilbury on October 29, 1855 and fought for 23 minutes before being interrupted by the local magistrates. Four days later they renewed their hostilities at Long Reach, and after another 20 minutes of fighting, Travers was declared the winner when Baker could not come to scratch to begin the 11th round. It was considered a good win for Bob, who was still judged a novice, but it was universally recognized after the fight that Travers had merely beaten a second rate man. Less than five months later, "Langham's Black" as Travers was now being called, entered the ring with the durable Jesse Hatton whom he defeated in 39 rounds at Coombe Bottom. Langham was ecstatic with the performance of his protégé but there were still those who felt Bob had a great deal to prove. *Bell's Life* remarked, "Langham's new black did smart work to the nob of Hatton, but the job was done by his damaging shots to the latter's wind. The Black counters well but his leads were generally rushed and off mark. If Hatton had been a man of better science the ending may have been quite different, for it is yet to be seen how the Black will take his gruel." Undeterred by the slight criticism he was receiving from the press, Bob continued to work on his game, enlisting his old teacher Jemmy Massey, to refine his technique and better prepare him for the stiffer competition he was bound to face.

Two months of training and hard work were rewarded with another match, this time in the form of a powerful challenger named George Crockett. A native of Borough, Crockett had figured in 10 prize ring battles, prior to fighting Travers, and had only experienced defeat once. His reputation was solid and *Bell's* reported that some of the "knowing ones" felt that, "Langham and his Black must be mad", for taking on such a challenger. The men agreed to fight at 135 pounds for a 50 pounds per side. The day prior to the match, both the fighters and their parties met at The Cambrian Stores where each weighed in under the subscribed limit. Travers, full of confidence and trained to the minute by Jemmy Massey, unveiled his color's, red and gold tartan handkerchiefs, which he sold for 2 shillings a piece. The following day all involved and interested parties traveled to Epham where a ring was pitched and a litany of ceremonies where completed prior to Bob and George entering the ring. Travers' body showed the effects of his time with Massey, as his shoulders and arms presented a far heavier muscle tone than in his prior appearances. Crockett was a shade taller and also formed an impressive figure as he stripped and readied for battle. When the men toed the line and set-to at near noon, betting was brisk and 2-1 in favor of the more experienced Crockett.

The fight was fairly one sided from the beginning, and Travers astonished even his most ardent supporters with the manner in which he dominated Crockett. Being the faster man, he chose to demonstrate that he could indeed lead, and opened the fight by stabbing his man continually with his left hand. Using this blow also as a range finder, Travers would set, and when in range, let go of his right hand to either the rib cage or the side of George's head. Bob spent the first 12 rounds using this one-two combination to punish Crockett and then settled into his more comfortable, counter-punching mode as the middle rounds approached. George did his best work when in close corners, landed some telling blows of his own, but Travers' tremendous countering told a dreadful tale on his opponent's visage whenever the former attempted to punch freely. By the 33 round, Crockett was a beaten man, but came to the scratch for three more frames until being downed for good in the 114th minute of the fight.

Bob Travers' victory over the well-experienced Crockett earned him universal respect and admiration from the fighting public as well as the press. *Bell's* remarks spoke glowingly of Travers' abilities stating, "He is as quick as lightning and extraordinary must be the skill of the man who can get on to him without receiving a smartish crack in return. The punishment he submitted to was quite sufficient to remove the doubts of most decided cavilers on the subject of his game; he stood it all without wincing and that there was plenty of it his appearance on the following day amply testified. The Black is one of the best men of his day and he has not his equal in the art of countering. In conclusion, we must content ourselves by stating, the he bids fair to be a dangerous customer to all men under 10 stone (140 pounds) and it will be his own fault if he is not ere long crowned with the title of Champion of the Lightweights." Travers' was now a star in pugilistic circles and there were many who felt that he was the best of the lightweights in England. He took several benefits at Nat Langham's where he was not only rewarded with fine compliments and high praise but substantial amounts of money as well. Bob took all of his praise in fairly good measure but an air of cockiness began to show in his nature. At one benefit he refused to spar with a novice because he stated, "it would be beneath a man of my level to show with an amateur." Most of the Fancy took Bob's action as little more than playful banter, but there were those, such as Jemmy Massey, who were noticing a more destructive problem at work.

When Travers was matched in July to battle Job Cobley, "The Enthusiastic Pot Boy", for a 50-pound side stake, he was immediately taken to Highgate with Massey to begin training. The men had stipulated that they would weigh in at no more than 133 pounds the day before the fight, a lighter weight than Bob had ever fought at, and Jemmy instituted a vigorous regime of daily work for Travers to follow. The idea was for Bob to shed weight without sacrificing strength. Bob, however, was supremely confident that he had nothing to fear from Cobley, and argued with Massey constantly about the necessity of such a rigorous schedule.

Eventually a fight ensued and Jemmy left Travers' camp at Highgate. Nat Langham immediately sent the veteran David Ingram to supplant Jemmy as chief trainer, but his presence did little to change Bob's attitude. Cobley was put under the care of Thomas Welsh, the aforementioned Young Sambo, and retired to Leicester, where his training schedule ran as planned.

That Travers was confident that Cobley would be easy pickings was not surprising. It was generally accepted that Job was a novice. He had taken part in only one contest in the London area, defeating Webb in 35 rounds at Coombe Bottom, and even on that occasion he had given little indication that he was a force to be reckoned with. However, many of the Fancy, and even Bob himself, were unaware that "The Pot Boy" had also taken part in four prize ring contests prior to his initial bow to the London sports. These battles, along with his recorded ring contest, led *Bell's* to comment that, "Cobley, despite his 24 years, is not a novice at all, but an experienced man with good science and knowledge of the art."

Bob Travers and his backers along with Cobley and his supporters appeared at Ben Caunt's the day prior to the fight to weigh in and sell their colors. It was genial event and most of the London Fancy supported Travers' chances with heavy betting. Job and his faction however were also noticed to be partaking in brisk wagering, and Cobley himself hawked his personal pocket watch so that he could lay a 3-pound bet. Both men weighed in at the prescribed 133 pounds, but while The Pot Boy looked tight and taunt, *Bell's* noticed that Travers, "lacked the extreme hardness about his bust and muscles which we have before noticed".

It was drizzling and cold on August 19, 1856 when Travers and Cobley met at the scratch on a small patch of land known as the Halfway House outside of London. At 12:50pm the men set to and little time was wasted in sparring. Travers followed his usual tactic of allowing his foe to lead and then countering with hard shots to the body and head. Cobley, who was the taller man, paid dearly for the punches he landed but seemed to be giving as much as he was taking. In the seventh round, Job scored the first knockdown of the fight when he felled Travers with a good right hand to the "sniffer". However, in the tenth frame The Pot Boy showed signs of weakening, and Langham's Black took over. For the next several rounds it seemed that those who had counted on Cobley's inexperience being his downfall were correct, as he seemed unable to deal with Bob's speed or strength. But as Job continued to weaken it was Travers who made a tactical era.

Bob began to lead, attempting to finish off his injured foe. However in doing so he both exhausted himself and allowed Cobley to use his own countering skills to ward off his demise. Travers had been criticized in the past for his lack of refinement when leading off, and his unfamiliarity with such tactics clearly showed in this match. His timing seemingly defunct, Travers was punished dreadfully by Cobley as his wild swings consistently missed their mark and left him open to drastic counter shots. The men fought on for over an hour with little to choose between them. Travers lack of condition began to tell as early as the 70th round when *Bell's* reported that he, "seemed to be growing slower and slower". The fortunes of each man continued to ebb and flow as the bout grew into a marathon. By the 90th round both of Bob's eyes were closed due to the tremendous hits of Cobley, and it seemed as if his chances were dwindling. Still Travers managed to punish Job further, doing most of his blind work to the ribs of his foe. Both men were near exhaustion by the 100th round, but The Pot Boy had the advantage of remaining vision in both his eyes. In the 107th round the ring was temporarily broken, evidently by some supporters of Travers who, seeing their man on the verge of defeat, hoped to alter the now inevitable ending. The ring "whips" squelched the short riot, and upon order being restored the battle continued. In the 110th round, Travers blind and bewildered, was led out to the scratch by his second Jemmy Welsh were he attempted to punch Cobley. The latter avoided the blow with little effort, and humanely pushed Bob to the ground. Welsh, upon seeing his man was insensible, conceded defeat. The fight had lasted 3 hours and 27 minutes.

Travers' defeat was met with astonishment by the Fancy. They had in no way envisioned such an outcome. But, as *Bell's Life* had so ominously stated in their prior descriptions of Travers', "it will be his own fault if he is not ere crowned Champion of the Lightweights." Indeed, Bob had no one to blame but himself. As *Bell's* noted in it comments on the Cobley battle, "Bob Travers from the first, held his opponent too cheap and neglected his training until too late. The consequence was that after he had got his man well in hand he gradually fell off himself, got slower and slower and in the end became as weak as Cobley who, in having two eyes open, had sufficient advantage over his game opponent to enable him to pull through." Travers' lack of training had certainly cost him dearly but *Bell's* also noted that his strategy during the fight also left him a step behind. "Bob too on many occasions forced the fighting and led off—a style of milling to which he was totally unaccustomed—and thus laid himself open to severe punishment." Despite these criticisms, Travers did win accolades for the determined and brave manner in which he "stood the gaff" while blinded. His reputation, while somewhat damaged by the defeat, was also, in the eyes of many, inflated due to his demonstration of guts and bottom.

Travers rested for the remainder of the year and did not enter the ring again until January 20, 1857, when he met the clever veteran Bill Cleghorne. In this contest, it was obvious that Travers had learned both the importance of training as well as the fact that his skills as a fighter were best suited when counterpunching. When the fight began Travers' physique demonstrated that he had worked himself into perfect shape. As the match progressed his newfound prudence was also evident as Bob refused to lead and remained on the defensive, while counterpunching. He allowed Bill to come to him, and simply picked him apart with sharp counters. There was a great deal of frustration and disgust shown by the spectators who witnessed the bout. It must be remembered that fights then were to the finish, and men were expected to "mix it" with impunity. Stylish methods, that today might garner a fighter a win on points, were in general detested by the patrons of the prize ring, and seen as somewhat cowardly. In his battle with Cleghorne, Travers drew the ire of the crowd because many felt that with a bit of aggressiveness he could have ended the match several different times before he did so in the 87th minute. Perhaps feeling a bit gun shy, Travers instead stuck firmly to his game plan, and even when Cleghorne could barely stand in the final round, Bob waited for his foe to throw a punch before striking out with his own and ending the match.

Bell's was similarly unhappy with Travers' performance, and panned him in their pages. They commented that, "Unless a man will go in and mix with him it is next to an impossibility for him to make what could be considered a good fight." It was obvious that Travers had learned from his defeat at the hands of Cobley. However it was also clear that in some ways it played on his psyche as well. His bout with Cleghorne did not win him any new fans, but those "in the know" certainly felt that Bob was still one of the best men of his weight in England.

Travers' took the criticism he received to heart, and in his next bout, with Bill Hayes on May 13, 1857 at Medway, Bob threw caution to the wind in an effort to demonstrate that he was not a coward. From the start of the fight he was the aggressor and despite Hayes' use of the "hit and get down" tactic early on, Travers was the master of the situation. However, as the bout progressed, and Bob began to tire, his leads lost their effectiveness. Hayes, whose use of the illegal drop system left him the fresher of the two combatants, began to counter the now wild rushes of Travers' with accurate and damaging punches. Yet, as *Bell's* noted, "the devil seemed to be in the eyes of Travers and he would not relent. His "thinking box" was seemingly impervious to Hayes' nobbing and the continuous visitations of the black's punches to Bill's body began to take their toll. Langham's darkey grew bolder and rash with impunity continually went up and planted his left and right without return." As if in a trance, Travers proved impervious to his opponents punching, and simply began to over power him. In the later stages of the fight he switched his attack to Hayes' body and began to punish his ribs dreadfully. In fact it was a severe right hand to the "short ribs" of Hayes that caused him to, "step back, wince and then drop insensible with pain". Bill's corner realized that there man was finished, and after a bout lasting 3 hours and 45 minutes, Bob Travers was declared the winner.

The victory over Hayes was undoubtedly the high point of Bob Travers' career up until this point. He had not only won, but did it in a manner that was pleasing to his supporters, and most importantly, his detractors. He took some time away from the ring, and with the exception of a benefit in his honor, at the plush Rotunda in London that netted him close to 100 pounds, Travers remained out of the public eye for close to six months. He returned to the ring in January of 1858 to fight with Bob Brettle in what would ultimately turn out to be the first of several disturbing incidents in his career.

The men met at Appledore on January 26, 1858 and fought evenly for an hour and five minutes before being interrupted by the authorities. The next day the men met again, this time at Shell Haven where they battled on for over two hours, Brettle finally being declared the winner when Travers was disqualified for falling without being hit. The fight itself was a fairly even affair, and up until the late rounds fought with a cleanliness and general action that all who witnessed dubbed first rate. However, in the 80th round Travers began hitting and then falling away to avoid punishment. Despite repeated warnings he continued this stratagem until finally, in the 100th round, the referee, left with little choice, awarded the bout and the stakes to Brettle.

Word quickly spread that the fight was a "cross", and that Bob had deliberately fouled out of the match on the demand of his backers. This of course was never proven, and Bob himself claimed that he had injured his left hand early in the fight and simply could not stand and fight any longer. Even this excuse angered many, for again, it was felt that Travers, even though injured, had shown the "white feather", and had not done his best to support his backer's interest. Either way, Travers name again fell under a black cloud, and he was now labeled as a cheat and a quitter.

Bob was now 26 years of age, and a veteran of many long and hard fights. His career had been neither fully successful, nor had it been a complete failure. His reputation had certainly suffered from his recent failing, but despite the general public's opinion of him as a fighter, prospective opponents and their backers alike, still considered him a dangerous foe. Oddly enough however, there was never any racist spin placed on Bob's shortcomings. The prevailing stereotypes of the "inferior black", which were popular at that time, never found their way into any description of Bob Travers. His reputation, although somewhat soiled, remained impervious to any racial criticisms. However, in his next match, Bob would have his first professional encounter with racism.

Johnny Walker was a unique individual. Despite loosing most of his bouts, and being suspected on more than one occasion of fixing a fight in order to swindle his backers, he was, in 1858, a well-respected pugilist. Claiming the Lightweight Championship of England in 1842, he had earned a reputation of making and then backing out of matches. His excuses were often thinly veiled, varying from sickness to unprepared ness, and often left in their wake a feeling of skullduggery. He had traveled to America in 1848 with his brother Alf, and spent five years there sparring and touring before returning to England in 1853. True to form he instantly made a match, with Bill Hayes, and then pulled out at the last moment, claiming he had injured on his legs in a riding incident. The men were re-matched a few months later, and fought to a draw. It was then that Walker turned his attention to Travers, challenging him to fight for 100 pounds a side. Bob accepted the match, and the two were scheduled to meet on May 26, 1858 at Gravesend.

The day of the match arrived and the men both boarded the same vessel that would take them down the Thames from London to the spot chosen for the battle. When the men took to the turf, and all the preliminary ceremonies were completed, Travers retired to his corner were he began to strip for battle. Walker did not. He instead walked to the center of the ring and stated that he would not fight. The crowd, Travers and especially Walker's backers were astonished. An explanation was requested and according to *Bell's Life*, Walker, pointing towards Bob, replied, "I object to fighting a colored man." The spectators were stunned and Walker was nearly mobbed as he pushed his way through the sea of angry men back towards the shores of the river. Travers simply packed up his things and returned to the launch quietly, knowing he was 90 pounds richer due to Walker's forfeit for failure to fight. *Bell's* did not handle the situation so well, and annihilated Walker in its columns. "Walker ", they wrote, "is a dastardly coward! His excuse of not meeting a colored man was paltry in the extreme, as he had no right at all to make the match with Travers if he had entertained such sentiments. His allowing the match to proceed and the stakes to be risen and the parties brought down to the scene of action, stamps him as a complete scoundrel!" Although obviously angered by the actions of Walker, *Bell's* was seemingly more upset with Walker for his methods than the reasons behind them. That he would not fight Travers because he was black may have been acceptable, although not commendable. However, the fact that he made the match and then acted as if he truly wanted to go through with the bout until the last moment, thereby wasting the money of his backers and cheating the paying public, was intolerable. Perhaps, *Bell's* was more keenly aware of Walker's reason's than they let on, for it is doubtful that Walker truly did not fight Travers because he was a black man. Bob was a famous man in fighting circles and even his nickname betrayed his color. It is implausible therefore that Walker did not know that Travers was indeed black. It may be safer to assume that either upon seeing Bob in person the day of the fight or by some other fit of panic, Walker thinking he had no chance to win, declined to fight. His seemingly racist reasoning was probably more of an effort to camouflage his cowardice than a true act of bigotry.

Bob returned to action the following spring and redeemed some of his lost luster by decisively beating the heavier Mike Madden in 97 minutes at Ashford. Madden had been heavily favored to win the bout and it was suspected by many that Bob stood nary a chance. But in a supreme effort, one that called on all of his skill, wit and determination, Travers proved his mettle. By all accounts it was a masterful performance and one in which Bob displayed what *Bell's* referred to as, "all the first rate fighting qualities that the Black was thought to possess but had never been asked to call upon against such a formidable foe." After such a stirring victory, Travers found difficulty in landing another match and rested for nearly nine months before again entering the lists.

Jem Mace is today remembered as one of England's great champions. He was born in Norfolk in 1831 and began his pugilistic career at the age of 18. Fighting at around 140 pounds "The Gypsy", as Mace was known, won 11 of his first 13 battles and was considered one of the finest technical fighters to have ever competed in the ring. His methods of attack and defense were superb and considered quite advanced for his day. However, when Mace signed to fight Bob Travers in early 1860, his reputation was anything but solid.

His problems began in October of 1857 when he agreed to fight the redoubtable Mike Madden for 100 pounds a side. Mysteriously however, for reasons known only to Mace, when the men entered the field of battle, Jem refused to fight sighting his objection to the selection of Dan Dismore as referee. That Mace and Madden had already agreed on Dismore weeks before was a mute point to Jem and he simply left the field of battle. Most accused the Gypsy of cowardice and his name instantly fell into ill-repute. He and Madden were again matched to fight in May of 1858 however, on the day of the fight Mace was nowhere to be found. It was later reported that he simply left town rather than go through with the fight. It was the second time in six months that he had left "ould Mike" on the field of battle waiting in vain. His next bout only further damaged his reputation. Matched with Bob Brettle, for what was deemed the Welterweight Championship of England, Mace was beaten in less than three and a half minutes during which only two rounds were fought. Most observers felt that the bout was fixed and that Mace did not try in the least to fight, further casting doubts about his honesty and courage. Just a few weeks later, Brettle offered to back his "Novice" against Posh Price, a very good fighter and the owner of an unblemished record, for one 100 pounds a side. Price accepted, but only when he showed up for the fight did he learn that Brettle's "Novice" was in fact Jem Mace. It was a horrid piece of trickery by both Bob and Jem, but Posh, being a man of extreme pride and character, went ahead with the bout only to be defeated by Mace in 11 rounds. Jem had won the bout but his character and reputation were so soiled at this point, that no one would dare go near, to either fight or back him. Undeterred, Mace turned publican and opened the Swan Inn tavern at Norwich were he ran a successful business for over a year. However, the lure of the ring seemed too great to resist and despite his previous troubles, Jem again decided to enter the lists. He published a challenge in *Bell's Life* on January 12, 1859 that challenged any man to fight him for 100 pounds a side at 151 pounds. Bob Travers accepted the challenge.

Travers was not a true welterweight. His best fighting weight had always been at or around 135 pounds. However he felt little discomfort in giving away poundage to Mace, for Bob was certain that his skill would offset any physical disadvantage Jem might present. Indeed, not only was the Gypsy heavier but he was also the taller man by 3 full inches and possessed a reach far greater than that of "Langham's Black". Both men trained diligently and when they stripped there was a general feeling of satisfaction that the pair were indeed prepared for a long and hard battle. Bob was actually the betting favorite and his supporters wagered freely on his chances, offering in some cases, odds of 2 to 1 on their man. The crowd was a large one and filled with dignitaries of both the ring and society. John C. Heenan, the American Champion who was in preparation for his fight with Tom Sayers, was in attendance but remained discreetly hidden beneath a large hat and coat in order to dissuade bringing any unwanted attention to his person.

In the first round of the fight, it was clear that Travers was not at his best. According to *Bell's Life* he seemed nervous and "uncomfortable with himself." Mace won the first two rounds handily and Bob was unable to use his countering measures with any degree of success. In the third round, as Mace backed him against the ropes, Travers purposefully dropped to the ground to avoid Jem's onslaught. The crowd voiced their displeasure with the tactic, and when Travers did it again in the fourth round, a cry of "foul!" went up among the backers of Mace. The referee ordered the men to fight on, which they did, until the sixth round when a shout of "Police!" went up and the men scattered. Ordered to return to the field of battle the next morning, Mace and Travers set to again with an even larger crowd present. The fight seemingly picked up where it left off, and at no point did Bob illustrate that he had any desire to mix it with Mace. Travers attempted to prolong the battle by using the unsavory "dropping system", but by the 57th round the referee had seen enough and disqualified Bob for falling without a blow being landed. Unbelievably, Travers challenged the decision and begged all who would listen to allow him to fight on. Mace crossed the ring and offered his hand to his irate opponent in a gesture of sportsmanship, but Bob was seeing red and slapped it away. A general row next occurred with Bob's supporters nearly mobbing the referee who in order to escape, half-heartedly changed his decision. However the next day, he again reversed the decision and justly awarded the stakes to Mace.

Jem Mace would go on to capture the Heavyweight Championship of England in 1862 and the Heavyweight Championship of the World in 1870. His active prize ring career would last until 1882, when thereafter he toured the world as a teacher of the pugilistic arts. Mace was instrumental in helping boxing make the quatum leap from the bare-knuckle era to the gloved and was later called "the Father of Modern Boxing". In 1897, nearly 37 years after their famous battle, Jem Mace and Bob Travers would appear in an exhibition bout together in London.

Despite his showing against Mace, Travers remained a popular fighter. Bob himself always claimed that his disqualification was unjust and that it was merely the loose sod of the fight locale that made him fall repeatedly. Many believed Travers and he continued to receive backing whenever a challenge presented itself. On April 30, 1861, Bob met Badger Crutchley, a full-fledged middleweight who scaled near 170 pounds outside of London. Travers, weighing a burdensome 151 pounds, (the heaviest weight of his career), was slow and off the mark, but still dominated Badger for the 3 rounds that they fought. Police interference brought a halt to the bout and the referee ordered the men to another location. When the men and their backers arrived, Crutchley offered to draw the stakes with Travers, but the latter refused evidently feeling that victory was imminent. When the men again stripped and prepared for battle, Badger refused to fight and Bob was declared the winner.

Travers would round out his year with another victory, scoring a 63 minute conquest over the well-respected Johnny "Bos" Tyler on December 12. *Bell's* commented, "Travers never looked a finer fighter. He used his left hand to a fine play on Tyler's upper works and his right with devastating affect on his ribs. That the darkey is not the same man of a few years past may be evident, but his hitting powers were never more apparent. His crashes against Tyler were of a sensational fashion and it was a fine mug that Bos wore after the fight had ended. He was cut and punished, his face and ribs swollen with alarming redness. Travers is still a man to be taken on with the utmost seriousness."

Travers again took some time away from the ring and with an eye to the future used his savings to open his own tavern called the Sun and Thirteen Cantons, which was located on Castle street in Leicester square, not far from Nat Langham's Cambrian Stores on the same thoroughfare. It was a successful business venture for Bob but not necessarily good for his fighting condition. It was considered in bad taste for the keeper of the bar not to drink with his customers, and therefore Bob was often times called upon to partake in the liquid pleasures of the Castle. Travers, who was never known to be a big drinker, took to his role as the jovial host like a duck to water, and soon his weight ballooned to over 160 pounds. A challenge from Patsy Reardon in the summer of 1862 reeled Bob in a bit, but upon accepting the fight he announced that he would be doing his training at his own tavern. Many of the sporting fraternity scoffed at such a statement and dubbed the bout a farce. It was felt that if Bob did not care to take his training seriously than he would stand little chance with such a fine fighting man as Reardon was reputed to be.

Those who had doubted Travers' resolve were quite surprised when he weighed in at Nat Langham's the day before his bout with Reardon at 135. *Bell's* noted that, "Traver's skin looked to carry that deep mahogany color that it had brandished when he was a younger man, his chest and arms thick with muscle, and his attitude, cool and resolved." Bob certainly was ready for Reardon, and when the two men met on July 15, 1862 at Hampshire, it was Langham's Black who was in control early on. The first day of the contest the men fought for 37 minutes, during which Travers was well in charge. As always, he did some terrific bodywork, and his countering was sharp and punishing. He seemed on the verge of victory, when in the 7th round the police came upon the scene, and chased the participants from the ring. The men met the next day not more than five miles from the scene of the previous day's action, and restarted the hostilities. Again,

Bob was well in control until the 40th round when the skies opened and the rain began to fall in torrents. As the men battled and the fight entered its third hour of the second day, Travers was noticed to be having an adverse reaction to the chilling rain and wind. *Bell's* noted, "his body shook violently against the cold, and despite the warm and liquid attempts of his seconds, Travers could not seem to control his forceful contortions of his limbs." Adding to his misery was the fact that Bob's left hand, which he had broken in the 33 round, was now swollen "to the size of a full club", and was offering him little in the way of use. Reardon, who was badly beaten, but handling the grueling weather a bit steadier than his foe, took advantage and began to turn the tide of the battle. By the 53 round, Bob was a trembling hulk and nearly insensible. The fight had now lasted over 4 hours and Travers, who could simply could not fight anymore, signaled his surrender.

There were those who stated that the weather had beaten Travers and not Reardon, however, the climate that supposedly defeated Bob did little to hamper his opponent. It is more likely that Bob Travers, who was now 30 years old and had been fighting in the prize ring for over 7 years, owed his defeat more to his age and eroding skills than to the rain. Furthermore, Travers had broken his left hand, an injury from which he had never suffered. Without its use, he was open to the attacks of Reardon, who was younger and the naturally bigger man. Those who wanted to deny Patsy his just victory were simply overlooking the fact that Bob Travers, although not beaten by a better man, was outlasted by a younger, stronger fighter.

Travers spent the early part of 1863 tending to both his business and personal affairs. He married a white woman from a respectable Manchester family, who helped run the Sun and Thirteen Cantons and gave birth to the couples' first child in early 1863(they would eventually have 5 children). It was a quiet life and one that Travers enjoyed very much. However, the lure of the ring was too much to resist and when the famous cockney lightweight Jem Dillon issued a 200 pounds a side challenge, Bob accepted.

Dillon and Travers had at one time both been under the patronage of Nat Langham and were in the least well-acquainted, if not good friends. Jem, who was born in Limerick, Ireland in 1839, was a broad, flat faced man whose two favorite things in the world were fighting and drinking. However, Dillon did not mix the two, and when in training for a bout he, unlike many in his profession, abstained from partaking in the pleasure of alcohol. The men had two common opponents, Patsy Reardon, who defeated both, and Job Cobley, who beat Travers, but had been defeated by Dillon. It was generally thought that the men were equally matched with the exception of Travers' being the elder of the two by a margin of seven years. Betting on the fight was nearly non-existent, and those men who did wager did so at even odds.

Dillon and Travers met Twyford, which could be reached by a private train that had been chartered for the event. Once upon the selected ground, *Bell's* reported that the repartee between Dillon and Travers betrayed their friendship: "'How do, Bob?' inquired Jem. 'Oh, I'm well.' Answered the dark un' and with a broad grin upon their warrior-like visages they at once proceeded to toss for corners." Prior to the fight it was believed that Bob, who had ballooned in weight to over 160 pounds during his layoff, might have been weakened by his "training down". However, those fears were quickly dismissed when Travers stripped for battle. *Bell's* noted, "Travers was as black as a well polished boot and every muscle stood out like polished ebony. Reports had been put about that Bob had neglected his training, and was worse for the life he led as a landlord of a hostelry in Castle Street, but when he did hold up his hands, the condition he exhibited was a canton. Every muscle showed like a bronze statue and the tendons and lesser muscles were plainly visible under the skin." Jem Dillon also looked as if he had trained with intent and *Bell's* stated that, "his condition when stripped created a buzz of admiration from the ringside."

Travers took control of the bout early, both hurting Dillon to the body with right hand leads and cutting his face with sharp counters. Bob's left hand was quick and accurate, and he displayed little concern about the break which had so dearly cost him in his fight with Reardon. Jem was not a man to go lightly however, and despite Bob's excellent tactics, Dillon was able to land his own blows to the chest and head of his foe. The battle waged on for over an hour and a half when the shout of "police" rang through the crowd and all parties involved scampered for safety. The men agreed to meet the next day at Wargrave Ferry, where they figured they would be safe from any further interference. Dillon was the worse for wear, but seemed eager to continue the fray. Travers, on the other hand, seemed almost reluctant to again enter the ring, but did so and immediately re-claimed his dominant position in the fight. In the 42 round, Dillon closed with Travers and in attempting to throw his foe, instead lost his balanced and accidentally kicked Bob in the groin. The backers of Travers tried to claim a foul, but the referee stated that the blow had been unintentional. Bob came out for the next round with a concentrated look of pain on his face, but succeeded in dropping Dillon with a right hand counter on the chest as the latter was rushing in. Travers continued to punish Dillon about the body until the 50th round, when again Jem attempted to close and throw his opponent. This time he was successful, but in the tumble, Dillon again struck Bob in the groin, this time with his knee and the full weight of his body. A foul was again claimed and yet again the referee announced it to be unintentional and therefore not grounds for disqualification. Travers returned to his corner in agony. When the call of time went up, he was barely able to the leave the knee of his second and resume the battle. He did however, and managed to shoot his left with enough accuracy and power to keep the ever-rushing Dillon off him. But Travers was merely buying time as the pain in his lower abdomen was fierce and did not allow him to move or punch freely. In the 53rd round, after more than two hours of fighting, the call of "police" again rattled the throng and scattered the participants and the crowd.

Bob was immediately brought to the home of physician Henry Sheppard in Twyford, where he was examined and treated. His wife, who had learned of her husband's unfortunate condition, met him less than two hours after his arrival. The blows to his groin area had done serious harm and there was concern that permanent damage could result if Bob were to return to the field of battle the next day as the referee had ordered. He instead sent Alec Keene in his stead, armed with a letter from Dr. Sheppard that stated, "I certify that I have examined Robert Travers and consider him suffering from an injury, and not capable of being removed from where he is at the present, and also that he is not in proper condition to renew the contest." Keene presented the letter to the referee, who along with Dillon, his backers and the rest of the mob had re-convened at Twyford for the renewal of the battle. However, after reading the letter and considering the blows that had caused Travers' injury, the referee still awarded the stakes to Dillon in consequence of Bob not being present at the allotted time and place to fight on.

This was the inglorious end of Bob Travers' fighting career. It is unclear as to whether or not the injuries that he suffered during his bout with Dillon were the cause of his retirement, however, they certainly had some sort of impact. It is more than likely that Travers' given his age, simply decided that there was a better way to make a living. The 13 Cantons had certainly put him in a financial situation that allowed him to make a comfortable living, but he was also able to supplement that income by touring, appearing at benefits, and teaching, as well as, backing other fighters.

It is unknown how Bob lived out his days. He undoubtedly kept his interests in the Thirteen Cantons, but whether or not it remained his main source of income is also not known. As late as 1904, when he would have been well into his late 60's, Bob was reported to be living in relative comfort and good health. How Travers eventually died is also a mystery, as is the date and location of his demise.

Bob's career as a fighter was certainly not unblemished. He lost quite a few fights, and was more than once accused of un-sportsmanlike behavior. However, with the exception of his fights Patsy Reardon and Job Cobley, Bob was rarely out fought or beaten outright. Up until late in his career he was considered one of the best men at his weight, and despite some of the questions surrounding many of his most famous matches, he was always held in high esteem by the fight crowd. It seems too, that despite the uneven record he accumulated, Travers skills were considered to be some of the best of his time.

It is interesting to note that Bob Travers was both a prizefighter and a boxer. Unlike most of the fighters of his time, his skills would have transferred fairly well to the modern ring. His ability to counterpunch like none before him and his unparalleled use of a left jab served him well throughout his career and would have proven invaluable in modern combat. In this vein, Bob was very much a symbol of his times and the slow change in fighting styles that was beginning to turn prizefighting into boxing.

11

The Undefeated

Robert Delaney was born in Baltimore, Maryland in 1840. He claimed to have come into the world as a freeman, the son of a vagrant father and a servant mother. Raised among seven brothers and three sisters, he received no schooling and was working in an oyster shop by the time he was ten. As a teen, he took to the sea, enjoying the rigors of the sailor's life for several years. When he reached the age of twenty, he left the service of his ship and found work in London docks as a stevedore. Becoming bored with heavy labor, he literally ran away to the circus, joining the famous Mander's Menagerie where he served in the capacity of "keeper of the beasts". Traveling with the Menagerie, Delaney was able to trek throughout England, visiting every major metropolis and village in Britain.

It was in Liverpool that a dispute arose between Bob and one of his fellow circus mates over a gambling debt. The men decided to settle the matter in the

"English way", and fought with their fists in an open field. Delaney proved quite proficient at fighting and settled the matter in less than five minutes. Bob's career as a fighter may have ended there had it not been for the presence of Jem Clarke, a noted pugilist and publican, who happened to be enjoying the menagerie when the fight broke out. Clarke thought Delaney had the makings of a real fighter and invited the latter to visit him at his hostelry The Houghton Abbey located in Liverpool. Bob, figuring he had nothing to loose, did so the next day, and further impressed Clarke with his sparring displays. Clarke offered to back Bob in a real prizefight and Delaney, learning of the money that he could make, readily agreed.

Delaney's first match took place in Liverpool on July 2, 1863. His opponent was a man named simply, "the Liverpool Greyhound"; which was hardly an appropriate nickname for a fighter who weighed close to 185 pounds and moved in ponderous and heavy sequences. Delaney, who weighed a mere 148 pounds and stood a shade over 5'7", seemed slight next to his large opponent, but once the fighting began it was clear that size would be of little consequence. Bob moved in straight and sharp paths, cutting his man to ribbons with short and effective blows. For a smallish man, he delivered punches with alarming affect and soon had the "Greyhound" at his mercy. It took Delaney less than 15 minutes to end the battle and afterwards he displayed nary a mark to signify that he had taken part in his first prize-ring encounter.

When the Mander's Menagerie left Liverpool, Bob Delaney stayed behind. Clarke had convinced him that he had both the talent and backing to make a living with his fists. Delaney settled into the Houghton Abbey where he studied the finer points of fighting with Clarke daily. Mysteriously he also started referring to himself as Bob Smith, and asked others to do the same. For what reason Delaney developed this alias is unclear, however, from that point forward Smith remained his surname.

Clarke was enamored with Smith's abilities as a fighter, and even brought Bob Travers to Liverpool to work with his new black protegee on counterpunching. Jem felt that Travers could help smooth out some of Bob's defensive deficiencies, and assist in making him a better counter-puncher. Smith liked Travers but could not grasp the timing of the veteran's counterpunching methods. Smith was an offensive fighter and after watching his young charge struggle with Travers' system, Clarke abandoned the idea of fiddling any further with his style.

Displaying his faith in his new man, Clarke hastily made a match for Smith with Harry Burgess, a Liverpool man of some repute, for 50 pounds. Burgess and Smith met at Point of Ayr on September 15, 1863 during a terrible rain and hailstorm. Burgess hurt Smith in the third round with a vicious right hand to the throat that both dropped and stunned Bob. Barely able to rise at the call of time to begin the fourth frame, Smith weathered the storm and slowly began to regain his head. By the eleventh round he was in control of the fight, landing tremendous right hand shots to the ribs and head of Burgess. In the 26th Smith grassed Harry with another well-timed, straight right hand that shook the latter so badly that he attempted to leave the ring, being forced back to the scratch only by the loud threats of his angry backers. Harry was all but done and continued to take punishment from Smith until Bob ended the fight with a full throw in the 41st round.

Smith's second essay into the prize ring was certainly a success, but despite the victory, there was a general feeling that he had quite a bit to learn about fighting. The Illustrated Sporting News noted in its remarks on the fight that, "Smith is a very hard hitter and uses his right very effectively, and though very lightly built, he is possessed of extraordinary propelling powers. He certainly has a great deal more knowledge to attain before he can hope to shine as a star in the profession he has now commenced."

The Sporting News could not have been more accurate in its assessment of Smith's boxing skill. He had only a rudimentary education in the "art" of fighting. Bob had won his bout with Burgess in true puncher's style. He weathered an early storm, and used his tremendous strength and powerful right hand to work his way back to a victory. There was nothing fancy about his methods. He was a natural fighter, who had been gifted with the ability to punch extremely hard. As he had demonstrated with his inability and reluctance to learn the methods of Travers, which relied heavily on defense, timing and counterpunching, Smith was not about style. He was purely and simply about power and strength.

Jem Clarke was thrilled with Smith's victory and threw his charge a benefit less than a week later at the plush Strawberry Gardens which netted both men a considerably larger sum of money than had been won with the triumph over Burgess. His coiffeurs full, Bob was able to remain inactive for close to six months, while Jem attempted to match him for another fight. He and Clarke had become fast friends and Smith assisted his benefactor with the day-to-day activities of the Houghton Abbey. These chores put Bob in contact with some of the lesser social elements of Liverpool society. Drunks, whores and gamblers, along with a fair faction of the Liverpool Fancy, filled Clarke's watering hole and Smith exposure to them was far from uneventful. Twice he was involved in altercations that brought him before the local magistrates and once he had been involved in a supposed assault on a prostitute. Smith was fined for his involvement in the two street fights but cleared of the latter charge of assaulting the "professional woman". However he had gained himself a reputation as both a temperamental and violent man. *Bell's Life* noted in 1864 that, "Smith is a gallus moke, and although a good fighter, he carries himself in a manner which many find uncommon for one of his race." It was also felt that Smith, in his deeds and actions, proved himself to be a bit of a social snob and somewhat of a racist. He detested the poor white women who threw themselves at the black sailors and laborers, and frowned upon the fact that interracial marriage between lower class white women and black men was commonplace in Liverpool at the time. He never took a wife and seemed to have never been involved with a woman in any way. His aforementioned altercation with the prostitute was more likely a case of Smith bouncing her from the Houghton Abbey than his wanting to purchase her services. Despite all of this however, Bob Smith was a popular man about town, and was treated as any other public dignitary. His association with Clarke no doubt helped endear him to the public, for Clarke's reputation as a fighter, publican and gentleman was impeccable.

In February of 1864, Clarke finally succeeded in finding a match for his "Ebony Youth", as Smith was sometimes called. The man was Harry Allen, brother of the more famous Tom Allen. Harry, who hailed from Birmingham, was a veteran of 7 fights when he and Smith were matched to meet on March 1 at Point of Ayr, not far from downtown Liverpool, for 60 pounds a side, at a weight limit of 146 pounds. Allen, although involved in some curious contests, had met with only one official defeat, (his being detained by the police being the cause of this blemish), when he and Smith set-to on a terribly cold and rainy early spring morning.

The fight was a grueling affair, and marred by the ugly behavior of a large contigent of pro-Allen, Birmingham roughs. True to form, Bob did most of his damage with his powerful right hand, swelling the left side of Allen's head to grotesque proportions. Harry did his share of harm as well, using his superior skill to work good combinations to the head and body of his American opponent. However, in contrast to Allen, who *Bell's* reported, "gave an audible cry every time he was struck by the Ebony's right hand", Smith seemed unfazed by Harry's blows. By the 60th minute of the fight Bob had taken control and worked on finishing his job. In the 49th round, Smith advanced and threw Allen with terrific force, and it was loudly proclaimed by the provincial crowd that the fight had been won. However, before the time of call to begin the 50th round could be sounded, a group of Birmingham roughs broke the outer ring, and stormed the fight grounds claiming that Allen had been "spiked" by Smith while the former was on the ground. A wild melee ensued and raged on for 20 minutes at which point the referee declared the bout over. He announced the he would give his decision on the affair later in the day when, "the environment would be more appropriate." The next day, the referee, from the safety of the Strawberry Gardens, announced that he would award the stakes and the victory to Smith who he deemed, "would have won outright if not for the unseemly actions of the crowd". Allen's backers objected voraciously, Allen himself demonstrating the cuts and bruises he claimed to have been the product of Bob's "spikes", but made little headway in pleading their case. They returned to Birmingham muttering that they had received little fair play in Liverpool.

Smith was un-daunted by the fight's conclusion. He felt that his victory had been a fair and good one, and despite the inglorious ending, that he had demonstrated his superiority. Allen and his backers were not of the same feeling. In fact, Tom Allen, who had been one of his brother's seconds for the fight, took the matter personally. He announced publicly that he would avenge the mistreatment of his brother by challenging and defeating Smith himself.

Tom Allen was still young in his professional career when he challenged Bob Smith for 100 pounds a side in 1864. In fact, he had taken part in only six contests against less than stellar competition, and had proven victorious only four times. He was however, considered a better pugilist than his brother, and the general feeling was that where Harry had failed in stopping the dreadful right hand of Smith, Tom would succeed.

The men agreed to meet at 150 pounds at Fiddler's Ferry on June 2, 1864 for a stake of 100 pounds and a side bet of 20. Allen was the taller man, but Smith his superior in reach and physique. That Tom was fighting for the honor of his family and with an urgent sense of revenge was evident the moment he took his position at the scratch. He glared at Smith coolly and according to *Bell's* stated, "you will need more than a spiked shoe to beat me darkey!" Bob took the comment in stride and assumed his fighting posture calmly. At the call of time, Allen leapt forward with such ferocity that despite the fact that his punches missed their mark, the weight of his body crashing into Smith caused the latter to stumble backwards and fall flat on his backside with considerable force. Tom smiled blissfully at his fallen foe, seemingly pleased with his work. Smith returned the smile, acknowledging that he had been caught off guard and made to look somewhat silly. The incident would prove to be the high water mark of the fight for Allen however, as Smith immediately went to work with his right hand in the second round. Tom's assumption that he would be able to nullify Bob's vaunted right hand with his own superior speed and defense proved to be woefully incorrect. Smith used his favorite weapon with alarming frequency and effectiveness. After just an hour of fighting, Allen was terribly punished and seemed near defeat. However, by employing his own hit and get down style he managed to last out for well over three full hours before finally succumbing to the dreadful effects of Smith's superior punching. When his brother Harry finally threw up the sponge in the 50th round, Tom was insensible. The bout lasted 2 hours and 49 minutes.

Tom Allen would go on to have a fine career as a fighter, winning the Middleweight Championship of England in 1865 and then emigrating to the United States in 1867 and capturing the Heavyweight Championship of America in 1873. He would return to England and win the British version of the Heavyweight title in 1877, fighting under the still fledgling Queensbury rules, and held that title until he retired in 1879. He returned to America in 1882 and settled in St. Louis where he died in 1904.

The Allen feud seemingly behind him, Bob Smith rested on his laurels for quite some time. His victories over the well-respected brothers earned him the wholly enviable yet difficult reputation as the best middleweight in England. Cashing in on his status, Smith earned his money appearing at benefits and fair booths, all the while maintaining his position as Jem Clarke's apprentice. He consistently upheld his reputation as a staunch moralist as well, refusing to take part in any gathering or activity that would be associated in the least with wanton gambling or drinking. Interestingly enough, Smith also detested street fighting and disliked the notoriety that came with his reputation. That his career in prizefighting, as well as his association with the Houghton Abbey, was so closely linked with all of these vices seems to have created a bit of struggle for Bob. But with few potential matches on the horizon, and his interest in the game waning, by mid 1865 Bob Smith was considering quitting the prize ring altogether: until Harry Allen came calling again.

Harry Allen was evidently still fuming about his March 1864 defeat at the hands of Smith when he and a few of his Birmingham friends came to Liverpool in the late Spring of 1865. Still complaining that the location of the bout and the partiality of the crowd and the referee had cost him a victory, he demanded another fight with Smith, stating that a neutral fight location would prove to be Bob's undoing. Smith, despite the recent uncertainty regarding his future in the ring, immediately accepted the challenge, but demanded a 120 pound a side stake. Allen, who seemingly had the backing of all Birmingham, consented.

The men agreed to fight at 146 pounds at a location not more than 20 miles from London. Allen and his backers felt that they would get a fair shake in the "Metropolis" and none of the interference or supposed rule infractions of the first bout would be allowed by the knowledgeable sports that made up the London

Fancy. Smith was unconcerned with the location of the fight. As mentioned, he felt he had won the first fight fair and square, and he saw no reason why a change in locale would make the outcome of the second match any different. He was correct.

Despite the fact that it took twice as long, Bob Smith once again defeated Harry Allen. In contrast to the first bout, Bob concentrated his efforts to his opponent's body, doing yeoman like work to Allen's ribs. It was this dreadful punishment in the early part of the fight that allowed Smith to work freely to Harry's head as the match reached its latter stages. Allen did not go quietly, and reached Bob with a considerable amount of punches, swelling the left side of his head and nearly closing his left eye. But in the end, Smith's strength was too much for Allen, and when he could not answer simple questions from his brother Tom at the end of the 29th frame, the latter threw in the sponge. Harry protested mildly after learning that his brother had conceded the match, but several minutes had already passed and Smith had long left the ring. Despite the remonstrations of Harry Allen it was a clear and clean victory for the "Ebony Youth".

The Illustrated Sporting News summarized the bout by stating, "a capital battle had been fought between these provincial battlers, and with a degree of fairness and gameness alike, honorable to both parties. That Smith, (who is entitled to take the highest position in pugilistic circles), is the better man has been abundantly proved by the present encounter". To his credit Harry Allen later admitted a superior man had beaten him. A few days after the fight, Bob and Harry were given a joint benefit at Nat Langham's Cambrian Stores when Allen made a short speech during which he acquiesced that Smith was his master. In response, Smith shook Allen's hand and vowed his loyal friendship. The crowd responded with hearty applause after which Langham presented Smith with a timepiece commemorating his victory over Allen.

Bob was now at the pinnacle of his career. Undefeated and unchallenged he again considered retiring from the ring. Unfortunately he would not get the opportunity to make such a decision. In September of 1865, Smith took ill and was bed ridden for close to six months. Doctors informed him that he had contracted bronchitis but he was truly suffering from the far more deadly Tuberculosis. Recovering briefly in the summer of 1866, Bob took work with Chucky Harris' sparring troupe with which he toured for several months. His chief sparmate on the tour was the famed Ned O'Baldwin. Despite his weakened condition, Bob kept Ned honest and rarely did the future contender have an easy night. In October of 1866, Smith left the tour due to his illness, which had placed him in such a weakened state that he could no longer go through the motions. He returned to Liverpool, destitute and dying. His old friend Jem Clarke took Smith in and cared for him until the latter finally passed on January 19, 1867. His cause of death was listed as complications due to Bronchitis.

Bell' Life ran an obituary for Bob Smith in their April 25, 1867 edition. They lamented the loss of such a fine fighter, briefly highlighting his life and career. Interestingly they noted the supposed circumstances which led to Bob contracting his illness stating, "he had been ailing since his first contest with Harry Allen, the severity of the weather at the time setting the seed of the disease that terminated his career and life." *Bell's* also noted Smith's staunch personality and social snobbery, while complimenting his fistic talents and personal behavior, stating "Like the majority of most colored gentlemen, Bob was quite conceited, and in his own estimation a long way ahead of the "white trash". However, Smith was a fine fighter and in his personal life he stood on his own dignity." But perhaps the most fascinating aspect of *Bell's* write-up was their noting that; "many Americans who have visited Liverpool will remember him when they read this." Whether or not Bob's American friends were sailors and seamen, wealthy vacationers, visiting dignitaries or mixture of all, is unclear. That he had developed such relationships, no matter whom with, is indicative of both his personal attractiveness and his fame as an athlete. In the end it was abundantly clear that all who knew him, and even those who merely knew of him, respected Bob Smith.

As a fighter Bob Smith was clearly superlative. Despite lacking some of the polish that is usually associated with championship fighters, Bob certainly deserves consideration as one of the best of his time. His power was unparalleled, his strength unyielding and his will indomitable. Despite his rather short career, he proved himself capable of beating first-rate men, as both Allen brothers must certainly be considered. At the time of his forced retirement, Smith was considered the best man of his weight in the world and even during his illness, remained unchallenged. That he died at such a young age further illustrates the harsh reality of the 19th century and the risks of his chosen trade. In the end however, Bob Smith the pugilist, can only be judged by his fighting record—and that remains unblemished to this day.

Appendix A

Fight Records

George Brown "Young Molineaux"

Born: Based out of Chicago, IL

Died:

Height:

Weight:

1854

Dec 15   Tom Davis, Boston, MA   D

—The purse for this bout was $60.

1857

May 30   John Mackey, Chicago, IL   EXH3

Jun 10   Young Sambo, Chicago, IL   EXH3

Sep 5   Richard Plume, Chicago, IL   W11(20min)

—The purse for this bout was $50.

1858

Jul 26   John Powers, Chicago, IL   EXH3

1859

Jul 4   Andy Foster, Cleveland, OH   W45(33min)

—The purse for this bout was $50.

1860

Feb 6	Andy Foster, Cleveland, OH	WF33

—The purse for this bout was $25.

May 14	John Mackey, Cleveland, OH	EXH3

1861

Jul 24	Ed Heddy, New York, NY	W23(51min)

—The Purse for this bout was $25

Aug 2	Johnny Lazurus, New York, NY	EXH3

Cain's Black

Born:

Died:

Height:

Weight: 168

1843

May 20	Hurley, Liverpool	W

—The purse for this bout was 10 pounds.

1844

Aug 30	Bill Butler, Bucknell Sumersett	L30(45min)

—The purse for this bout was 10 pounds.

Young Congou "Norley's Black"

Born: 1829

Died:

Height: 5'4"

Weight: 112

1847

Jul 27   Harrigan, Woodhead, Chesire   W189(4hr40min)

1848

         Moore   L

George Crowhurst "The Black"

Born:

Died:

Height:

Weight:

1854

Apr 10   Jim Malvern, Throstle Neck, Manchester   W65(90min)

—The purse for this bout was 10 pounds.

Daniels "The Black"

Born:

Died:

Height:

Weight:

1822

Oct 7   George Croft, Weybridge   L13

—The purse for this bout was 40 pounds.

Davis "The Black"

Born:

Died:

Height:

Weight: 170

1837

May 2   George Church, Colcey Hatch   L37(53min)

Dobson "Holden's Nigger"

Born:

Died:

Height: 5'3"

Weight: 103 pounds

1848

Feb 12   Butler, Hodge Hill, Birmingham   W50(90min)

—The purse for this bout was 20 pounds.

Oct 2   Tom Jinks, Hodge Hill, Birmingham   W47(52min)

—The purse for this bout was 20 pounds.

1853

Jan 10   Longmore, Purferay Green   W33(70min)

Bill Evans "The Black"

Born:

Died:

Height:

Weight:

1857

Aug 17   George Beasley, Worcester Road   W43(70min)

—The purse for this bout was 10 pounds.

Edward Green "Jem Burn's Black"
A.K.A. John Augustus Edward Plantagenet Green
A.K.A "Billy Croft's Black"

Born:

Died:

Height:

Weight:

1851

Jul 15   Fred Dickenson, Horley   L149(269min)

—The purse for this bout was 20 pounds.

1853

Jun 1   Shylock(Patton's Waiter), Brandon   W (20min)

1854

Feb 11   Jerry Noon, Woolrich Reach   L34(82min)

1857

Dec 23   Jesse Hatton, London   W78(118min)

Aaron Hewlett "Molineaux"

Born:

Died: 1871

Height: 5'9"

Weight: 156

1851

| Jun 11 | Timmon's Black Boy, Brooklyn, NY | W3(21min) |

1852

| Aug 13 | WM Hastings "Dublin Tricks", New York, NY | W36(110min) |

1853

| Jun 23 | Mingo, Brooklyn, NY | W15(11min) |
| Dec 6 | Caesar Coit, Brooklyn, NY | D(50min) |

—This was a wrestling macth.

1854

| Feb 24 | Caesar Coit, Brooklyn, NY | W10(35min) |

—Coit had previously defeated Hewlitt in a wrestling match.

Mar 18	Young Brian, Brooklyn, NY	EXH
Apr 14	Jack Killfeather, New York, NY	EXH
Apr 28	Harry Gribben, New York, NY	EXH
May 5	Matt Davis, Brooklyn, NY	W4(5min)
Oct 22	Harry Gribben, New York, NY	EXH
Nov 13	Tom Davis, New York, NY	EXH
Dec 25	Harry Gribben, New York, NY	EXH

1859

May 23   Sam Freeman, New York, NY   EXH

Oct 16   Harvard University announced the appointment of Hewlett
         as its first director of physical education culture.

Jemmy Johnson "Jemmy The Black"

Born:

Died:

Height:

Weight:

1820

Mar 3   C. Smith (The Waterman), Banstead Downs   W3

—The purse for this bout was 10 pounds.

1821

Jul 17   Jem Garroll, Mousley Hurst   L86(105min)

—The purse for this bout was 12 guineas.

1822

Aug 21   Nixon, Marshfield Common   W9

—The purse for this bout was 10 Pounds

1823

Jan 1 Harry Fowler, Wycomb   *L12(120min)*

—The Purse for this bout was 20 Pounds.

Jan 28   Tod Harris, Caxton Heath   W15(140min)

—The Purse for this bout was 15 Pounds.

Feb 15   Rickers, Somesburg Warren   W16(40min)

—The Purse for this bout was 10 Pounds.

Jul 31   C. Smith (The Waterman), Elstree Herts   W6(22min)

—The Purse for this bout was 20 Guineas

Aug 20   Jem Ward, Southhampton   L8(18min)

—This bout was fought for a subscription purse.

Oct 1   Harry Griffin, Newport, Pagnel   L10

—The Purse for this bout was 50 Pounds.

Nov 13   Phil Crossley, Mattingley Park   W25

—The Purse for this bout was 50 Pounds

1824

Jan 28   Bishop Harris, Bradwell, Oxford   W57(70min)

—The Purse for this bout was 50 Pounds

Apr 23   Jewin(The Navigator), Sussex   W27(37min)

—The Purse for this bout was 40 Pounds

John Kendrick"Massa Kendrick"

Born: St. Kitts 1798

Died: 1844

Height:

Weight:

Manager:

1819

May 11   George Cooper, Peter Street, Westminster   L69(65min)

—The purse for this bout was 50 guineas. This was an improtu match.

May 28	Tom Oliver, Epsom Races	L30(70min)

—The purse for this match was 50 pounds.

Aug 24	Harry Boone, Mousley Hurst	SCH

—Boone did not appear

Dec 23	Harry Sutton, Blindlow Heath	L12(17min)

—The purse for this bout was 25 guineas.

1821

Dec 18	Dick Acton, Mousley Hurst	W17(25min)

—The purse for this bout was 40 guineas.

1822

Mar 8	Dick Acton, Mousley Hurst	L32(35min)

—The purse for this bout was 50 guineas

Kendrick "The Black"

Born:

Died:

Weight: 178

Height: 5'11"

1840

Jan 13	Josh Burgin, Surrey	W17(72min)

—The purse for this bout was 20 pounds.

1842

Mar 7	Dawes, Cambridge	W7

—The purse for this bout was 50 pounds.

Daniel Knox

Born: Unknown

Died: Unknown

Height: 5'10"

Weight: 165

1842

Jun 1   Sam Briggs, Hoboken, NJ   W7(18min)

—The purse for this bout was $50.

—Described as being for the "Colored Championship".

1843

Apr 10   Butcher Mack, Hoboken, NJ   W2(10min)

Joe Lashley "The African Black"

Born:

Died:

Height:

Weight:

1791

Jun 13   Tom Treadway, Marylebone Fields   W (35min)

1796

           Stewey "The Breakman"   W

—Stewey supposedly died from his injuries.

Ned Myers

Born:

Died:

Height: 5'9"

Weight: 175

1862

| Jan 14 | Joshua Williams, Toronto, Can | W21(45min) |

Tom Molineaux "The Terrible Black"

Born: Georgetown, South Carolina

Died: August 4, 1818 Galway, Ireland

Height:5'8½"

Weight:185

1810

| Jul 24 | Jack Burrows, Tothill Fields, Westminster | W (65min) |

—This purse for this bout was 50 pounds.

| Aug 21 | Tom "Tough" Blake, Epple Bay, near Margate | W8 |

—The purse for this bout was 100 guineas.

| Dec 18 | Tom Cribb, Copthall Common | L40(55min) |

—The purse for this bout was 200 guineas.

1811

Jan	Bill Richmond, Fives Court, London	EXH
Apr 2	Isaac Bitton, Fives Court, London	EXH
Apr 2	Tom Belcher, Fives Court, London	EXH
Apr 2	Ben Bunr, Fives Court, London	EXH

May 21	Rimmer, Mousley Hurst	W21

—The purse for this bout was 100 guineas.

Sep 28	Tom Cribb, Thistleton Gap	L11(19min)

—The purse for this bout was 600 pounds.

—

Power, London	W (17min)

This bout was an impromptu match fought on the street.

1812

Jul 27	John Snow	EXH

This was a wrestling match at the Exeter Fair

1813

Mar 31	Jack Carter

—This fight did not take place as Tom was arrested for debt to Bill Richmond.

Apr 23	Jack Carter, Sanbury, England	W25

The purse for this bout was 100 guineas.

1814

May 27	William Fuller, Glasgow, Scotland	NC8

The sheriff interrupted this fight.

May 31	William Fuller, Paisley, Scotland	WF2(68min)

—The purse for this bout was 100 guineas.

1815

Mar 10	George Cooper, Edinburgh, Scotland	L14(20min)

—The purse for this fight was 100 guineas.   Exh.
  —Abraham Deniston

Massa Morgan "Josh Hudson's Black"

Born:

Died:

Height: 5'10"

Weight:

1827

Jun 21	Fisher(The Oxford Champ), Tennis Court, London	EXH3
Jun 21	Young Gas (Johnathan Bissell), Tennis Court	EXH3

—Morgan knocked Bissell twice.

Jul 3	Abbinet, Ranscombe Range	W11(11min)

—The purse for this bout was 10 pounds.

1829

Mar 24	Fleming, Market Deeping	W1(2min)

—The purse for this bout was 40 pounds.

John Perry "The Black"

Born: Annapolis, Nova Scotia

Died:

Height: 6'1"

Weight: 182

1845

Oct 12	Unknown, Bradford, England	W
Dec	Harry Broome, London, England	EXH

1846

Jan 20   Bill Burton, London, England   W(25min)

—The purse for this match was 15 pounds.

1847

Apr   Perry is convicted at Winchester Assizes for passing forged 20
           pound notes, sentenced to 14 years transportation and sent to
           Australia.

1849

Dec 10   Goerge Hough, Cummons Points, Australia   W4(5min)

1850

Jan   Perry goes on exhibition tour of New South Wales

Jun   Perry challenges all comers at Sydney for 100 pounds.

1857

Jun   Perry appears in a production of Othello

1858

Jan 11   Bob McLaren, Windsor, Australia   SCH

—Perry was scheduled to fight McLaren, but the latter did not show.

1859

May 14   Harry Sellars, Sydney, Australia   SCH

—This bout fell through because of purse differences

Bill Richmond "The Black Terror"

Born: Cuckold's town, Richmond (Staten Island), NY, Aug 5, 1763

Died: Dec. 29, 1829, England

Height: 5'6"

Weight: 150–156

Undated early fights

—	"George "Dockey" Moore, York Racetrack	W (25min)
—	Inniskillin Dragoon, York Racetrack	W
—	Inniskillin Dragoon, York Racetrack	W
(Above two fights on same day)		
—	Unknown Blacksmith, York (The Groves)	W
—	Frank Meyers, York (The Groves)	W

1804

Jan 23	George Maddox, Wimbledon Commons	L 3

1805

Apr 12	Whipmaker Green, Islington Fields	W (10min)
May 21	"Youssop, the Jew", Blackheath	W 6(59min)
Jul 8	Jack Holmes, Cricklewood Green	W28(50min)
Oct 8	Tom Cribb, Hailsham, Sussex	L (90min)

1808

Apr 14	Carter, Epsom Downs	W (29min)

The purse for this bout was 15 guineas.

Jun 11	Atkinson, Golder's Green	W (20min)

1809

Apr 11	Isaac Wood, Combe Wood	W23
—	A Baker, near Wildsen Green	W (2min)
Aug 9	George Maddox, Recuivers	W52(52min)

—The purse for this bout was 100 guineas.

1810

| May 1 | Jack Power, Castle Tavern | W7 (15min) |

—The purse for this bout was 18 pounds.

1814

| May 3 | Jack Davis, Coombe Wood | W13(20min) |

—The purse for this bout was 50 pounds.

1815

| Aug 11 | Tom Shelton, Moulsey Hurst | W23(29min) |

—The purse for this bout was 25 pounds.

1816

May 23	Hall	Exh
May 23	Tom Oliver	Exh
Dec 20	Unknown	Exh

1817

Feb 12	Harry Harmer	Exh
Mar 11	Harry Harmer	Exh
Apr 15	Harry Harmer	Exh

1818

Nov 12   Jack Carter, Chancery Lane, London   W 3

—This match was an impromptu event.

1821

Apr 25   Unknown   Exh

James "Jem" Robinson "The Ebony Phenomenon" "Norley's Black"

Born: August 8, 1829

Died: June 11, 1849, Manchester, England

Height: 5'5.5"

Weight: 122–126

Manager:

1846

Jan 12   Jem Millwood, Manchester   Exh

Sep 8   James Evans, Madeley Station   W59(59min)

—The purse for this bout was 50 pounds.

1847

Mar 9   Johnny Peach, Buxton   W58(109min)

—The purse for this bout was 60 pounds.

Jun 15   Charley Mullett, Manchester   W47(73min)

1848

Jun 13   Enoch Horridge, Saltersbrook, York   W24(67min)

—The purse for this bout was 120 pounds.

Sam Robinson

Born: New York, NY May 23 1778

Died:

Height: 6'

Weight: 190

Manager:

1816

Jan 11	Tom Crockery	W7
Mar 14	Alf Butcher, Coombe Warren	W44(47min)

—The purse for this bout was 10 guineas.

| Apr 24 | Jack Carter, Mousley Hurst | L12(18min) |

—The purse for this bout was 50 guineas.

| May 28 | Joe Stephenson, Coombe Warren | W68(72min) |

—The purse for this bout was 40 guineas.

| Jun 26 | Jack Carter, Coombe Warren | L13(28min) |

—The purse for this bout was 50 pounds.

| Sep 26 | Harry Sutton, Doncaster, England | L26(38min) |

—There was no purse for this bout.

| Dec | Tom Taylor, Yorkshire | W (19min) |

1817

Feb 24	George Cooper, Edinburgh, Scotland	L7
Jun 27	Alexander Fangill, Ayshire, Scotland	W20(40min)
Dec 5	Dent, Greta Green	W (23min)

Harry Sellars

Born: Baltimore, MD 1820

Died:

Height: 160

Weight: 5'9.5"

1858

Oct 19	Joe Kitchen, Victorian Goldfields, Aus	L32

—The purse for this bout was 300 pounds.

1859

Jun 21	Dick Hunt, Victorian Goldfields, Aus	W3(4min)

—The purse for this bout was 240 pounds.

1860

Apr 22	Tom Curran, Victorian Goldfields, Aus	LF26

—The purse for this bout was 300 pounds.

—For the vacant Heavyweight Championship of Australia.

1861

Jun 12	John Carstairs, Forbes, Aus	W4

—For the Middlweight Championship of Australia.   W
  Paddy Broomfield

1862

	George Belcher	W
	Tom Curran, Victorian Goldfields	W37

—For the Heavyweight Championship of Australia.

1878

Sep 16   John Thompson, Mace's Hall, NSW, Aus   EXH4

1879

          Larry Foley, Redfern, NSW, Aus   EXH3

Jun 23   Peter Newton, Mace's Hall, NSW, Aus   EXH

Robert Delaney a.k.a. Bob Smith "The Ebony Youth"

Born: March 11, 1840, Washington, DC

Died: January 16, 1867, Liverpool, England
(died of Bronchitis and complications due to consumption)

Height: 5'10"

Weight: 148–150

1863

Jul 2   Liverpool Greyhound, Liverpool   W7(14min)

Sep 15   Harry Burgess, Point of Ayr, Liverpool   W41(53min)

—The purse for this bout was 50 pounds.

1864

Mar 1   Harry Allen, Point of Ayr, Liverpool   W49(75min)

—The purse for this bout was 60 pounds.

Jun 2   Tom Allen, Windbury Island   W50(169min)

—The purse for this bout was 100 pounds.

1865

Feb 21   Harry Allen, London, England   W29(139min)

—The purse for this bout was 120 pounds.

Joe Stephenson

Born: 1786, Harve de Grace, MD

Died:

Height: 5'10.5"

Weight: 185

1816

| Feb 6 | Jack Carter, Coombe Warren | L18 |

—The purse for this bout was 25 guineas. The combatants also wagered 25 guineas a side.

| May 28 | Sam Robinson, Coombe Warren | L68(72min) |

—The purse for this bout was 40 guineas.

Harry Sutton "Sutton the Black"

Born: Baltimore, MD

Died: 1823, Consumption

Height: 6'1"

Weight: 165—190

Manager:

1816

| May 28 | Cropley's Black, Coombe Wood, England | W3 |

—The purse for this bout was 25 guineas.

Jun 6	Tom Spring, Fives Court, London, England	EXH
Jun 6	George Cooper, Fives Court, London, England	EXH
Sep 26	Sam Robinson, Doncaster Races, England	W26(38min)

—There was no purse for this bout.

1817

Jul 23	Ned Painter, Mousley-Hurst, England	W40

—The purse for this bout was 50 guineas.

Dec 16	Ned Painter, Bungay, Suffolk, England	L15(102min)

—The purse for this bout was 50 guineas.

1819

Apr 1	Harry Harmer, Fives Court, London, England	EXH
Dec 23	Massa Kendrick, Blindlow Heath, England	W12

—The purse for this bout was 25 guineas.

Sambo Sutton

Born:

Died:

Height: 5'10"

Weight: 168

1836

May 27	Nick Ward, Tottenham	W12

—The purse for this bout was 5 pounds.

Dec 20	Harry Preston, Woodstock	L53(95min)

—The purse for this bout was 50 pounds.

1838

Mar 27	Nick Ward, Bicester	D

—The purse for this bout was 50 pounds. It was interrupted by the police.

1842

Oct 25   John Gorrick (The Bungaree), Milbourne Heath   L72(71min)

—The purse for this bout was 100 pounds.

1843

Jan   John Gorrick(The Bungaree)   W

Bob Travers "The Black Wonder"

Born: June 21, 1832

Died: Unknown

Height: 5'6" (other sources report 5'5½")

Weight: 136–138 (other sources report 168)

1855

Oct 29   George Baker, Tilbury   D10(23min)

—The police stopped this contest.

Nov 3   George Baker, Long Reach   W10(20min)

—The purse for this bout was 50 pounds.

1856

Feb 5   Jesse Hatton, Coombe Bottom   W39(76min)

—The purse for this bout was 50 pounds.

May 13   George Crockett, Egham,   W37(114min)

—The purse for this bout was 100 pounds.

Aug 19   Job Cobley, Halfway House,   L100(3hr27min)

—The purse for this bout was 100 pounds.

1857

Jan 20   Bill Cleghorne, Long Reach, Medway   W36(87min)

—The purse for this bout was 200 pounds.

May 13   Bill Hayes, Medway   W78(3hr45min)

—The purse for this bout was 200 pounds.

1858

Jan 26   Bob Brettle, Appledore   D42(65min)

—The police stopped this bout.

Jan 27   Bob Brettle, Shell Haven   LF100(2hr5min)

—The purse for this bout was 200 pounds.

—Travers was accused of falling without a blow and disqualified.

May 26   Johnny Walker   SCH

—Travers received a forfeit of 90 pounds when Walker would not fight.

1859

Apr 5   Mike Madden, Ashford   W45(97min)

—The purse for this bout was 200 pounds.

1860

Feb 21   Jem Mace, Thames   D6(21min)

—Police intervened

Feb 22   Jem Mace Thames   LF51(91min)

—Referee awarded the stakes to Mace when Travers fell without being hit.

—The purse for this bout was 200 pounds.

1861

Apr 30   Badger Crutchley, Essex Coast   W3

—Police intervened and when the bout was moved to another location, Crutchley refused to continue. The referee awarded the stakes to Travers.

Dec 12   Bos Tyler, Kent   W17(63min)

—The purse for this bout was 100 pounds.

1862

Jul 15   Patsy Reardon, Hampshire   D7(37min)

—The police intervened.

Jul 16   Patsy Reardon, Hampshire   L53(4hr5min)

—The purse for this bout was 200 pounds.

1863

Aug 11   Jem Dillon, Twyford   D28(1hr46min)

—The police intervened. The referee ordered the fighters to meet at Wargrave Ferry.

Aug 11   Jem Dillon, Wargrave Ferry   L53(2hr2min)

—Police intervened and the referee ordered the fighters to return to Twyford. Dillon appeared but Travers did not.

Thomas Welsh "Young Sambo"

Born:

Died:

Height:

Weight: 136

Manager:

1839

Jan 18   Jemmy Shaw   L(40min)

1843

Jan 9   Brighton Jack Sears, Plumstead Marshes   W39(45min)
—The purse for this bout was 20 pounds.

1844

Mar 26   Bill Jones, Norfleet   W48(105min)
—The purse for this bout was 100 pounds.

Jun 24   Tom Verdun,

1845

Jan 21   Billy Jordan, Purfleet,   WF34(93min)
—The purse for this bout was 100 pounds.

Mar 11   Billy Jordan, Norley   W113(3hrs58min)
—The purse for this bout was 100 pounds.

1848

Jun 20   Alec Keene, New Market   L6(19min)

1850

Dec 10   Jem Cross, Long Reach   D64(2hrs28min)
—Each man given 50 pounds.

1852

Jun 1   Jem Cross, Long Reach   W29(2hrs20min)
—The purse for this bout was 100 pounds.

James Wharton "Young Molineaux" "Jemmy The Black"

Born: March 3, 1813

Died: April 25, 1856

Height: 5'9"

Weight: 154 pounds

1833

Apr 16   Tom McKeever, Whetstone,   W38(51min)
—The purse for this bout was 10 Pounds per side.

1834

Oct 21   Evans, Green St. Green, Kent   W8(14min)
—The purse for this bout was 5 Pounds per side.

1835

Jan 20   Wilsden, Colney Heath   W12(22min)
—The purse for this bout was 10 Pounds.

Nov 24   Bill Fisher, Staffodshire   W49(70min)
—The purse for this bout was 25 pounds per side.

1836

Feb 9   Tom Britton, Staffodshire   D200(4hrs,7min)
—The purse for this bout was 50 Pounds.

1837

Apr 18   Harry Preston, Newcastle   W16(61min)
—The purse for this bout was 100 Pounds per side.

Jun	Exhibition Tour in Scotland	
Oct 31	Wil Renwick, Cambo	Stpd. Police
Oct 31	Wil Renwick, Middleton Ridge	W86

—The purse for this bout was 50 Pounds per side.

1838

| May | Toured Scotland and Ireland, giving exhibitions. | |

1839

| Jun 18 | Will Renwick, Shap Fell, Westmoreland | W14(65min) |

—The purse for this bout was 100 Pounds per side.

1840

| Jun 9 | Hammer Lane, Worksop, Notts | W53(72min) |

The purse for this bout was 100 Pounds per side.

Joshua Williams

Born:

Died:

Height: 5'9"

Weight: 175

1862

| Jan 14 | Ned Myers, Toronto, Can | L21(45min) |

APPENDIX B

BROUGHTON'S RULES (1743)

I. That a square of a yard be chalked in the middle of the stage, and on every fresh set-to after a fall, or being parted form the rails, each Second is to bring his Man to the side of the square, and place him opposite to the other, and till they are fairly set-to at the Lines, it shall not be lawful for one to strike at the other.

II. That, in order to prevent any Disputes, the time a Man lies after a fall, if the Second does not bring his Man to the side of the square, within the space of half a minute, he shall be deemed a beaten Man.

III. That in every main Battle, no person whatever shall be upon the Stage, except the Principals and their Seconds, the same rule to be observed in bye-battles, except that in the latter, Mr. Broughton is allowed to be upon the Stage to keep decorum, and to assist Gentlemen in getting to their places, provided always he does not interfere in the Battle; and whoever pretends to infringe these Rules to be turned immediately out of the house. Every body is to quit the Stage as soon as the Champions are stripped, before the set-to.

IV. That no Champion be deemed beaten, unless he fails coming up to the line in the limited time, or that his own Second declares him beaten. No Second is to be allowed to ask his man's Adversary any questions, or advise him to give out.

V. That in bye-battles, the winning man to have two-thirds of the Money given, which shall be publicly divided upon the Stage, notwithstanding any private agreements to the contrary.

VI. That to prevent Disputes, in every main Battle the Principals shall, on coming on the Stage, choose from among the gentlemen present two Umpires, who shall absolutely decide all Disputes that may arise about the Battle; and if the two Umpires cannot agree, the said Umpires to choose a third, who is to determine it.

VII. That no person is to hit his Adversary when he is down, or seize him by the ham, the breeches, or any part below the waist: a man on his knees to be reckoned down.

As agreed to by several Gentlemen at Broughton's Ampitheatre, Tottenham Court Road, August 16, 1743.

London Prize Ring Rules, as revised by the British Pugilistic Association (1838)

1. That the ring shall *be* made on turf and shall be four-and-twenty feet square, formed of eight stakes and ropes, the latter extending in double lines, the uppermost line being four feet from the ground and the lower two feet from the ground. That in the center of the ring a mark be formed, to be termed "the scratch"; and that at two opposite comers, as may be selected, spaces be enclosed by other marks sufficiently large for the reception of the seconds and bottleholders, to be en-titled "the corners."

2. That each man shall be attended to the ring by a second and a bottleholder, the former provided with a sponge and the latter with a bottle of water. That the combatants, on shaking hands, shall retire until the seconds of each have tossed for choice of position, which adjusted, the winner shall choose his comer according to the state of the wind or sun and con-duct his man thereto, the loser taking the opposite corner.

3. That each man shall be provided with a handkerchief of a color suitable to his own fancy, and that the seconds proceed to entwine these handkerchiefs at the upper end of one of the center stakes. That these handkerchiefs shall be called the "colors," and that the winner of the battle at its conclusion shall be entitled to their possession as the trophy of victory.

4. That two umpires shall be chosen by the seconds or backers to watch the progress of the battle and take exception to any breach of the rules hereafter stated. That a referee shall be chosen by the umpires, unless otherwise agreed on, to whom all disputes shall be referred; and that the decision of this referee, whatever it may be, shall be final and strictly binding on all parties, whether as to the matter in dispute or the issue of the battle. That the umpires shall be provided with a watch for the purpose of calling time; and that they mutually agree upon whom this duty shall devolve, the call of that umpire only to be attended to, and no other person whatever to interfere in calling time. That the referee shall withhold all opinion till appealed to by the umpires, and that the umpires strictly abide by his decision without dispute.

5. That, on the men being stripped, it shall be the duty of the seconds to examine their drawers, and if any objection arise as to insertion of improper substances therein, they shall appeal to their umpires, who, with the concurrence of the referee, shall direct what alterations shall be made.

6. That in future no spikes be used in fighting boots except those authorized by the Pugilistic Association, which shall not exceed three eighths of an inch from the sole of the boot and shall not be less than one eighth of an inch broad at the point; and it shall be in the power of the referee to alter, or file in any way he pleases, spikes which shall not accord with the above dimensions, even to filing them away altogether.

7. That, both men being ready, each man shall be conducted to that side of the scratch next his corner previously chosen; and the seconds on the one side, and the men on the other, having shaken hands, the former shall immediately return to their corners, and there remain within the prescribed marks till the round be finished, on no pretense whatever approach-ing their principals during the round, under a penalty of five shillings for each offense, at the option of the referee. The penalty, which will be strictly enforced, to go to the funds of the Association. The principal to be responsible for every fine inflicted on his second.

8. That at the conclusion of the round, when one or both of the men shall be down, the seconds and bottleholders shall step forward and carry or conduct their principal to his corner, there affording him the necessary assistance, and that no person whatever be permitted to interfere in this duty.

9. That on the expiration of thirty seconds the umpire ap-pointed shall cry "Time," upon which each man shall rise from the knee of his bottleholder and walk to his own side of the scratch unaided; the seconds and bottleholders remaining at their corner; and that either man failing so to be at the scratch within eight seconds shall be deemed to have lost the battle. This rule to be strictly adhered to.

10. That on no consideration whatever shall any person be permitted to enter the ring during the battle nor till it shall have been concluded; and that in the event of such unfair practice, or the ropes or stakes being disturbed or removed, it shall be in the power of the referee to award the victory to that man who, in his honest opinion, shall have the best of the contest.

11. That the seconds and bottleholders shall not interfere, advise, or direct the adversary of their principal and shall re-frain from all offensive and irritating expressions, in all respects conducting themselves to the diligent and careful discharge of their duties to their principals.

12. That in picking up their men, should the seconds or bottleholders wilfully injure the antagonist of their principal, the latter shall be deemed to have for-feited the battle on the decision of the referee.

13. That it shall be a fair "stand-up fight," and if either man shall wilfully throvv himself down without receiving a blow, *whether blows shall have previously been exchanged or not,* he shall be deemed to have lost the battle; but that this rule shall not apply to a man who in a close slips down from the grasp of his opponent to avoid punishment or from obvious accident or weakness.

14. That butting with the head shall be deemed foul, and the party resorting to this practice shall be deemed to have lost the battle.

15. That a blow struck when a man is thrown or down shall be deemed foul. That a man with one knee and one hand on the ground, or with both knees on the ground, shall be deemed down; and a blow given in either of those positions shall be considered foul, provided always that, when in such position, the man so down shall not himself strike or attempt to strike.

16. That a blow struck below the waistband shall be deemed foul, and that in a close seizing an antagonist below the waist, by the thigh, or otherwise, shall be deemed foul.

17. That all attempts to inflict injury by gouging, or tearing the flesh with the fingers or nails, and biting, shall be deemed foul.

18. That kicking or deliberately falling on an antagonist with the knees or other-wise when down shall be deemed foul.

19. That all bets shall be paid as the battle money, after a fight, is awarded.

20. That no person, under any pretense whatever, shall be permitted to approach nearer the ring than ten feet, with the exception of the umpires and referee and the persons appointed to take charge of the water or other refreshments

for the com-batants, who shall take their seats close to the corners selected by the seconds.

21. That due notice shall be given by the stakeholder of the day and place where the battle money is to be given up, and that he be exonerated from all responsibility upon obeying the direction of the referee; that all parties be strictly bound by these rules, and that in future all articles of agreement for a contest be entered into with a strict and willing adherence to the letter and spirit of these rules.

22. That in the event of magisterial or other interference, or in case of darkness corning on, the referee shall have the power to name the time and place for the next meeting, if possible on the same day, or as soon after as may be.

23. That, should the fight not be decided on the day, all bets shall be drawn, unless the fight shall be resumed the same week, between Sunday and Sunday; in which case the bets shall stand and be decided by the event. The battle money shall remain in the hands of the stakeholder until fairly won or lost by a fight, unless a draw be mutually agreed upon.

24. That any pugilist voluntarily quitting the ring previous to the deliberate judgment of the referee being obtained shall be deemed to have lost the fight.

25. 2$. That on an objection being made by the seconds or um-pire, the men shall retire to their corners and there remain until the decision of the appointed authorities shall be ob-tained; that if pronounced "foul," the battle shall be at an end; but if "fair," "time" shall be called by the party appointed, and the man absent from the scratch in eight seconds after shall be deemed to have lost the fight. The decision in all cases to be given promptly and irrevocably, for which purpose the umpires and the referee should be invariably close together.

26. That if in a rally at the ropes a man steps outside the ring to avoid his antagonist or to escape punishment, he shall for-feit the battle.

27. That the use of hard substances, such as stone or stick, or of resin in the hand during the battle shall be deemed foul, and that on the requisition of the seconds of either man, the accused shall open his hands for the examination of the referee.

28. That hugging on the ropes shall be deemed foul. That a man held by the neck against the stakes, or upon or against the ropes, shall be considered down, and all interference with him in that position shall be foul. That if a man in any way makes use of the ropes or stakes to aid him in squeezing his adversary, he shall be deemed the loser of the battle; and that if a man in a close reaches the ground with his knees, his ad-versary shall immediately loose him or lose the battle.

29. That all stage fights be as nearly as possible in con-formity with the foregoing rules

Appendix C

Illustrations

Chapter One: Saint George de Chevalier

Chapter Two: Bill Richmond

Chapter Three: Tom Molineaux

Chapter Four: Harry Sutton versus Dolly Smith

Chapter Five: Joe Stephenson versus Sam Robinson

Chapter Six: Jemmy Johnson

Chapter Seven: James Wharton versus Hammer Lane

Chapter Eight: John Perry versus George Hough

Chapter Nine: Aaron Molineaux Hewlett

Chapter Ten: Bob Travers

Chapter Eleven: Bob Delaney

APPENDIX D

Glossary of Terms

Blackamoor	-a black person
Bottom	-courage, ability to take punishment
Claret	-blood
Conk	-nose
Cross	-a fixed fight
Dial	-the face
Dice	-teeth
Duds	-clothing
Facer	-a punch to the face
Fancy	-the sporting crowd; those who attended, arranged or participated in prize-fights or sparring
Gams	-legs
Ivories	-teeth
Knee	-a second or cornerman
Mauleys	-boxing gloves or bare fists
Mill	-a prizefight; or to fight
Mufflers	-boxing glove
Muzzler	-an uppercut type punch; usually a finisher
Ogles	-eyes
Peepers	-eyes
Phiz	-the face
Pimple	-the head
Ruby	-blood
Trap	-the mouth

Wet   -a drink

Whip   -guards at a prizefight who protected the inner ring from invasion

Winder   -a body punch

Bibliography

Books

Arthur Ashe Jr., *A Hard Road To Glory*

Capt. Godfrey, *A Treatise on the Useful Art of Self-Defence*

"An Amateur," *Recollections of Pugilism and Sketches of the Ring*

"Jon Bee" (Jonathan Badcock) *Lives off the Boxers*

Pierce Egan, *Boxiana* 3 vols., 5 vols.

Bill Oxberry, *Pancratia, or a History of Pugilism*

John Ford, *Prizefighting: The Age of Regency Boximania*

Reid, *Bucks and Bruisers: Pierce Egan and Regency England*

Peter Corris, Lords of the Ring

Fred Henning, *Fight for the Championship*

Nat Fleischer, *Black Dynamite Volume One*

Richard Fox, *The Lives and Battles of Famous Black Pugilists*

TB Sheppard, *The Noble Art*

Denzil Batchelor, *British Boxing*

Alexander Johnston, *Ten and Out!*

Frank Dowling, *Fistiana; or The Oracle of the Ring, 1841, 1861*

Jeffrey Farnol, *Famous Prize Fights*

James Butler, *What Do You Know About Boxing?*

Tom Sawyer, *Noble Art*

Elliot J. Gorn, *The Manly Art*

James Brady, *Strange Encounters, Tales of Famous Fights and Fighters*

Patrick Myler, *Regency Rogue*

Charles Saunders, *Sweat and Soul*

J.A. Rogers, *World's Great Men of Color*

Melvin D. Adleman, *A Sporting Time: New York and the Rise of Modern Athletics 1820-1870*

Richard Holt, *Sport and The British*

Alan Lloyd, *The Great Prize Fight*

Tony Gee, *Up to Scratch*

James Weldon *Johnson, Black Manhattan*

An Amateur, *The Battle:An Impartial and Scientific Account of the Battle Between Cribb and Molineaux*

Henry Downes Miles, *Pugilistica: The History of British Boxing*

John B. McCormick, *The Square Circle; Or Stories of the Prize Ring*

Newspapers

The Sporting Magazine

Bell's Weekly Messenger

Bell's Life

Weekly Dispatch

The Daily Register (which became *The Times* in 1788)

The London Times

The New York Clipper

The Brooklyn Eagle

Articles

Carl B. Cone, *The Molineaux-Cribb Fight 1810: Wuz Tom Molineaux Robbed?* *(The Journal of Sports History, Vol 9, No 3 Winter 1982)*

Michael Harris Goodman, *The Moor vs. The Black Diamond (Virginia Calvalcade, XXIX: 4 Spring 1980)*

Randy Roberts, *Morals and Maulers: the Ethics of Early Pugilism (The Journal of Sports History, Vol 12, No 2 Summer 1985)*

Index

0-595-28884-7

Printed in Great Britain
by Amazon